W9-AGK-786

Canon® EOS Digital Rebel XTi/400D Guide to Digital SLR Photography

David D. Busch

THOMSON

COURSE TECHNOLOGY

Professional ■ Technical ■ Reference

© 2008 Thomson Course Technology, a division of Thomson Learning Inc. All rights reserved. No part of this book may be reproduced or transmitted in any form or by any means, electronic or mechanical, including photocopying, recording, or by any information storage or retrieval system without written permission from Thomson Course Technology PTR, except for the inclusion of brief quotations in a review.

The Thomson Course Technology PTR logo and related trade dress are trademarks of Thomson Course Technology, a division of Thomson Learning Inc., and may not be used without written permission.

Canon is a registered trademark of Canon Inc. All other trademarks are the property of their respective owners.

Important: Thomson Course Technology PTR cannot provide software support. Please contact the appropriate software manufacturer's technical support line or Web site for assistance.

Thomson Course Technology PTR and the author have attempted throughout this book to distinguish proprietary trademarks from descriptive terms by following the capitalization style used by the manufacturer.

Information contained in this book has been obtained by Thomson Course Technology PTR from sources believed to be reliable. However, because of the possibility of human or mechanical error by our sources, Thomson Course Technology PTR, or others, the Publisher does not guarantee the accuracy, adequacy, or completeness of any information and is not responsible for any errors or omissions or the results obtained from use of such information. Readers should be particularly aware of the fact that the Internet is an ever-changing entity. Some facts may have changed since this book went to press.

Educational facilities, companies, and organizations interested in multiple copies or licensing of this book should contact the Publisher for quantity discount information. Training manuals, CD-ROMs, and portions of this book are also available individually or can be tailored for specific needs.

ISBN-10: 1-59863-456-9

ISBN-13: 978-1-59863-456-3

Library of Congress Catalog Card Number: 2007931835

Printed in the United States of America

08 09 10 11 12 BU 10 9 8 7 6 5 4 3 2

Publisher and General Manager, Thomson Course Technology PTR:
Stacy L. Hiquet

Associate Director of Marketing:
Sarah O'Donnell

Manager of Editorial Services:
Heather Talbot

Marketing Manager:
Jordan Casey

Executive Editor:
Kevin Harreld

Marketing Assistant:
Adena Flitt

Project Editor:
Jenny Davidson

Technical Reviewer:
Michael D. Sullivan

PTR Editorial Services Coordinator:
Erin Johnson

Interior Layout Tech:
Bill Hartman

Cover Designer:
Mike Tanamachi

Indexer:
Sharon Hilgenberg

Proofreader:
Sandi Wilson

THOMSON

COURSE TECHNOLOGY

Professional ■ Technical ■ Reference

Thomson Course Technology PTR, a division of Thomson Course Technology
25 Thomson Place ■ Boston, MA 02210 ■ http://www.courseptr.com

For Teryn

Acknowledgments

Once again thanks to the folks at Course Technology, who have pioneered publishing digital imaging books in full color at a price anyone can afford. Special thanks to executive editor Kevin Harreld, who always gives me the freedom to let my imagination run free with a topic, as well as my veteran production team including project editor Jenny Davidson and technical editor Mike Sullivan. Also thanks to cover designer Michael Tanamachi and my agent, Carole McClendon, who has the amazing ability to keep both publishers and authors happy.

About the Author

David D. Busch has written nine bestselling guidebooks for specific digital SLR models, and a half-dozen other popular books devoted to dSLRs, including *Mastering Digital SLR Photography, Second Edition* and *Digital SLR Pro Secrets*. As a roving photojournalist for more than 20 years, he illustrated his books, magazine articles, and newspaper reports with award-winning images. He's operated his own commercial studio, suffocated in formal dress while shooting weddings-for-hire, and shot sports for a daily newspaper and upstate New York college. His photos have been published in magazines as diverse as *Scientific American* and *Petersen's PhotoGraphic*, and his articles have appeared in *Popular Photography & Imaging, The Rangefinder, The Professional Photographer*, and hundreds of other publications. He's also reviewed digital cameras for CNet and *Computer Shopper*.

When **About.com** recently named its top five books on Beginning Digital Photography, occupying the #1 and #2 slots were Busch's *Digital Photography All-In-One Desk Reference for Dummies* and *Mastering Digital Photography*. During the past year, he's had as many as five of his books listed in the Top 20 of Amazon.com's Digital Photography Best Seller list—simultaneously! Busch's 90-plus other books published since 1983 include bestsellers like *QuickSnap Guide to Digital SLR Photography*.

Busch earned top category honors in the Computer Press Awards the first two years they were given (for *Sorry About The Explosion* and *Secrets of MacWrite, MacPaint and MacDraw*), and he later served as Master of Ceremonies for the awards.

Contents

Chapter 3
Setting Up Your Canon EOS Digital
Rebel XTi   31

Chapter 4
Getting the Right Exposure   75

Chapter 5
Advanced Shooting with Your Canon EOS
Digital Rebel XTi   101

Chapter 6
Working with Lenses   131

Chapter 7
Working with Light   167

Chapter 8
Downloading and Editing Your Images   193

Chapter 9
Canon Digital Rebel XTi: Troubleshooting and Prevention 211

Preface

You've unpacked your Canon EOS Digital Rebel XTi digital SLR (known as the Canon EOS 400D outside the United States and Canada). The slim little book included in the box is complete, but it's difficult to wade through. You know everything you need to know is in there, somewhere, but you don't know where to start. In addition, the camera manual doesn't offer much information on photography or digital photography. Nor are you interested in spending hours or days studying a comprehensive book on digital SLR photography that doesn't necessarily apply directly to your XTi.

All you want at this moment is a guide that explains the purpose and function of the XTi's basic controls, how you should use them, and why. Ideally, there should be information about file formats, resolution, aperture/priority exposure, and special autofocus modes available, but you'd prefer to read about those topics only after you've had the chance to go out and take a few hundred great pictures with your new camera. Why isn't there a book that summarizes the most important information in its first two or three chapters, with lots of illustrations showing what your results will look like when you use this setting or that?

Now there is such a book. If you want a quick introduction to the XTi's focus controls, flash synchronization options, how to choose lenses, or which exposure modes are best, this book is for you. If you can't decide on what basic settings to use with your camera because you can't figure out how changing ISO or white balance or focus defaults will affect your pictures, you need this guide.

Introduction

I sincerely believe that this book is your best bet for learning how to use your new camera, and for learning how to use it well.

If you're a Canon EOS Digital Rebel XTi owner who's looking to learn more about how to use this great camera, you've probably already explored your options. There are DVDs and online tutorials—but who can learn how to use a camera by sitting in front of a television or computer screen? Do you want to watch a movie or click on HTML links, or do you want to go out and take photos with your camera? Videos are fun, but not the best answer.

Of course, there's always the manual furnished with the camera. It's compact and filled with information, but there's really very little about *why* you should use particular settings or features, and its organization may make it difficult to find what you need. Multiple cross-references may send you flipping back and forth between two or three sections of the book to find what you need. The basic manual is also hobbled by black-and-white line drawings and tiny monochrome pictures that aren't very good as examples of what you can do.

Also available are third-party guides to the XTi, like this one. I haven't been happy with some of these guidebooks, which is why I wrote this one. The existing books range from skimpy and illustrated by black-and-white photos to lushly illustrated in full color but too generic to do much good. Photography instruction is useful, but it needs to be related directly to the Canon Digital Rebel XTi as much as possible.

I've tried to make *Canon EOS Digital Rebel XTi/400D Guide to Digital SLR Photography* different from your other XTi learn-up options. The roadmap sections use larger, color pictures to show you where all the buttons and dials are, and the explanations of what they do are longer and more comprehensive. I've tried to avoid overly general advice, including the two-page checklists on how to take a "sports picture" or a "portrait picture" or a "travel picture." Instead, you'll find tips and techniques for using all the features of your Canon Digital Rebel XTi to take *any kind of picture* you want. If you want to know where you should stand to take a picture of a quarterback dropping back to unleash a pass, there are plenty of books that will tell you that. This one concentrates on teaching you how to select the best autofocus mode, shutter speed, f/stop, or flash capability to take, say, a great sports picture under any conditions.

Rest assured that this book is *not* a rewritten version of an earlier Digital Rebel guidebook. This is an all-new edition, written from scratch specifically for the Canon Digital Rebel XTi. Nor is this book a lame rehash of the manual that came with the camera. Some folks spend five minutes with a book like this one, spot some information that also appears in the original manual, and decide, "Rehash!" without really understanding the differences. Yes, you'll find information here that is also in the owner's manual, such as the parameters you can enter when changing your XTi's operation in the various menus. Basic descriptions—before I dig in and start providing in-depth tips and information—may also be vaguely similar. There are only so many ways you can say, for example, "Hold the shutter release down halfway to lock in focus." But not *everything* in the manual is included in this book. If you want a large table showing which settings are available in each of the various Basic Zone and Creative Zone modes, you'd better have the Canon Function Availability Table available in the original manual. But if you need advice on when and how to use the most important functions, you'll find the information here.

Canon EOS Digital Rebel XTi/400D Guide to Digital SLR Photography is aimed at both Canon and dSLR veterans as well as newcomers to digital photography and digital SLRs. Both groups can be overwhelmed by the options the XTi offers, while underwhelmed by the explanations they receive in their user's manual. The manuals are great if you already know what you don't know, and you can find an answer somewhere in a booklet arranged by menu listings and written by a camera vendor employee who last threw together instructions on how to operate a camcorder.

Once you've read this book and are ready to learn more, I hope you pick up one of my five other guides to digital SLR photography. Three of them are offered by Thomson Course Technology PTR, each approaching the topic from a different perspective. They include:

Quick Snap Guide to Digital SLR Photography Consider this a prequel to the book you're holding in your hands. It might make a good gift for a spouse or friend who may be using your XTi, but who lacks even basic knowledge about digital photography, digital SLR photography, and Canon EOS photography. It serves as an introduction that summarizes the basic features of digital SLR cameras in general (not just the XTi), and what settings to use and when, such as continuous autofocus/single autofocus, aperture/shutter priority, EV settings, and so forth. The guide also includes recipes for shooting the most common kinds of pictures, with step-by-step instructions for capturing effective sports photos, portraits, landscapes, and other types of images.

Mastering Digital SLR Photography, Second Edition This book is an introduction to digital SLR photography, with nuts-and-bolts explanations of the technology, more in-depth coverage of settings, and whole chapters on the most common types of photography. While not specific to the Digital Rebel XTi, this book can show you how to get more from its capabilities.

Digital SLR Pro Secrets This is my more advanced guide to dSLR photography with greater depth and detail about the topics you're most interested in. If you've already mastered the basics in *Mastering Digital SLR Photography, Second Edition,* this book will take you to the next level.

Why the Canon Digital Rebel XTi Needs Special Coverage

There are many general digital photography books on the market. Why do I concentrate on books about specific digital SLRs like the Digital Rebel XTi? One reason is that I feel dSLRs are the wave of the future for serious photographers, and those who join the ranks of digital photographers with single lens reflex cameras deserve books tailored to their equipment.

When I started writing digital photography books in 1995, digital SLRs cost $30,000 and few people other than certain professionals could justify them. As recently as 2003 (before the original Digital Rebel was introduced), the lowest-cost dSLRs were priced at $3,000 or more. Today, anyone with around $600 can afford a sophisticated model like the Canon EOS Digital Rebel XTi/400D. The digital SLR is no longer the exclusive bailiwick of the professional, the wealthy, or the serious photography addict willing to scrimp and save to acquire a dream camera. Digital SLRs have become the favored camera for anyone who wants to go beyond point-and-shoot capabilities. And Canon cameras have enjoyed a dominating position among digital SLRs because of Canon's innovation in introducing affordable cameras with interesting features and outstanding performance (particularly in the area of high ISO image quality). It doesn't hurt that Canon also provides both full frame and smaller format digital cameras and a clear migration path between them (if you stick to the Canon EF lenses that are compatible with both).

You've selected your camera of choice, and you belong in the avid photographer camp if you fall into one of the following categories:

- Individuals who want to get better pictures, or perhaps transform their growing interest in photography into a full-fledged hobby or artistic outlet with a Canon Digital Rebel XTi and advanced techniques.

- Those who want to produce more professional-looking images for their personal or business website, and feel that the Digital Rebel XTi will give them more control and capabilities.

- Small business owners with more advanced graphics capabilities who want to use the Digital Rebel XTi to document or promote their business.

- Corporate workers who may or may not have photographic skills in their job descriptions, but who work regularly with graphics and need to learn how to use digital images taken with a Canon Digital Rebel XTi for reports, presentations, or other applications.

- Professional Webmasters with strong skills in programming (including Java, JavaScript, HTML, Perl, etc.) but little background in photography, but who realize that the XTi can be used for sophisticated photography.

- Graphic artists and others who already may be adept in image editing with Photoshop or another program, and who may already be using a film SLR (Canon or otherwise), but who need to learn more about digital photography and the special capabilities of the XTi.

Who Am I?

You may have seen my photography articles in *Popular Photography & Imaging* magazine. I've also written about 2,000 articles for (late, lamented) *Petersen's PhotoGraphic*, plus *The Rangefinder, Professional Photographer*, and dozens of other photographic publications. First and foremost, I'm a photojournalist and made my living in the field until I began devoting most of my time to writing books. Although I love writing, I'm happiest when I'm out taking pictures, which is why I took 10 days off late last year for a solo visit to Toledo, Spain—not as a tourist, because I've been to Toledo no less than a dozen times in the past—but solely to take photographs of the people, landscapes, and monuments that I've grown to love.

Like all my digital photography books, this one was written by someone with an incurable photography bug. My first Canon SLR was a Pellix back in the 1960s, and I've used a variety of newer models since then. I've worked as a sports photographer for an Ohio newspaper and for an upstate New York college. I've operated my own commercial studio and photo lab, cranking out product shots on demand and then printing a few hundred glossy 8 × 10s on a tight deadline for a press kit. I've served as a photo-posing instructor for a modeling agency. People have actually paid me to shoot their weddings and immortalize them with portraits. I even prepared press kits and articles on photography as a PR consultant for a large Rochester, N.Y., imaging company. My trials and travails with imaging and computer technology have made their way into print in book form an alarming number of times, including a few dozen on scanners and photography.

Like you, I love photography for its own merits, and I view technology as just another tool to help me get the images I see in my mind's eye. But, also like you, I had to master this technology before I could apply it to my work. This book is the result of what I've learned, and I hope it will help you master your Digital Rebel XTi digital SLR, too.

Chapter Outline

Chapter 1: Shooting Your First Digital Rebel XTi Picture

Just what you need to know to take your camera out of the box, make basic settings, and begin shooting good pictures within minutes.

Chapter 2: Canon EOS Digital Rebel XTi Roadmap

This chapter is a guided tour of the external buttons, dials, and controls of the Digital Rebel XTi.

Chapter 3: Setting Up Your Canon EOS Digital Rebel XTi

Here you'll learn how to make all the key menu settings needed to customize and tailor the operation of your Digital Rebel XTi.

Chapter 4: Getting the Right Exposure

Learn how to use the Digital Rebel XTi's metering modes, select the best ISO setting, and use exposure compensation and histograms to fine-tune your exposure.

Chapter 5: Advanced Shooting with Your Canon EOS Digital Rebel XTi

This chapter explains autofocus modes, white balance, continuous shooting, and custom image parameters.

Chapter 6: Working with Lenses

Everything you need to know about Canon lenses, compatibility, choosing and using prime lenses and zooms, and much more.

Chapter 7: Working with Light

This chapter includes Canon Digital Rebel XTi flash basics, as well as tips for working with other types of illumination, including studio flash.

Chapter 8: Downloading and Editing Your Images

There are plenty of good Photoshop books available, and this isn't one of them. Instead, you'll find the information you need for choosing the right editing software, noise reduction utilities, RAW converters, and other aids as you learn how to modify and print your images.

Chapter 9: Canon Digital Rebel XTi: Troubleshooting and Prevention

This chapter provides some tips for bringing a dead camera back to life, troubleshooting common problems, and ways to maintain the health of your XTi and its accessories.

Glossary

Want a quick definition of an unfamiliar word? You'll find it here.

1

Shooting Your First Digital Rebel XTi Picture

If you're like me, the first time you laid your hands on your Canon EOS Digital Rebel XTi, you couldn't wait to use it. I would have taken some shots on the way home from the camera store if I'd remembered to bring a Compact Flash card along with me. It's likely the battery didn't have much juice in it, but I would have tried anyway. The XTi is quite tempting right out of the box, especially if you've previously used either of its predecessors, the original Digital Rebel or the Digital Rebel XT. All three cameras are similar enough that a veteran Digital Rebel owner can use, at least, the basic features of the Digital Rebel XTi with very little prompting.

However, it's also possible that you're upgrading to the Digital Rebel XTi from a point-and-shoot digital camera, a film SLR, or a digital SLR offered by a different manufacturer. In any of these cases, you'll find the XTi to be a strange beast, with lots of dials and buttons and settings that might not make sense to you at first, but will surely become second-nature after you've had a chance to use the camera for a while.

But don't fret about needing to wade through a manual in order to find out what you need to take those first few tentative snaps. I'm going to help you hit the ground running with this brief chapter, which will help you set your camera up and begin shooting in minutes. You won't find a lot of detail in this chapter. Indeed, I'm going to tell you just what you absolutely must know. I'll go into more depth and even repeat some of what I explain here in later chapters, so you don't have to memorize everything you see. Just relax, follow a few easy steps, and then go out and take your best shots—ever.

Getting Ready to Shoot

There's a lot of stuff in the box, including booklets, CDs, and lots of paperwork. The most important components are the camera and lens, battery, battery charger, and, if you're the nervous type, the neckstrap. You'll also need to buy a Compact Flash memory card, because one is not included. If you purchased your Digital Rebel XTi from a camera shop, the store personnel probably attached the neckstrap for you, ran through some basic operational advice that you've already forgotten, tried to sell you another Compact Flash card, and then, after they'd given you all the help you could absorb, sent you on your way with a handshake.

If you bought your XTi from a "Big Box" retailer that also sells refrigerators, you might have gotten only the handshake and a hard-sell pitch to purchase an extended warranty. (Now you know why the mass retailers can charge a little less—those extended warranties are very lucrative.) If your camera arrived from a mail order/Internet source in a big brown truck, it's possible your only interaction when you took possession of your camera was to scrawl your signature on an electronic clipboard.

Now what?

While you're trying to figure out how to fasten the neckstrap, you might as well charge the battery. Recharging the NB-2LH battery (the same one used in the Digital Rebel XT) takes about an hour or two, and you can easily spend that long attaching the neckstrap just the way you like it. The battery furnished with your XTi probably arrived at least partially discharged. Lithium Ion power packs of this type typically lose a few percent of their charge every day, even when the camera isn't turned on. These cells lose their power through the chemical reaction that continues when the camera is switched off.

Several battery chargers are available for the Digital Rebel XTi. The compact CB-2LT, shown in Figure 1.1, is the most convenient, because it requires no cord; the charger itself plugs directly into your power strip or wall socket. The CB-2LWE requires a cord. A charger for AA batteries can come in handy if you're using the XTi's optional BG-E3 battery grip, which can use AA rechargeable batteries (with a supplied adapter) as well as one or two NB-2LH packs. The BGM-E3L can charge two NB-2LH battery packs at once, so you can always have fresh power.

When the battery is inserted into the charger properly (it's impossible to insert it incorrectly), a Charge light begins glowing orange-red and remains a steady green when the battery is fully charged about two hours later. When the battery is charged, flip the lever on the bottom of the camera and slide the battery in (see Figure 1.2).

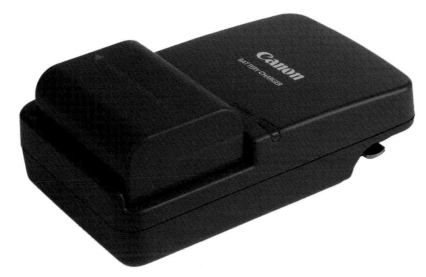

Figure 1.1 The status light indicates that the battery is being charged.

Figure 1.2 Insert the battery in the camera; it only fits one way.

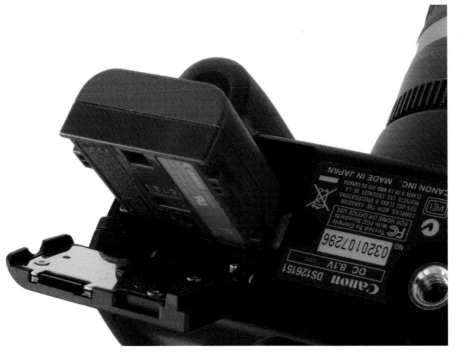

If your XTi has no lens attached, mount one by removing the body and rear lens caps, then matching the indicator on the lens barrel (red for EF lenses and white for EF-S lenses) with the red or white dot on the camera's lens mount, and rotating until the lens seats securely (see Figure 1.3). (You can find out more about the difference between EF and EF-S lenses in Chapter 6.) Set the focus mode switch on the lens to AF (autofocus).

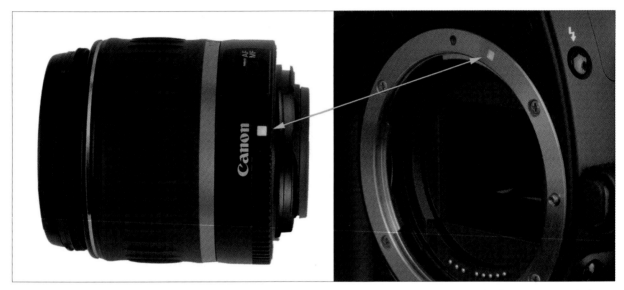

Figure 1.3 Match the white dot on EF-S lenses with the white dot on the camera mount to properly align the lens with the bayonet mount. For EF lenses, use the red dots.

If you want to change the XTi's vision-correction adjustment, press the shutter release to illuminate the indicators in the viewfinder, and then rotate the diopter adjustment wheel next to the viewfinder while looking through the viewfinder until the indicators appear sharp.

The final step is to insert a Compact Flash card. Slide the door cover on the right side of the body toward the back of the camera to release it, and then open the door. Insert the memory card with the label facing the back of the camera, and insert the edge with the double row of tiny holes into the slot, as shown in Figure 1.4. Close the door, and your preflight checklist is done! (I'm going to assume you remember to remove the lens cap when you're ready to take a picture!)

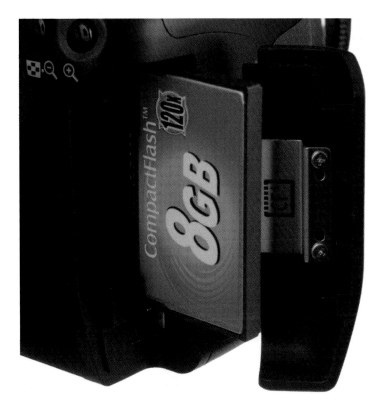

Figure 1.4 The Compact Flash card is inserted with the label facing the back of the camera.

Selecting a Shooting Mode

The Canon Digital Rebel XTi has seven Basic Zone shooting modes, in which the camera makes virtually all the decisions for you (except when to press the shutter), and five Creative Zone modes, which allow you to provide input over the exposure and settings the camera uses. You'll find a complete description of both Basic Zone and Creative Zone modes in Chapter 4.

Turn your camera on by flipping the power switch next to the Mode Dial to On, as shown in Figure 1.5. Next, you need to select which shooting mode to use. If you're very new to digital photography, you might want to set the Mode Dial on the camera to Auto (the green frame on the Mode Dial) or P (Program mode) and start snapping away. Either mode will make all the appropriate settings for you for many shooting situations. If you have a specific type of picture you want to shoot, you can try out one of the other Basic Zone modes—indicated on the Mode Dial with appropriate icons and shown in Figure 1.6.

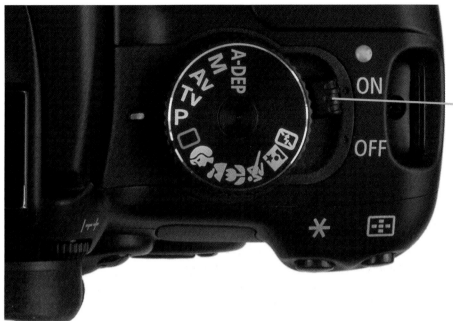

Figure 1.5 Flip the power switch on to activate the camera.

Power Switch

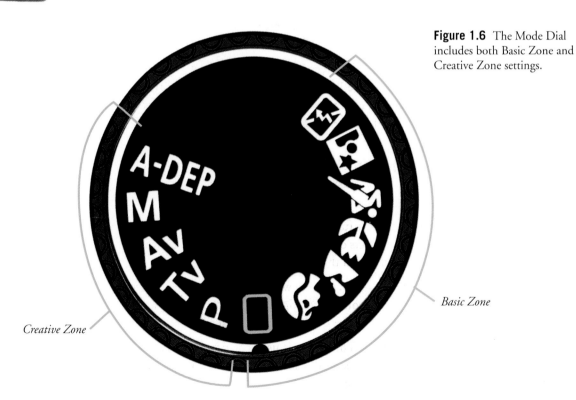

Figure 1.6 The Mode Dial includes both Basic Zone and Creative Zone settings.

Basic Zone

Creative Zone

Note that with any of the Basic Zone modes, you can't make most exposure or other changes manually:

- **Auto.** The camera makes all the settings for you.

- **Portrait.** Use this mode when you're taking a portrait of a subject standing relatively close to the camera and you want to de-emphasize the background, maximize sharpness, and produce flattering skin tones.

- **Landscape.** Select this mode when you want extra sharpness and rich colors of distant scenes.

- **Close Up.** This mode is helpful when you are shooting close-up pictures of a subject from about one foot away or less.

- **Sports.** Use this mode to freeze fast-moving subjects.

- **Night Portrait.** Choose this mode when you want to illuminate a subject in the foreground with flash, but still allow the background to be exposed by the available light. Be prepared to use a tripod or an image stabilized (IS) lens to reduce the effects of camera shake. (You'll find more about IS and camera shake in Chapter 6.)

- **Flash Off.** This is the mode to use in museums and other locations where flash is forbidden or inappropriate.

If you have more photographic experience, you might want to opt for one of the Creative Zone modes, also shown in Figure 1.6. These, too, are described in more detail in Chapter 4. These modes all let you apply a little more creativity to your camera's settings. These modes are indicated on the Mode Dial by letters A-DEP, M, Av, Tv, and P:

- **A-DEP (Automatic depth-of-field).** Choose this mode if you want to allow the XTi to select an f/stop that will maximize depth-of-field for the subjects in the frame.

- **M (Manual).** Select when you want full control over the shutter speed and lens opening, either for creative effects or because you are using a studio flash or other flash unit not compatible with the XTi's automatic flash metering.

- **Av (Aperture Priority/Aperture value).** Choose when you want to use a particular lens opening, especially to control sharpness or how much of your image is in focus. The XTi will select the appropriate shutter speed for you.

- **Tv (Shutter Priority/Time value).** This mode is useful when you want to use a particular shutter speed to stop action or produce creative blur effects. The XTi will select the appropriate f/stop for you.

- **P (Program).** This mode allows the XTi to select the basic exposure settings, but you can still override the camera's choices to fine-tune your image.

Choosing a Metering Mode

You might want to select a particular metering mode for your first shots, although the default Evaluative metering (which is set automatically when you choose a Basic Zone mode and cannot be changed) is probably the best choice as you get to know your camera. To change metering modes, press the left cross key (it's the directional key located to the immediate left of the Set button on the right side of the camera back) to produce a list of available modes on the LCD. Press the left/right cross keys to cycle among them, and then press Set to lock in your choice among the trio shown in Figure 1.7:

- **Evaluative metering.** The standard metering mode; the XTi attempts to intelligently classify your image and choose the best exposure based on readings from 35 different zones in the frame, with emphasis on the autofocus points.

- **Partial metering.** Exposure is based on a central spot, roughly nine percent of the image area.

- **Center-Weighted Averaging metering.** The XTi meters the entire scene, but it gives the most emphasis to the central area of the frame.

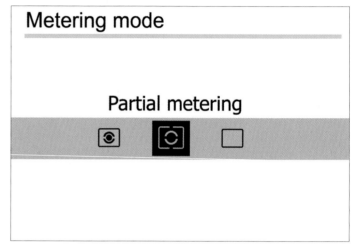

Figure 1.7 Metering modes (left to right Evaluative, Partial, Center-Weighted).

You'll find a detailed description of each of these modes in Chapter 4.

Choosing a Focus Mode

You can easily switch between automatic and manual focus by moving the AF/MF switch on the lens mounted on your camera. However, if you're using a Creative Zone shooting mode, you'll still need to choose an appropriate focus mode. (You can read more on selecting focus parameters in Chapter 5.) If you're using a Basic Zone mode, the focus method is set for you automatically.

Press the AF button (the right cross key) and spin the Main Dial (located just behind the shutter release button) or press the left/right cross keys to choose from the three modes that appear on the color LCD (see Figure 1.8). Press Set to lock in your choice. (The AF/M switch on the lens must be set to AF before the autofocus mode you select takes effect.)

The three choices are

- **One Shot.** This mode, sometimes called *single autofocus*, locks in a focus point when the shutter button is pressed down halfway, and the focus confirmation light glows in the viewfinder. The focus will remain locked until you release the button or take the picture. If the camera is unable to achieve sharp focus, the focus confirmation light will blink. This mode is best when your subject is relatively motionless. Portrait, Night Portrait, and Landscape Basic Zone modes use this focus method exclusively.

- **AI Focus.** In this mode, the XTi switches between One Shot and AI Servo as appropriate. That is, it locks in a focus point when you partially depress the shutter button (One Shot mode), but switches automatically to AI Servo if the subject begins to move. This mode is handy when photographing a subject, such as a child at quiet play, which might move unexpectedly. The Flash Off Basic Zone mode uses this focus method.

- **AI Servo.** This mode, sometimes called *continuous autofocus*, sets focus when you partially depress the shutter button, but continues to monitor the frame and refocuses if the camera or subject is moved. This is a useful mode for photographing sports and moving subjects. The Sports Basic Zone mode uses this focus method exclusively.

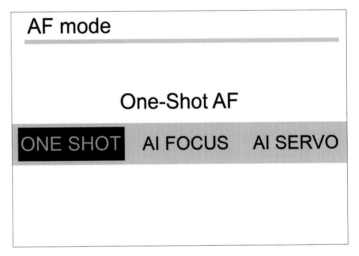

Figure 1.8 Set autofocus mode.

Selecting a Focus Point

The Canon Digital Rebel XTi uses nine different focus points to calculate correct focus. In A-DEP, or any of the Basic Zone shooting modes, the focus point is selected automatically by the camera. In the other Creative Zone modes, you can allow the camera to select the focus point automatically, or you can specify which focus point should be used.

You can change which of the nine focus points the Canon Digital Rebel XTi uses to calculate correct focus (see Figure 1.9), or allow the camera to select the point for you. To set the focus point manually, look through the viewfinder and then press the AF point selection button on the extreme upper-right corner of the back of the camera, marked with a square icon with four square dots arranged in a cross shape, and use either the cross keys (which move highlighting directly to a point) or the Main Dial (which rotates through all the points in turn) to select the zone you want to use. As you cycle among the focus points, each will be illuminated individually, and then all at one time (see Figure 1.10). Press the Set button to switch back and forth between the center autofocus point and automatic selection.

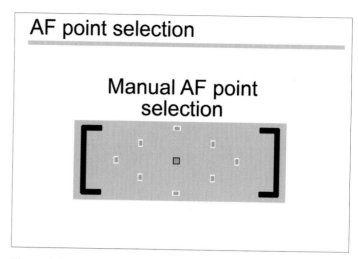

Figure 1.9 Set the autofocus point using the LCD screen.

Figure 1.10 Select a focus point.

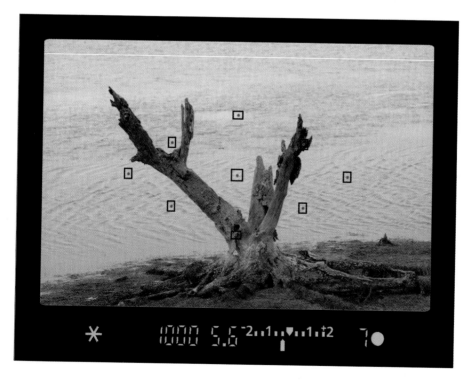

Other Settings

You can adjust a few other settings if you're feeling ambitious, but don't feel ashamed if you postpone using these features, which aren't available in Basic Zone modes anyway, until you've racked up a little more experience with your Digital Rebel XTi.

Adjusting White Balance and ISO

If you like, you can custom-tailor your white balance (color balance) and ISO sensitivity settings. To start out, it's best to set white balance (WB) to Auto, and ISO to ISO 100 or ISO 200 for daylight photos, and ISO 400 for pictures in dimmer light. You'll find complete recommendations for both of these settings in Chapter 4. Set the white balance by pressing the White Balance button (the down cross key), and choosing a white balance from the menu of choices that appears on the color LCD with the left/right cross keys or by rotating the Main Dial. Press Set to confirm your choice.

To adjust ISO sensitivity, press the ISO button (the up cross key) and choose the setting you want from the menu of choices that appears on the color LCD. Use the up/down cross keys or rotate the Main Dial to highlight your selection, and then press the Set button to lock it in.

If you've been playing with your camera's settings, or your XTi has been used by someone else, you can restore the factory defaults by choosing Clear Settings in the Set-up 2 menu, and then selecting Clear All Camera Settings, or Clear All Custom Functions. (I'll show you how to navigate the menu system in Chapter 3.)

Using the Self-Timer

If you want to set a short delay before your picture is taken, you can use the self-timer. Press the Drive button (located to the right of the LCD and marked by three icons representing continuous shooting, a self-timer, and remote control), and press the left/right cross keys or rotate the Main Dial until the self-timer icon appears on the Drive mode screen. Canon supplies a rubber eyepiece cover, which attaches to your camera strap and can be slid over the eyepiece in place of the rubber eyecup. This prevents light from entering through the eyepiece, which can confuse the exposure meter. I've found that extraneous light is seldom a problem unless a bright light source is coming from directly behind the camera, in which case I use my hand to shield the viewfinder.

Press the shutter release to lock focus and start the 10-second timer. The self-timer lamp will blink and the beeper will sound (unless you've silenced it in the menus) until the final two seconds, at which time the lamp remains on and the beeper beeps more rapidly. To cancel the self-timer and choose another shooting mode, press the Drive button again and press the left/right cross keys to select a different mode.

Reviewing the Images You've Taken

The Canon Digital Rebel XTi has a broad range of playback and image review options, and I'll cover them in more detail in Chapter 3. For now, you'll want to learn just the basics. Here is all you really need to know at this time (see Figure 1.11):

- Press the Playback button (marked with a blue right-pointing triangle) to display the most recent image on the LCD.

- Rotate the Main Dial or press the left/right cross keys to review additional images. Turn it counterclockwise to review images from most recent to oldest, or clockwise to start with the first image on the Compact Flash card and cycle forward to the newest.

- Use the Jump button to leap ahead 10 or 100 images.

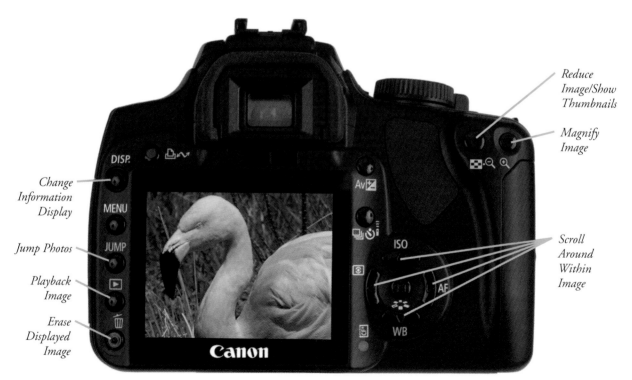

Figure 1.11 Review your images.

- Press the Disp. button repeatedly to cycle among overlays of basic image information, detailed shooting information, or no information at all.

- Press the Magnify button repeatedly to zoom in on the image displayed; the Reduce Image button zooms back out. Press the Playback button to exit magnified display. A graphic appears in the image that indicates the degree of magnification.

- Use the cross keys to scroll around within a magnified image.

You'll find information on viewing thumbnail indexes of images, jumping forward and backward 10 or 100 images at a time, automated playback, and other options in Chapter 3.

Transferring Photos to Your Computer

The final step in your picture-taking session will be to transfer the photos you've taken to your computer for printing, further review, or image editing. Your XTi enables you to print directly to PictBridge-compatible printers and to create print orders right in the camera, plus you can select which images to transfer to your computer. I'll outline those options in Chapter 3.

For now, you'll probably want to transfer your images either by using a cable transfer from the camera to the computer, or by removing the Compact Flash card from the XTi and transferring the images with a card reader. The latter option is usually the best, because it's usually much faster and doesn't deplete the battery of your camera. However, you can use a cable transfer when you have the cable and a computer but no card reader (perhaps you're using the computer of a friend or colleague, or at an Internet café).

To transfer images from the camera to a Mac or PC computer using the USB cable:

1. Turn off the camera.

2. Pry back the rubber cover that protects the Digital Rebel XTi's USB port, and plug the USB cable furnished with the camera into the USB port.

3. Connect the other end of the USB cable to a USB port on your computer.

4. Turn the camera on. Your installed software usually detects the camera and offers to transfer the pictures, or the camera appears on your desktop as a mass storage device, enabling you to drag and drop the files to your computer.

To transfer images from a Compact Flash card to the computer using a card reader (see Figure 1.12), do the following:

1. Turn off the camera.

2. Slide open the Compact Flash card door, and press the black button, which ejects the card.

3. Insert the Compact Flash card into your memory card reader. Your installed software detects the files on the card and offers to transfer them. The card can also appear as a mass storage device on your desktop, which you can open and then drag and drop the files to your computer.

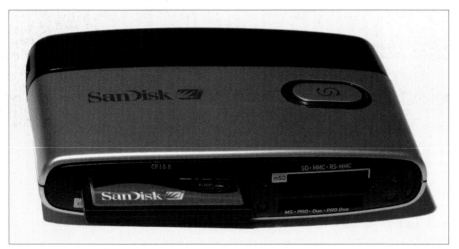

Figure 1.12 A card reader is the fastest way to transfer photos.

2

Canon EOS Digital Rebel XTi Roadmap

It's time for you to get to know your Canon EOS Digital Rebel XTi up close. Unfortunately, there are so many buttons and dials and knobs on this camera that many new owners—especially those coming to the XTi from point-and-shoot models—find the array of controls bewildering. What you really need is a roadmap, showing you where everything is and how it's used.

Unfortunately, the diagrams provided in the XTi's manual have more resemblance to a world globe than a roadmap: everything is there in great detail, but you almost have to know exactly what you're looking for to find it. You're supplied with two main black-and-white outline drawings that cover the front, back, two sides, and top and bottom of the camera in a single pair of views, adorned with several dozen labels per illustration. The print and drawings are so small and cramped that you might have some difficulty sorting out individual features. The only good thing about the manual's global view is that each label is supplemented with one to five page cross-references, so you can flip back and forth through the pages to retrieve the information you really wanted to know. Several of the third-party books aren't much better, featuring black-and-white photos of front, back, and top views, and lots of labels.

I'm out to atone for those deficiencies. In this chapter, I'm going to provide a street-level roadmap, rather than a satellite view, using several different views and lots of explanation, so that by the time you finish this chapter, you'll have a basic understanding of every control, and what it does. I'm not going into menu functions here—you'll find a discussion of your setup, shooting, and playback menu options in Chapter 3. Everything here is devoted to the button pusher and dial twirler in you.

The Canon Digital Rebel XTi's Public Face

The front of the XTi (see Figure 2.1) is the face seen by your victims as you snap away. For the photographer, though, the front is the surface your fingers curl around as you hold the camera, and there are really only three buttons to press, all within easy reach of the fingers of your left hand, plus the shutter button and Main Dial, which are on the top/front of the handgrip. Additional controls are on the lens itself. You'll need to look at several different views to see everything.

Figure 2.2 shows a three-quarters view of the left side of the Digital Rebel XTi (when viewed from the front). You can see the flash hot shoe on top and the door for the Compact Flash card at the left edge. The other components you need to know about are as follows:

- **Shutter button.** Angled on top of the handgrip is the shutter button. Press this button down halfway to lock exposure and focus (in One Shot Mode and AI Focus with non-moving subjects).

- **Main Dial.** This dial is used to change shooting settings. When settings are available in pairs (such as shutter speed/aperture), this dial will be used alone to make settings such as shutter speed, or used with other buttons to make additional settings such as f/stop.

- **Red-Eye Reduction/Self-Timer lamp.** When activated, this LED provides a blip of light shortly before a flash exposure to cause the subjects' pupils to close down, reducing the effect of red-eye reflections off their retinas. When using the self-timer, this lamp also flashes to mark the countdown until the photo is taken.

- **Infrared sensor.** This sensor activates the remote control features of the camera when a signal from an infrared remote control is received.

- **Handgrip.** This provides a comfortable handhold and also contains the XTi's battery.

Figure 2.1

Red Eye Reduction/
Self-Timer Lamp

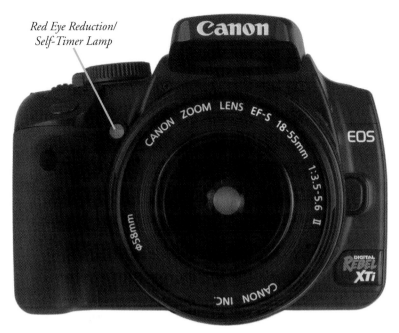

Figure 2.2

Main
Dial

Shutter
Release

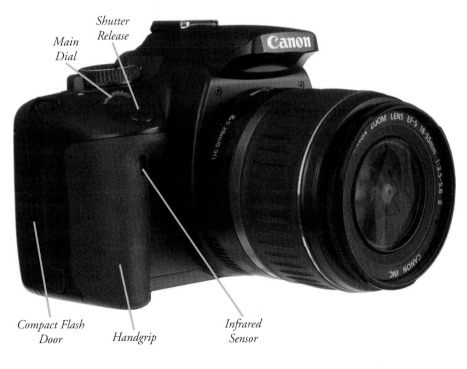

Compact Flash
Door

Handgrip

Infrared
Sensor

You'll find more controls on the other side of the XTi, shown in Figure 2.3. You can see the rubber cover on the side that protects the camera's USB, TV, and remote control ports. The main buttons shown include:

■ **Flash button.** This button releases the built-in flash so that it can flip up (see Figure 2.4) and starts the charging process.

Figure 2.3

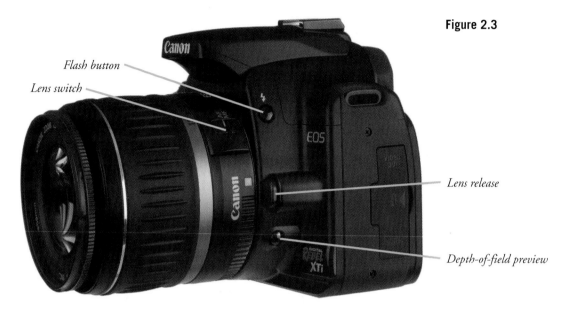

Flash button

Lens switch

Lens release

Depth-of-field preview

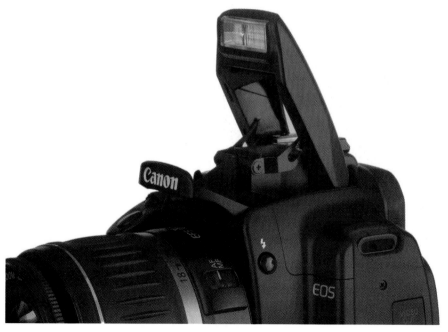

Figure 2.4 Pressing the Flash button pops up the built-in flash unit and starts the charging process.

- **Lens release.** Press and hold this button to unlock the lens so you can rotate the lens to remove it from the camera.

- **Depth-of-field preview.** This button adjacent to the lens mount stops down the lens to the taking aperture so you can see in the viewfinder how much of the image is in focus. The view grows dimmer as the aperture is reduced. It also displays exposure status information in the viewfinder.

- **Lens switches.** Canon autofocus lenses have a switch to allow changing between automatic focus and manual focus and, in the case of IS lenses, another switch to turn image stabilization on and off.

The main feature on this side of the Digital Rebel XTi is a rubber cover (see Figure 2.5) that protects the three connector ports underneath from dust and moisture. The three connectors, shown in Figure 2.6, are as follows:

- **USB port.** Plug in the USB cable furnished with your Digital Rebel XTi, and connect the other end to a USB port in your computer to transfer photos.

- **Video port.** You can link this connector with a television to view your photos on a large screen.

- **Remote control terminal.** You can plug various Canon remote release switches, timers, and wireless controllers into this connector.

Figure 2.5

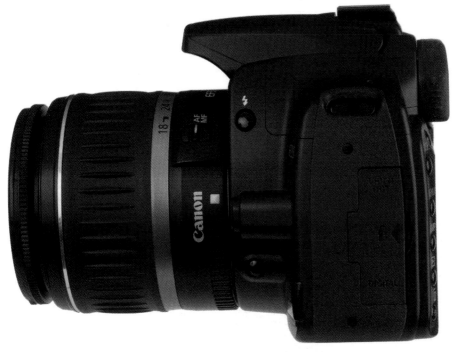

Figure 2.6

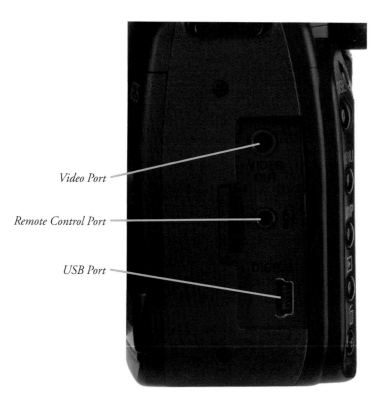

Video Port

Remote Control Port

USB Port

The Canon Digital Rebel XTi's Business End

The back panel of the Digital Rebel XTi (see Figure 2.7) bristles with more than a dozen different controls, buttons, and knobs. That might seem like a lot of controls to learn, but you'll find that it's a lot easier to press a dedicated button and spin a dial than to jump to a menu every time you want to change a setting.

You can see the controls clustered on the left side of the XTi in Figure 2.8. The key buttons and their functions are as follows:

- **Viewfinder.** This is your window to the through-the-lens view of your image. The rubber eyecup blocks extraneous light from entering when your eye is pressed up against the viewfinder. It can be removed and replaced by the cap attached to your neckstrap when you use the camera on a tripod to ensure that light coming from the back of the camera doesn't venture inside and possibly affect the exposure reading.

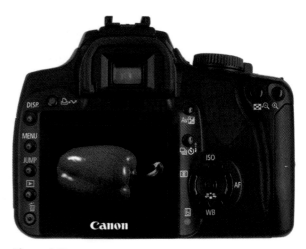

Figure 2.7

Figure 2.8

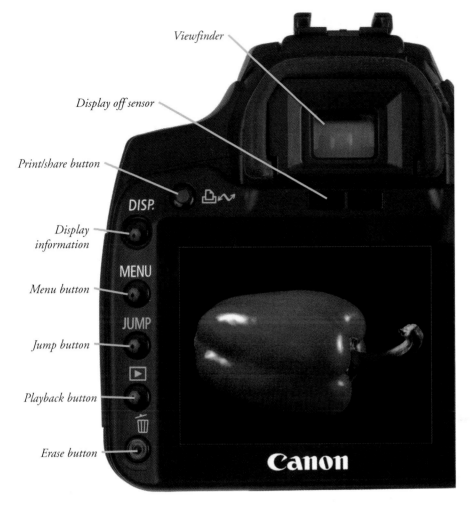

Viewfinder

Display off sensor

Print/share button

Display information

Menu button

Jump button

Playback button

Erase button

DISP.

MENU

JUMP

Canon

■ **Print/share button.** Press to select images for print orders.

■ **Display off sensor.** Senses when the camera is brought to your eye, and turns off the LCD display to save power. You can disable this feature in Setup Menu 1, as described in Chapter 3.

■ **Menu button.** Summons/exits the menu displayed on the rear LCD of the XTi. When you're working with submenus, this button also serves to exit a submenu and return to the main menu.

■ **Display Info button.** When pressed repeatedly, it changes the amount of picture information displayed on the LCD; from no information, brief information, and detailed information (including histograms).

- **Jump button.** Skips a specified number of images among the shots you've already taken; choose from 10 images, 100 images, or jump by date. After the Jump button is pressed, press the left/right cross keys to jump forward or back. To change the jump method, press the Jump button, and then press the up/down cross keys until the desired jump method is displayed.

- **Playback button.** Display the last picture taken. Thereafter, you can move back and forth among the available images by pressing the left and right cross keys. To quit playback, press this button again. The XTi also exits playback mode automatically when you press the shutter button (so you'll never be prevented from taking a picture on the spur of the moment because you happened to be viewing an image).

- **Erase button.** Press to erase the image shown on the LCD. A menu will pop up with Cancel, Erase, and All choices. Use the left/right cross keys to select one of the three actions, and then press the Set button to activate your choice. If you want to erase an image other than the one displayed, use the left/right cross keys to scroll to the image to be removed, and then press the Erase button.

- **LCD display.** Shows a review image of pictures you've taken; displays menus for changing camera settings; and shows current shooting status information, such as shutter speed, f/stop, and focus mode.

More buttons reside on the right side of the back panel, as shown in Figure 2.9. The key controls and their functions are as follows:

- **Diopter adjustment knob.** Rotate this knob to adjust the diopter correction for your eyesight.

- **AE/FE (auto exposure/flash exposure) lock/Thumbnail/Zoom Out button.** This button has several functions.

  In shooting mode, it locks the exposure or flash exposure that the camera sets when you partially depress the shutter button. The exposure lock indication (*) appears in the viewfinder. If you want to recalculate exposure with the shutter button still partially depressed, press the * button again. The exposure will be unlocked when you release the shutter button or take the picture. To retain the exposure lock for subsequent photos, keep the * button pressed while shooting.

  When using flash, pressing the * button fires a preflash that allows the unit to calculate and lock exposure prior to taking the picture.

  In playback mode, press this button to switch from single-image display to nine-image thumbnail index. Move among the thumbnails with the left/right cross keys. When an image is zoomed in, press this button to zoom out.

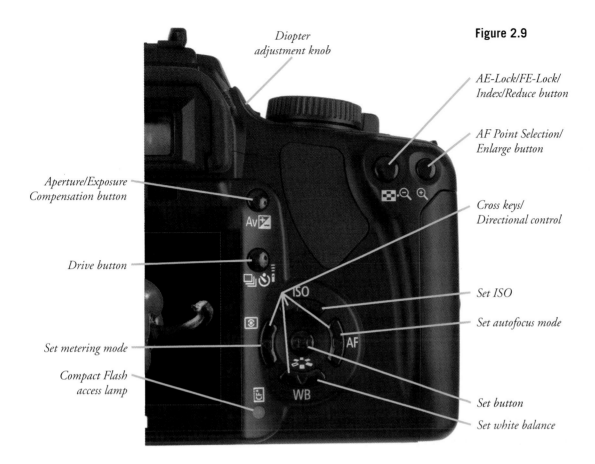

Diopter adjustment knob

Figure 2.9

AE-Lock/FE-Lock/ Index/Reduce button

AF Point Selection/ Enlarge button

Aperture/Exposure Compensation button

Cross keys/ Directional control

Drive button

Set ISO

Set autofocus mode

Set metering mode

Compact Flash access lamp

Set button

Set white balance

- **Aperture/Exposure Compensation button.** Tap the shutter release to turn on exposure information in the viewfinder. In Manual mode, press this button and turn the Main Dial to adjust the aperture. (To set the aperture in Av mode, just turn the Main Dial without holding down any button.) In P, Tv, Av, or A-DEP modes, hold this button and turn the Main Dial to add or subtract from the metered exposure.

- **Drive button.** Press repeatedly until single shot, continuous, self-timer/remote control icons appear in the LCD.

- **Cross keys.** Use the up/down/left/right cross keys to navigate on the color LCD screen. Each has a second function, too: up (ISO), down (White Balance), left (Metering mode), right (Autofocus mode).

- **AF Point Selection/Zoom In button.** In shooting mode, this button activates autofocus point selection. (See Chapter 4 for information on setting autofocus/exposure point selection.) In playback mode, this button zooms in on the image that's displayed or the highlighted thumbnail index image.

■ **Compact Flash Access lamp.** When lit or blinking, this lamp indicates that the Compact Flash card is being accessed.

■ **Set button.** Selects a highlighted setting or menu option.

Going Topside

The top surface of the Canon Digital Rebel XTi is fairly sparsely populated by controls. The key controls and components, shown in Figure 2.10, are as follows:

■ **Mode Dial.** Rotate this dial to switch among Basic Zone and Creative Zone modes. You'll find these modes described in more detail in Chapter 4.

■ **Sensor focal plane.** Precision macro and scientific photography sometimes require knowing exactly where the focal plane of the sensor is. The symbol on the top left side of the camera marks that plane.

Figure 2.10

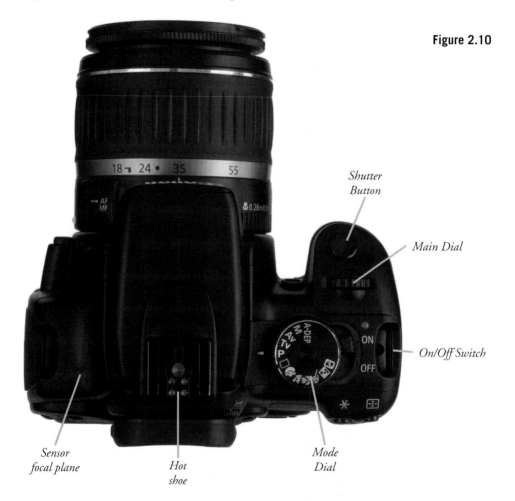

Shutter
Button

Main Dial

On/Off Switch

Sensor
focal plane

Hot
shoe

Mode
Dial

- **Hot shoe.** Slide an electronic flash into this mount when you need a more powerful speedlight. A dedicated flash unit, like those from Canon, can use the multiple contact points shown to communicate exposure, zoom setting, white balance information, and other data between the flash and the camera. There's more on using electronic flash in Chapter 7.

- **Main Dial.** This dial is used to select many shooting settings.

- **Shutter-release button.** Partially depress this button to lock in exposure and focus. Press all the way to take the picture. Tapping the shutter release when the camera has turned off the auto exposure and autofocus mechanisms reactivates both. When a review image is displayed on the back-panel color LCD, tapping this button removes the image from the display and reactivates the auto exposure and autofocus mechanisms.

LCD Panel Readouts

The back panel of the Digital Rebel XTi (see Figure 2.11) contains a color LCD readout that not only shows your pictures for review, and displays menus as you change settings, it provides a constant update of your current shooting settings when the metering system is active. This display turns off after a specified number of seconds (I'll show you how to do the specifying in Chapter 3), or, if you have the automatic display off feature activated, vanishes when the sensor under the viewfinder detects that you have brought the XTi to your eye. All of the information segments available are shown in Figure 2.12. I've color-coded the display

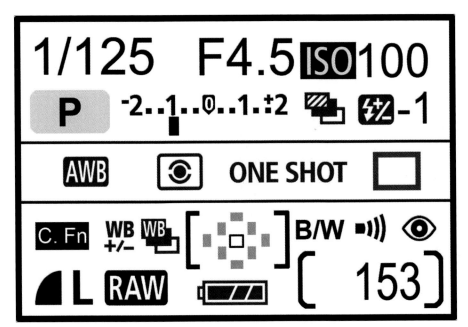

Figure 2.11

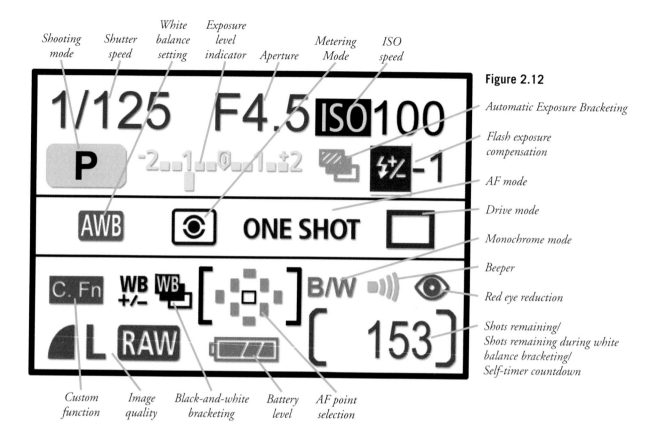

Figure 2.12

to make it easier to differentiate them; the information does *not* appear in color on the actual Digital Rebel XTi. Many of the information items are mutually exclusive (that is, in the White Balance area at left center shows AWB (automatic white balance), but if another setting is used that readout will be replaced by a different icon or text message). Some of the items on the status LCD also appear in the viewfinder, such as the shutter speed and aperture (pictured at top in blue in the figure), and the exposure level (in yellow just below the shutter speed/aperture).

Lens Components

The typical lens, like the one shown in Figures 2.13 and 2.14, has seven or eight common features:

- **Filter thread.** Lenses have a thread on the front for attaching filters and other add-ons. Some also use this thread for attaching a lens hood (you screw on the filter first, and then attach the hood to the screw thread on the front of the filter).

- **Lens hood bayonet.** This is used to mount the lens hood for lenses that don't use screw-mount hoods (the majority).

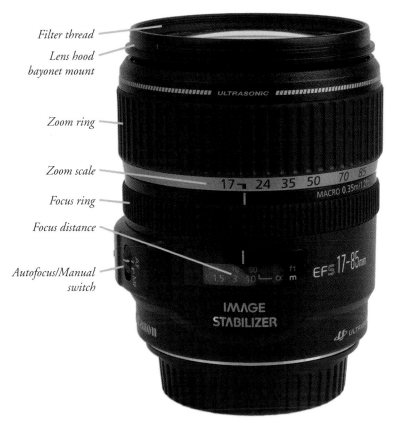

Figure 2.13

- **Zoom ring.** Turn this ring to change the zoom setting.

- **Zoom scale.** These markings on the lens show the current focal length selected.

- **Focus ring.** This is the ring you turn to manually focus the lens.

- **Distance scale.** This is a readout that rotates in unison with the lens's focus mechanism to show the distance at which the lens has been focused. It's a useful indicator for double-checking autofocus, and for roughly setting manual focus or depth-of-field.

- **Autofocus/Manual switch.** Allows you to change from automatic focus to manual focus.

- **Image stabilization switch (not shown).** Lenses with IS include a separate switch for adjusting the stabilization feature.

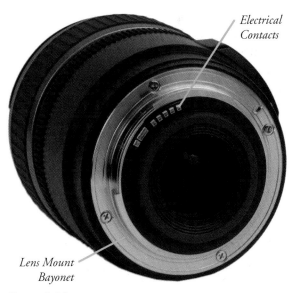

Figure 2.14

Looking Inside the Viewfinder

Much of the important shooting status information is shown inside the viewfinder of the Digital Rebel XTi. As with the status LCD above, not all of this information will be shown at any one time. Figure 2.15 shows what you can expect to see.

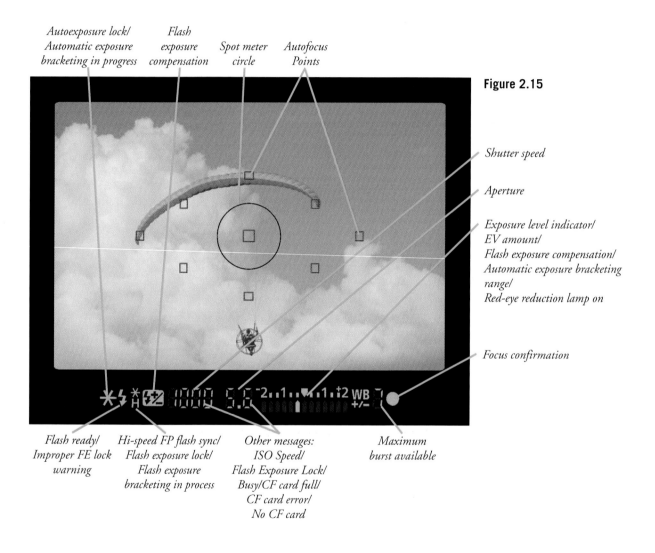

Autoexposure lock/ Automatic exposure bracketing in progress

Flash exposure compensation

Spot meter circle

Autofocus Points

Figure 2.15

Shutter speed

Aperture

Exposure level indicator/ EV amount/ Flash exposure compensation/ Automatic exposure bracketing range/ Red-eye reduction lamp on

Focus confirmation

Flash ready/ Improper FE lock warning

Hi-speed FP flash sync/ Flash exposure lock/ Flash exposure bracketing in process

Other messages: ISO Speed/ Flash Exposure Lock/ Busy/CF card full/ CF card error/ No CF card

Maximum burst available

Tap the shutter release to turn on the information in the viewfinder. These readouts include:

- **Autofocus zones.** Shows the nine areas used by the XTi to focus. The camera can select the appropriate focus zone for you, or you can manually select one or all of the zones, as described in Chapter 4.

- **Auto exposure lock.** Shows that exposure has been locked. This icon also appears when an automatic exposure bracketing sequence is in process.

- **Flash ready indicator.** This icon appears when the flash is fully charged. It also shows when the flash exposure lock has been applied for an inappropriate exposure value.

- **Flash status indicator.** Appears along with the flash ready indicator: the H is shown when high-speed (focal plane) flash sync is being used. The * appears when flash exposure lock or a flash exposure bracketing sequence is underway.

- **Flash exposure compensation.** Appears when flash EV changes have been made.

- **Shutter speed/aperture readouts.** Most of the time, these readouts show the current shutter speed and aperture. This pair can also warn you of Compact Flash card conditions (full, error, or missing), ISO speed, flash exposure lock, and a buSY indicator when the camera is busy doing other things (including flash recycling).

- **Exposure level indicator.** This scale shows the current exposure level, with the bottom indicator centered when the exposure is correct as metered. The indicator may also move to the left or right to indicate underexposure or overexposure (respectively). The scale is also used to show the amount of EV and flash EV adjustments, the number of stops covered by the current automatic exposure bracketing range, and is used as a red-eye reduction lamp indicator.

- **White balance correction.** Shows that white balance has been tweaked.

- **Maximum burst available.** Changes to a number to indicate the number of frames that can be taken in continuous mode using the current settings.

- **Focus confirmation.** This green dot appears when the subject covered by the active autofocus zone is in sharp focus.

Underneath Your Digital Rebel XTi

There's not a lot going on with the bottom panel of your Digital Rebel XTi. You'll find a tripod socket, which is also used to secure the optional battery grip. To mount the grip, slide the battery door latch to open the door, and then push down on the small pin that projects from the hinge. That will let you remove the battery door. Then slide the grip into the battery cavity, aligning the pin on the grip with the small hole on the other side of the tripod socket. Tighten the grip's tripod socket screw to lock the grip onto the bottom of your XTi. Figure 2.16 shows the underside view of the camera.

Figure 2.16

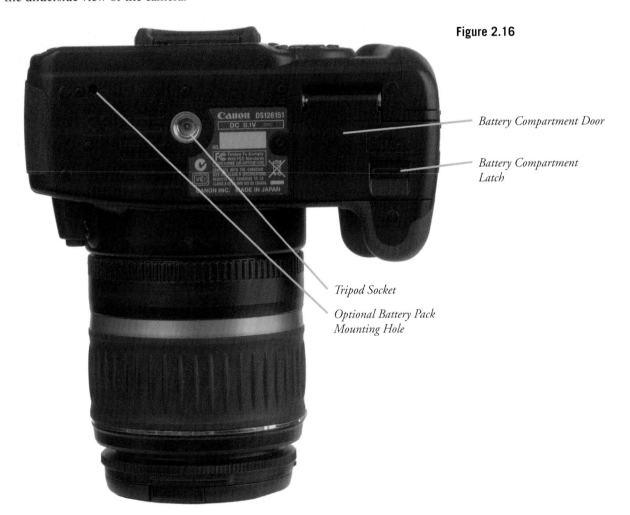

Battery Compartment Door

Battery Compartment Latch

Tripod Socket

Optional Battery Pack Mounting Hole

3

Setting Up Your Canon EOS Digital Rebel XTi

Menus, set-up, playback, and shooting options are what enable your Canon EOS Digital Rebel XTi to perform in ways that better suit the needs of a particular shooting session. The options available customize how your camera behaves, shoots photos, and displays the images you've taken, transforming it from a limited single-purpose tool into a versatile, do (almost) everything machine.

As I've mentioned before, this book isn't intended to replace the manual you received with your Digital Rebel XTi, nor have I any interest in rehashing its contents. There is, however, some unavoidable duplication between the Canon manual and this chapter, because I'm going to explain the key menu choices and the options you may have in using them. You should find, though, that this chapter

ALL MENUS ARE NOT CREATED EQUAL

In the discussions that follow, you'll find that some of the menu items are treated in a fair amount of detail, while others of equal nominal rank are given short shrift. Though this be madness, yet there is method in 't, as a Prince of Denmark once observed. As it turns out, some menu entries, such as Beep, allow a feature to simply be turned on or off, while others have limited options that can be summed up in a sentence or two. Other options, such as Picture Styles and Custom Functions require a bit more explanation. I'm even going to skip illustrations of some of the more mundane menu entries, granting you the opportunity to visualize the On or Off choices in your mind.

gives you the information you need in a much more useful form, with plenty of detail on why you should make some settings that are particularly cryptic. I'll start off with an overview of using the XTi's menus themselves.

Anatomy of the Digital Rebel XTi's Menus

To access a menu item, press the Menu button on the left side of the XTi to produce a display like the one shown in Figure 3.1. (If the camera goes to "sleep" while you're reviewing a menu, you may need to wake it up again by tapping the shutter-release button.) There are five menu tabs: Shooting 1, Shooting 2, Playback, Set-Up 1, and Set-Up 2. If you've scrolled down within a menu and want to skip to a different menu (say, from Shooting 1 to Shooting 2), you can scroll up to the top tab with the up cross key, and then press the left/right cross keys to move to a different tab. But it's usually much faster to simply press the Jump button to leap between menu tabs to get to the menu you want.

To select an item within a menu, move up or down each tab's menu list to highlight a particular item using either the up/down cross keys or the Main Dial. I find using the Main Dial to be faster, as my index finger is always poised near the dial and the shutter release, anyway. Here are the things to watch for as you navigate the menus:

- **Menu bar.** In the top row of the menu screen, the menu that is currently active will be highlighted in its default color: red for Shooting 1 or Shooting 2 (camera icons), blue for Playback (the right-pointing triangle), and yellow-orange for Set-Up 1 or Set-Up 2 (the "tool kit" icons).

- **Selected menu item.** The currently selected menu item will have a black background and will be surrounded by a box the same hue as its color code: red for the Shooting menus, blue for the Playback menu, and yellow-orange for the Set-up menus.

- **Other menu choices.** The other menu items visible on the screen will have a medium or dark gray background (alternating).

- **Current setting.** The current settings for visible menu items are shown in the right-hand column, until one menu item is selected (by pressing the Set key). At that point, all the settings vanish from the screen except for those dealing with the active menu choice.

When you've moved the menu highlighting to the menu item you want to work with, press the Set button to select it. The current settings for the other menu items in the list will be hidden, and a list of options for the selected menu item (or a submenu screen) will appear. Within the menu choices you can scroll up or down with the up/down cross keys, press Set to select the choice you've made, and press the Menu button again to exit.

Selected menu   *Selected menu item*

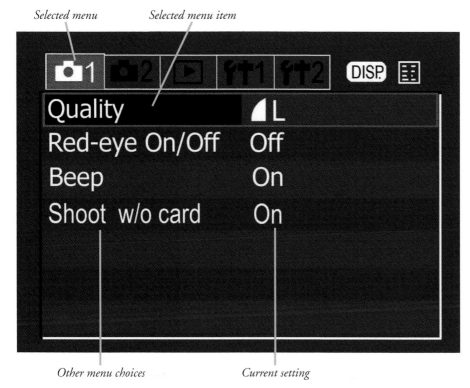

Other menu choices   *Current setting*

Figure 3.1 The Digital Rebel XTi's menus are arranged in a series of five tabs.

Shooting Menu 1/2 Options

The various direct setting buttons on the back panel of the camera, for autofocus mode, white balance, drive mode, ISO sensitivity, metering mode, and flash, along with exposure compensation (EV) adjustments are likely to be the most common settings changes you make, with changes during a particular session fairly common. You'll find that the Shooting menu options are those that you access second-most frequently when you're using your Digital Rebel XTi. You might make such adjustments as you begin a shooting session, or when you move from one type of subject to another. Canon makes accessing these changes very easy.

This section explains the Shooting menu options and how to use them. The options you'll find in this red-coded menu include:

- Quality
- Red-Eye On/Off
- Beep
- Shoot w/o card
- AEB (Automatic Exposure Bracketing)

- Flash exposure compensation
- WB SHIFT/BKT
- Custom White Balance
- Color space
- Picture Style
- Dust Delete Data

Quality Settings

You can choose the image quality settings used by the XTi to store its files. You have three choices to make:

- **Resolution.** The number of pixels captured determines the absolute resolution of the photos you shoot with your Digital Rebel XTi. Your choices range from 10 megapixels (Large, or L), measuring 3888 × 2592 pixels; 5.3 megapixels (Medium, or M), measuring 2816 × 1880 pixels; to 2.5 megapixels (Small, or S), measuring 1936 × 1288 pixels.

- **JPEG compression.** To reduce the size of your image files and allow more photos to be stored on a given Compact Flash card, the XTi uses JPEG compression to squeeze the images down to a smaller size. This compacting reduces the image quality a little, so you're offered the choice of Fine compression or Normal compression. The symbols help you remember that Fine compression (represented by a quarter-circle) provides the smoothest results, while Normal compression (signified by a stair-step icon) provides "jaggier" images.

- **JPEG, RAW, or both.** You can elect to store only JPEG versions of the images you shoot, or you can save your photos as uncompressed, loss-free RAW files, which consume more than twice as much space on your memory card. Many photographers elect to save *both* versions, so they'll have a JPEG version that might be usable as-is, as well as the original "digital negative" RAW file in case they want to do some processing of the image later. You'll end up with two different versions of the same file: one with a .jpg extension, and one with the .cr2 extension that signifies a Canon RAW file. When you choose RAW+JPEG, the JPEG file is always stored using the FINE compression setting.

To choose the combination you want, access the menus, scroll to Quality, and press the Set button. A screen similar to the one shown in Figure 3.2 will appear. Use the cross keys or Main Dial to cycle among the eight choices. In practice, you'll probably use only the Large-Fine, RAW+Large Fine, or RAW selections.

Why so many choices, then? There are some limited advantages to using the Medium and Small resolution settings and Normal JPEG compression setting. They allow stretching the capacity of your Compact Flash card so you can shoehorn quite a few more pictures onto a single memory card. That can come in useful when on vacation and you're running out of storage, or when you're shooting non-critical work that doesn't require a full 10 megapixels of resolution (such as photos taken for real estate listings, web page display, photo ID cards, or similar applications). Some photographers like to record RAW+JPEG so they'll have a moderate quality JPEG file for review only, while retaining access to the original RAW file for serious editing.

However, for most work, using lower resolution and extra compression is false economy. You never know when you might actually need that extra bit of picture detail. Your best bet is to have enough memory cards to handle all the shooting you want to do until you have the chance to transfer your photos to your computer or a personal storage device.

Reduced image quality can also sometimes be beneficial if you're shooting sequences of photos rapidly, as the XTi is able to hold more of them in its internal memory buffer before transferring to the Compact Flash card. Still, for most sports and other applications, you'd probably rather have better, sharper pictures than longer periods of continuous shooting.

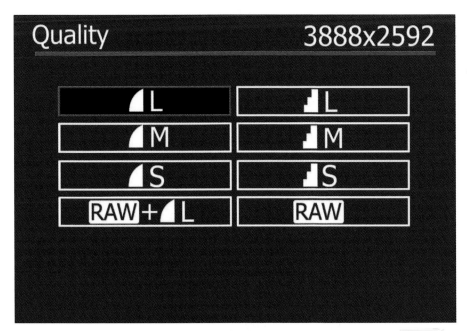

Figure 3.2 Choose your resolution, JPEG compression, and file format (Large/Fine JPEG in this case) from this screen.

JPEG vs. RAW

You'll sometimes be told that RAW files are the "unprocessed" image information your camera produces, before it has been modified. That's nonsense. RAW files are no more unprocessed than your camera film is after it's been through the chemicals to produce a negative or transparency. A lot can happen in the developer that can affect the quality of a film image—positively and negatively—and, similarly, your digital image undergoes a significant amount of processing before it is saved as a RAW file. Canon even applies a name (Digic II) to the digital image processing (DIP) chip used to perform this magic.

A RAW file is more similar to a film camera's processed negative. It contains all the information, captured in 12-bit channels per color (and stored in a 16-bit space), with no compression, no sharpening, no application of any special filters or other settings you might have specified when you took the picture. Those settings are *stored* with the RAW file so they can be applied when the image is converted to a form compatible with your favorite image editor. However, using RAW conversion software such as Adobe Camera Raw or Canon's Digital Photo Professional, you can override those settings and apply settings of your own. You can select essentially the same changes there that you might have specified in your camera's picture-taking options in creating a new file that leaves the original RAW file untouched.

RAW exists because sometimes we want to have access to all the information captured by the camera, before the camera's internal logic has processed it and converted the image to a standard file format. RAW doesn't save space like JPEG. But it preserves all the information captured by your camera after it has been converted from analog to digital form.

So, why don't we always use RAW? Although some photographers do save only in RAW format, it's more common to use either RAW plus one JPEG Fine, or just shoot JPEG and eschew RAW altogether. While RAW is overwhelmingly helpful when an image needs to be fine-tuned, in other situations working with a RAW file can slow you down significantly. RAW images take longer to store on the Compact Flash card, and they require more post-processing effort, whether you elect to go with the default settings in force when the picture was taken, or make minor adjustments.

As a result, those who depend on speedy access to images or who shoot large numbers of photos at once may prefer JPEG over RAW. Wedding photographers, for example, might expose several thousand photos during a bridal affair and offer hundreds to clients as electronic proofs for inclusion in an album. Wedding shooters take the time to ensure that their in-camera settings are correct, minimizing the need to post-process photos after the event. Given that their JPEGs are so good, there is little need to get bogged down shooting RAW. JPEG was invented as a more compact file format that can store most of the information in a digital image, but in a much smaller size. JPEG predates most digital SLRs, and was initially used to squeeze down files for transmission over slow dialup connections. Even if you were using an early dSLR with 1.3-megapixel files for news photography, you didn't want to send them back to the office over a modem at 1200 bps uncompressed.

But, as I noted, JPEG provides smaller files by compressing the information in a way that loses some image data. JPEG remains a viable alternative because it offers several different quality levels. At the highest quality Fine level, you might not be able to tell the difference between the original RAW file and the JPEG version, even though the RAW file occupies, by Canon's estimate, 9.8 MB on your memory card, while the Fine JPEG takes up only 3.8 MB of space. You've squeezed the image by more than half without losing much visual information at all. If you don't mind losing some quality, you can use more aggressive Normal compression with JPEG to cut the size in half again, to 2.0 MB. In my case, I shoot virtually everything at RAW+JPEG. Most of the time, I'm not concerned about filling up my memory cards, because I usually have a minimum of 15 GB worth of Compact Flash cards with me. If I know I may fill up all those cards, I have a tiny battery-operated personal storage device that can copy a 4 GB card in about eight minutes. Sometimes when shooting sports, I'll shift to JPEG FINE (with no RAW file) to squeeze a little extra speed out of my XTi's continuous shooting mode, and to reduce the need to wade through eight-photo bursts taken in RAW format. On the other hand, on my last trip to Europe, I took only RAW (instead of my customary RAW+JPEG) photos to fit more images onto my 60 GB personal storage device, shown in Figure 3.3, as I planned on doing at least some post-processing on many of the images for a travel book I was working on.

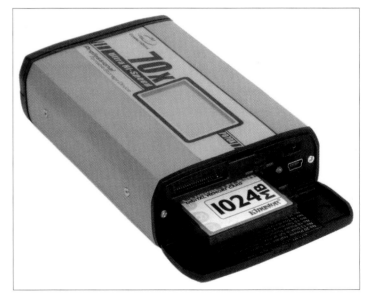

Figure 3.3 If RAW storage space is a concern, consider a portable storage device like this one.

MANAGING LOTS OF FILES

The only long-term drawback to shooting everything in RAW+JPEG is that it's easy to fill up your computer's hard drive if you are a prolific photographer. Here's what I do. My most recent photos are stored on my working hard drive in a num-bered folder, say XTi-01, with subfolders named after the shooting session, such as 080301Trees, for pictures of trees taken on March 1, 2008. An automatic utility copies new and modified photos to a different hard drive for temporary backup four times daily.

When the top-level folder accumulates about 30 GB of images, I back it up to DVDs and then move the folder to a 500 GB drive dedicated solely for storage of folders that have already been backed up onto DVD. Then I start a new folder, such as XTi-02, on the working hard drive and repeat the process. I always have at least one backup of every image taken, either on another hard drive or on a DVD.

Red-Eye Reduction

Your Digital Rebel XTi has a fairly effective Red-Eye Reduction flash mode. Unfortunately, your camera is unable, on its own, to *eliminate* the red-eye effects that occur when an electronic flash (or, rarely, illumination from other sources) bounces off the retinas of the eye and into the camera lens. Animals seem to suf-fer from yellow or green glowing pupils, instead; the effect is equally undesirable. The effect is worst under low-light conditions (exactly when you might be using a flash) as the pupils expand to allow more light to reach the retinas. The best you can hope for is to *reduce* or minimize the red-eye effect.

The best way to truly eliminate red-eye is to raise the flash up off the camera so its illumination approaches the eye from an angle that won't reflect directly back to the retina and into the lens. That alone is a good reason for using an external flash. While your XTi's built-in flash does elevate the strobe slightly (compared to point-and-shoot cameras) to further reduce the chance of red-eye effects, your only recourse may be to switch the Red-Eye Reduction feature on with the menu choice shown in Figure 3.4. It causes a lamp on the front of the camera to illu-minate, which may cause your subjects' pupils to contract, decreasing the amount of the red-eye effect. (You might need to ask your subject to look at the lamp to gain maximum effect.) Figure 3.5 shows the effects of wider pupils (left) and those that have been contracted using the XTi's Red-Eye Reduction feature.

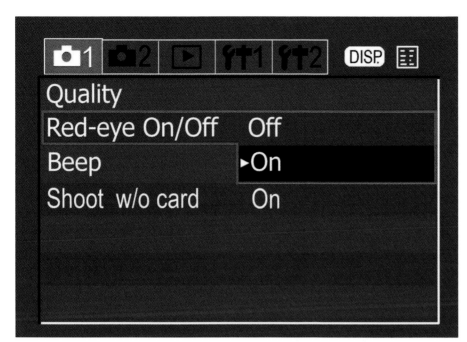

Figure 3.4 Turn on your camera's Red-Eye Reduction feature to help eliminate demon-red pupils.

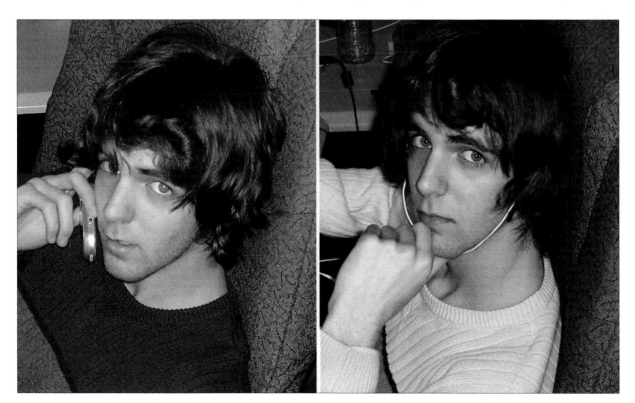

Figure 3.5 Same pose, same location (but different days) and red-eye is tamed (right), thanks to the Digital Rebel XTi's Red-Eye Reduction lamp.

Beep

The Digital Rebel XTi's internal beeper provides a helpful chirp to signify various functions, such as the countdown of your camera's self-timer. You can switch it off if you want to avoid the beep because it's annoying, impolite, or distracting (at a concert or museum), or undesired for any other reason. It's one of the few ways to make the XTi a bit quieter. (I've actually had new dSLR owners ask me how to turn off the "shutter sound" the camera makes; such an option was available in the point-and-shoot camera they'd used previously.) Select Beep from the menu, press Set, and use the up/down cross keys to choose On or Off, as you prefer, as shown in Figure 3.6. Press Set again to activate your choice.

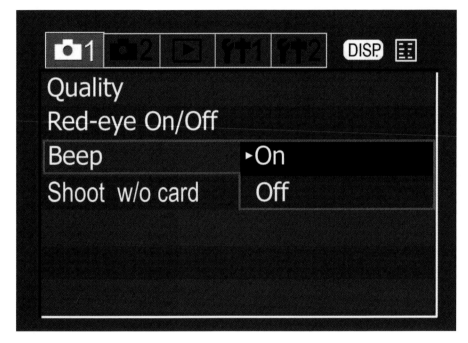

Figure 3.6 Silence your camera's beep when it might prove distracting.

Shoot Without Card

The last entry in the Set-Up 1 menu gives you the ability to snap off pictures without a Compact Flash card installed—or to lock up the camera if that is the case. It is sometimes called Play mode, because you can experiment with your camera's features or even hand your XTi to a friend to let them fool around, without any danger of pictures actually being taken. Back in our film days, we'd sometimes finish a roll, rewind the film back into its cassette surreptitiously, and then hand the camera to a child to take a few pictures—without actually wasting any film. It's hard to waste digital film, but Shoot Without Card mode is still appreciated by some. Choose this menu item, press Set, select On or Off, and press Set again to enable or disable this capability.

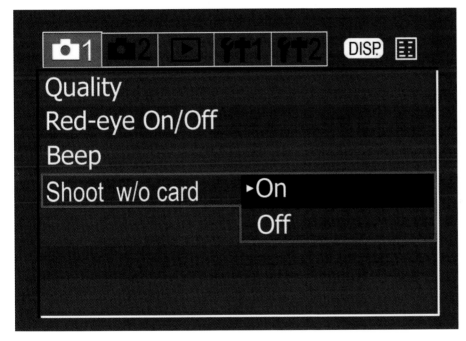

Figure 3.7 You can enable triggering the shutter even when no Compact Flash card is present.

Automatic Exposure Bracketing

The first entry on the Shooting 2 menu is AEB, or automatic exposure bracketing. Bracketing using the XTi's AEB feature is a way to shoot several consecutive exposures using different settings, to improve the odds that one will be exactly right. Select this menu choice, then use the left/right cross keys to spread or contract the three green dots on the -2/+1 scale until you've defined the range you want the bracket to cover, shown as one-stop jumps in Figure 3.8. When AEB is activated, the three bracketed shots will be exposed in this sequence: metered exposure, decreased exposure, and increased exposure. You'll find more information about exposure bracketing, including instructions on how to cancel it when you've finished using the feature, in Chapter 4.

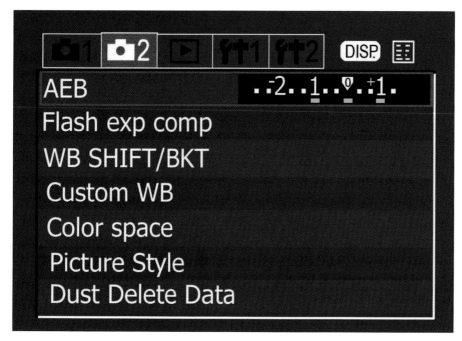

Figure 3.8 Set the range of the three bracketed exposures.

Flash Exposure Compensation

Use this menu choice to adjust the amount of additional or reduced exposure to be applied to images taken with electronic flash. You'll find a complete discussion of flash exposure in Chapter 7. When you've chosen this menu entry, use the left/right cross keys to select the desired amount, as shown in Figure 3.9. Moving the indicator to the left reduces flash exposure; to the right increases it. Press Set to lock in your exposure. Return to this menu to cancel flash exposure compensation when you no longer need it.

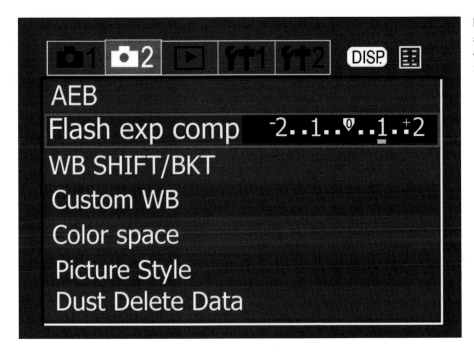

Figure 3.9 Dial in the amount of exposure compensation for electronic flash.

White Balance Shift and Bracketing

White balance bracketing can be performed in any JPEG-only mode (you can't use RAW or RAW+JPEG). This form of bracketing is similar to exposure bracketing, but with the added dimension of hue. When you select WB SHIFT/BKT, a screen like the one shown in Figure 3.10 appears. First, you turn the Main Dial to set the range of the shift in either the Green-Magenta dimension (turn the dial to the left to change the separation of the three dots representing the separate exposures), or in the Blue-Yellow/Amber dimension by turning the Main Dial to the right. Use the cross keys to move the bracket set around within the color space, and outside the Green-Magenta or Blue-Yellow/Amber axes.

Use the cross keys only after you've accumulated some experience in shifting around the white balance manually. In most cases, it's fairly easy to determine whether you want your image to be more green, magenta, blue, or yellow.

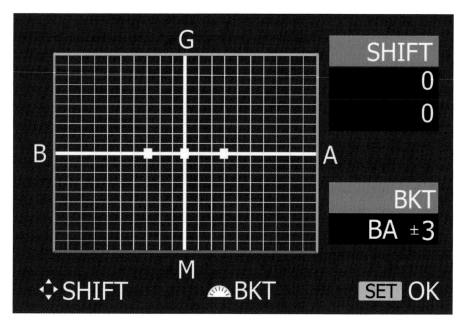

Figure 3.10 Use the cross keys to specify color balance bracketing using Green-Magenta bias or to specify Blue-Yellow/Amber bias.

Custom White Balance

If automatic white balance or one of the six preset settings available (Daylight, Shade, Cloudy/Twilight/Sunset, Tungsten, White Fluorescent, or Flash) aren't suitable, you can set a custom white balance using this menu option. The custom setting you establish will then be applied whenever you select Custom using the White Balance menu entry described earlier.

To set the white balance to an appropriate color temperature under the current ambient lighting conditions, focus manually (with the lens set on MF) on a plain white or gray object, such as a card or wall, making sure the object fills the center of the viewfinder. Then, take a photo. Next press the Menu button and select Custom WB from the Shooting 2 menu. Use the left/right cross keys until the reference image you just took appears, and press the Set button to store the white balance of the image as your Custom setting. You can use this custom white balance by pressing the WB button (the down cross key) and choosing Custom from the menu that appears on the LCD. You'll find more about setting white balance in Chapter 5.

A WHITE BALANCE LIBRARY

Shoot a selection of blank-card images under a variety of lighting conditions on a spare Compact Flash card. If you want to "recycle" one of the color temperatures you've stored, insert the card and set the Custom white balance to that of one of the images in your white balance library, as described in the previous section.

Color Space

You can select one of two color gamuts (the range of colors available to represent an image) using this menu entry, shown in Figure 3.11. Adobe RGB is an expanded color space useful for commercial and professional printing, and can reproduce a wider range of colors. Canon recommends against using this color space if your images will be displayed primarily on your computer screen or output by your personal printer. The sRGB setting is recommended for images that will be output locally on the user's own printer, as this color space matches that of the typical inkjet printer fairly closely. Strictly speaking, both color spaces can reproduce the exact same absolute number of colors (16.8 million when reduced to a 24-bit file from the original capture) but Adobe RGB spreads those colors over a larger space. Think of a box of crayons (the jumbo 16.8 million crayon variety). Some of the basic crayons from the original sRGB set have been removed and replaced with new hues not contained in the original box. Your "new" box contains colors that can't be reproduced by your computer monitor, but which work just fine with a commercial printing press.

BEST OF BOTH WORLDS

If you plan to use RAW+JPEG for most of your photos, go ahead and set sRGB as your color space. You'll end up with JPEGs suitable for output on your own printer, but you can still extract an Adobe RGB version from the RAW file at any time. It's like shooting two different color spaces at once—sRGB and Adobe RGB—and getting the best of both worlds.

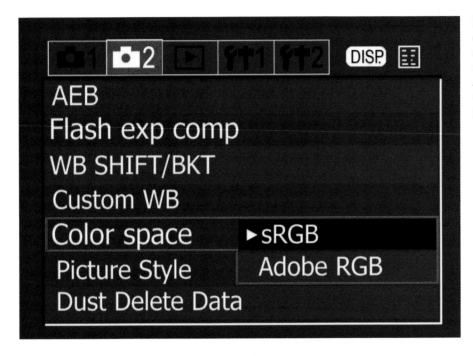

Figure 3.11 Use Color Space options to choose between sRGB (a display- and printer-friendly color gamut) and Adobe RGB (which can represent more colors for professional applications).

Picture Style

Picture styles let you choose a combination of sharpness, contrast, color saturation, and color tone settings that you can apply to all the pictures you take using a particular style. The Digital Rebel XTi has a "standard" picture style, plus preset styles for Portrait, Landscape, Neutral, and Faithful pictures (which can all be customized with your preferences), plus three user-definable settings you can apply to any sort of shooting situation you want, such as sports, architecture, or baby pictures. There is also a Monochrome picture style that allows you to adjust filter effects or add color toning to your black-and-white images.

The new Picture Styles feature is one of the most important upgrades the XTi has over the original XT, which had a Parameters setting that didn't allow as much customization. It had only two defined presets: Parameter 1 (used in Basic Zone modes by default, and designed to optimize images for printing directly from the camera), and Parameter 2, which was the default for Creative Zone modes, and was optimized for images displayed on computer monitors. The Rebel XT also had three user-definable Set 1, Set 2, and Set 3 parameters, and a B/W mode similar to the XTi's Monochrome picture style.

Picture styles are much more flexible. If you don't like one of the pre-defined styles, you can adjust it to suit your needs. You can also use those three User Definition files to create styles that are all your own. If you want rich, bright colors to emulate Velvia film or the work of legendary photographer Pete Turner, you can build your own color-soaked style. If you want soft, muted colors and less sharpness to create a romantic look, you can do that, too. Perhaps you'd like a setting with extra contrast for shooting outdoors on hazy or cloudy days.

After your styles are set up, picture styles are easy to access. Choose Picture Style from the Shooting Menu 2 and press Set to produce the menu screen shown in Figure 3.12. Use the Main Dial or up/down cross keys to scroll among the nine choices (the ones shown, plus Monochrome and User Def. 1, User Def. 2, and User Def. 3) and press Set to activate your choice. Then press the Menu button to exit the menu system. You can see that switching among picture styles is fast and easy enough to allow you to shift gears as often as you like during a shooting session.

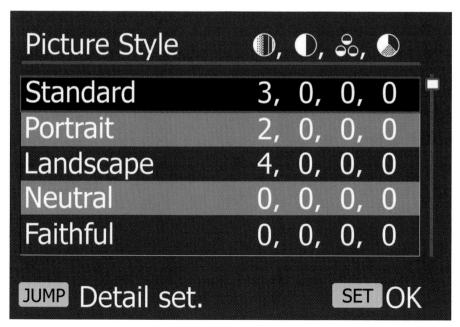

Figure 3.12 Nine different picture styles are available; these five plus four more not shown.

The Digital Rebel XT is smart enough to use picture styles on its own. When using one of the Basic Zone modes, the camera selects the Standard picture style automatically, except if you select the Portrait or Landscape modes. The Portrait and Landscape picture styles will be used (respectively) instead.

Defining Picture Styles

Canon makes interpreting current picture style settings and applying changes very easy. The current settings are shown as numeric values on the menu screen shown in Figure 3.12. Some camera vendors use word descriptions, like Sharp, Extra Sharp or Vivid, More Vivid that are difficult to relate to. The XT's settings, on the other hand, are values on uniform scales, with seven steps (from 1 to 7) for sharpness, and plus/minus four steps clustered around a zero (no change) value for contrast and saturation (so you can change from low contrast/low saturation, -4, to high contrast/high saturation, +4), as well as color tone (-4/reddish to +4/yellowish). The individual icons represent (left to right) Sharpness, Contrast, Saturation, and Color Tone. To change one of the existing picture styles, or to define your own, just follow these steps:

1. Access the Picture Style menu and use the Main Dial to scroll to the style you'd like to adjust.

2. Press the Jump button. The Main Dial can scroll among the four parameters, plus Default at the bottom of the screen, which restores the values to the preset numbers.

3. Press Set to change the values of one of the four parameters. If you're redefining one of the default presets, the menu screen will look like Figure 3.13, which represents the Landscape picture style.

4. Use the Main Dial to move the blue triangle to the value you want to use. Note that the previous value remains on the scale, represented by a gray triangle. This makes it easy to return to the original setting if you want.

5. Press the Set button to lock in that value, and then press the Menu button three times to back out of the menu system.

Any picture style that has been changed from its defaults will be shown in the Picture Style menu with blue highlighting the altered parameter. You don't need to worry about changing a picture style and then forgetting that you've modified it. A quick glance at the Picture Style menu will show you which styles and parameters have been changed. Figure 3.14 shows changes being made to a user-definable picture style.

Making changes in the Monochrome picture style is slightly different, as the Saturation and Color Tone parameters are replaced with Filter Effect and Toning Effect options. (Keep in mind that once you've taken a photo using a

Monochrome picture style, you can't convert the image back to full color.) You can choose from Yellow, Orange, Red, Green filters, or None, and specify Sepia, Blue, Purple or Green toning, or None. You can still set the Sharpness and Contrast parameters that are available with the other picture styles. Figure 3.15 shows filter effects being applied to the Monochrome picture style.

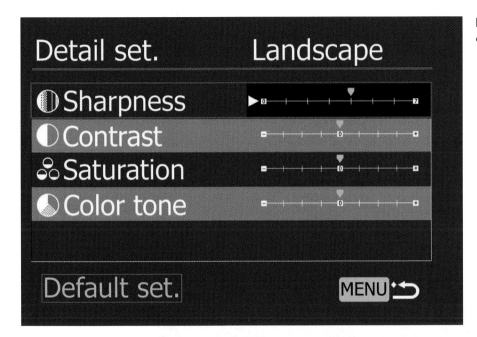

Figure 3.13 Each parameter can be changed separately.

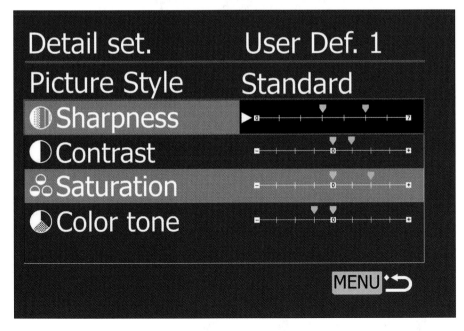

Figure 3.14 Set your own parameters for a user-definable style.

FILTERS VS. TONING

Although some of the color choices overlap, you'll get very different looks when choosing between Filter Effects and Toning Effects. Filter Effects add no color to the monochrome image. Instead, they reproduce the look of black-and-white film that has been shot through a color filter. That is, Yellow will make the sky darker and the clouds will stand out more, while Orange makes the sky even darker and sunsets more full of detail. The Red filter produces the darkest sky of all and darkens green objects, such as leaves. Human skin may appear lighter than normal. The Green filter has the opposite effect on leaves, making them appear lighter in tone. Figure 3.16 shows the same scene shot with no filter, then yellow, green, and red filters.

The Sepia, Blue, Purple, and Green toning effects, on the other hand, all add a color cast to your monochrome image. Use these when you want an old-time look or a special effect, without bothering to recolor your shots in an image editor.

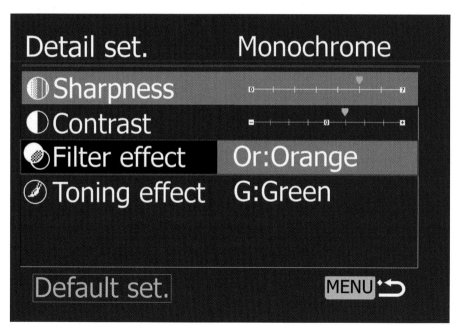

Figure 3.15 Select from among four color filters in the Monochrome picture style.

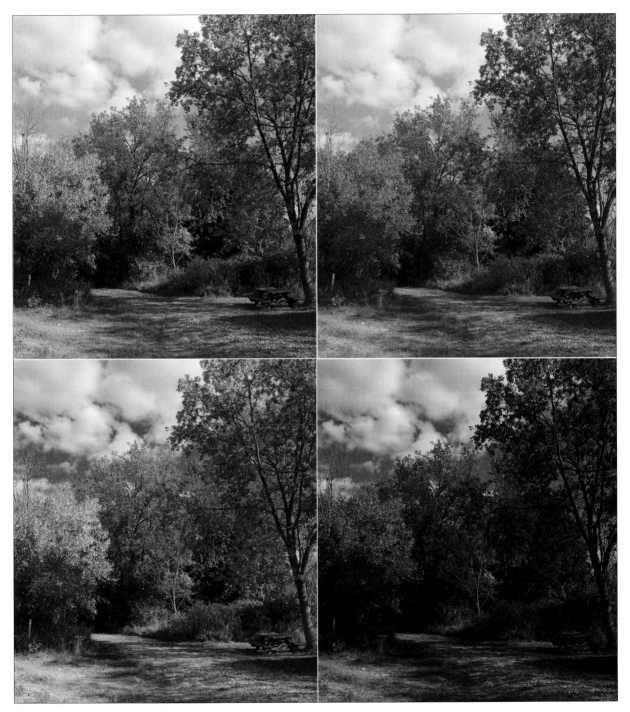

Figure 3.16 No filter (upper left); yellow filter (upper right); green filter (lower left); and red filter (lower right).

Dust Delete Data

This menu choice lets you "take a picture" of any dust or other particles that may be adhering to your sensor. The Rebel XTi will then append information about the location of this dust to your photos, so that Digital Photo Professional can use this reference information to identify dust in your images and remove it automatically. You should capture a Dust Delete Data photo from time to time as your final line of defense against sensor dust.

To use this feature, select Dust Delete Data to produce the screen shown in Figure 3.17. Select OK and press the Set button. The camera will first perform a self-cleaning operation by applying ultrasonic vibration to the low-pass filter that resides on top of the sensor. Then, a screen will appear asking you to press the shutter button. Point the XTi at a solid white card with the lens set on manual focus and rotate the focus ring to infinity. When you press the shutter release, the camera takes a photo of the card using aperture priority and f/22 (which provides enough depth-of-field (actually, in this case *depth-of-focus*) to image the dust sharply. The "picture" is not saved to your Compact Flash card but, rather, is stored in a special memory area in the camera. Finally, a "Data obtained" screen appears.

The Delete Dust Data information is retained in the camera until you update it by taking a new "picture." The XTi adds the information to each image file automatically.

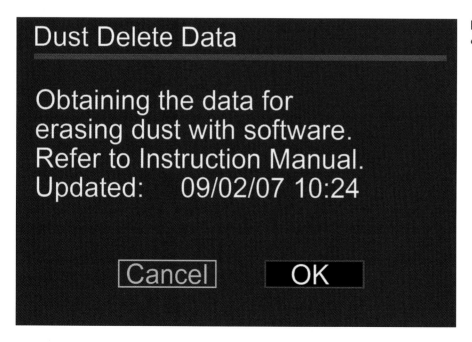

Figure 3.17 Capturing dust delete data.

Playback Menu Options

The blue-coded Playback menu (see Figure 3.18) is where you select options related to the display, review, and printing of the photos you've taken. The choices you'll find include:

- Protect
- Rotate
- Print Order
- Transfer Order
- Auto Play
- Review Time
- Histogram

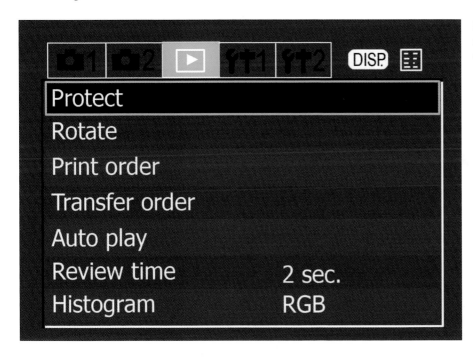

Figure 3.18 The Playback menu offers options for display, review, and printing.

Protect

If you want to prevent an image from being accidentally erased (either with the Erase button, or by using the Erase All feature), you can mark that image for protection. To protect one or more images, press the Menu button and choose Protect from the Playback menu. Then use the left/right cross keys or Main Dial to view the image to be protected. Press the Set button to apply the protection. A key icon will appear in the full information display. To remove protection, repeat the process. You can scroll among the other images on your memory card and protect/unprotect them in the same way. Image protection will not save your images from removal when the card is reformatted. I repeat: if you format your memory card, all images, including those that have been "protected" will be removed.

Rotate

While you can set the Digital Rebel XTi to automatically rotate images taken in a vertical orientation using the Auto Rotate option in the Set-Up menu, if you choose not to activate that feature, you can still manually rotate an image during playback using this menu selection. Select Rotate from the Playback menu, use the left/right cross keys or Main Dial to page through the available images on your memory card until the one you want to rotate appears, and then press Set. The image will appear on the screen rotated 90 degrees, as shown in Figure 3.19. Press Set again, and the image will be rotated 270 degrees.

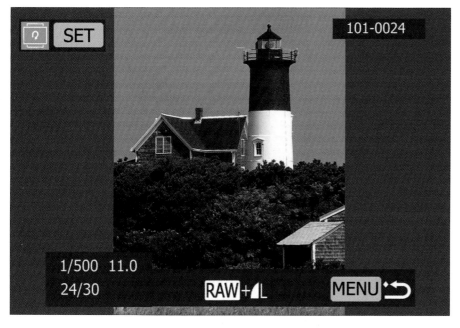

Figure 3.19 Vertically oriented shots can be rotated on the LCD using the Rotate command in the Playback menu.

Print Order

The Digital Rebel XTi supports the DPOF (Digital Print Order Format) that is now almost universally used by digital cameras to specify which images on your memory card should be printed, and the number of prints desired of each image. This information is recorded on the memory card, and can be interpreted by a compatible printer when the camera is linked to the printer using the USB cable, or when the memory card is inserted into a card reader slot on the printer itself. Photo labs are also equipped to read this data and make prints when you supply your memory card to them.

Transfer Order

You can specify which images are to be transferred to your personal computer when the Digital Rebel XTi is linked to the computer with the USB cable. Individual images are "marked" using a review and selection system similar to the one used to specify print orders. You'll find more about creating a transfer order in Chapter 8.

Auto Play

Auto Play is a convenient way to review images one after another, without the need to manually switch between them. To activate, just choose Auto Play from the Playback menu. During playback, you can press the Set button to pause the "slide show" (in case you want to examine an image more closely), or the Disp. button to change the amount of information displayed on the screen with each image. For example, you might want to review a set of images and their histograms to judge the exposure of the group of pictures. Press the Menu button to stop Auto Play.

Review Time

You can adjust the amount of time an image is displayed for review on the LCD after each shot is taken. You can elect to disable this review entirely, or choose display times of 2, 4, or 8 seconds. You can also set an indefinite display, which will keep your image on the screen until you use one of the other controls, such as the shutter button or Main Dial. Turning the review display off or choosing a brief duration can help preserve battery power. However, the Digital Rebel XTi will always override the review display when the shutter button is partially or fully depressed, so you'll never miss a shot because a previous image was on the screen. Choose Review Time from the Playback menu, and select Off, 2 sec., 4 sec., 8 sec., or Hold, as shown in Figure 3.20. If you want to retain an image on the screen for a longer period, but you don't want to use Hold as your default, press the Erase button under the LCD monitor. The image will display until you choose Cancel, Erase, or All from the menu that pops up at the bottom of the screen.

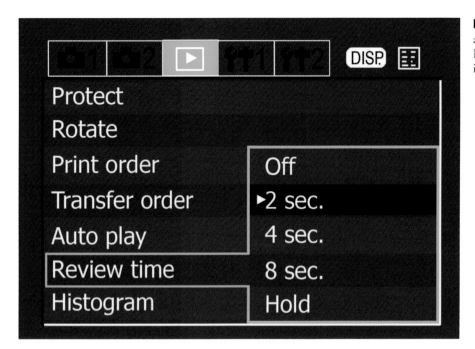

Figure 3.20 Adjust the time an image is displayed on the LCD for review after a picture is taken.

Histogram

The XTi can show either a Brightness histogram or set of three separate Red, Green, and Blue histograms in the full information display during picture review. Brightness histograms give you information about the overall tonal values present in the image. The RGB histograms can show more advanced users valuable data about specific channels that might be "clipped" (details are lost in the shadows or highlights). Select Histogram from the Playback menu and choose Brightness or RGB. You can read more about using histograms in Chapter 4.

Set-Up Menu Options

The orange-yellow-coded Set-Up 1 and Set-Up 2 menus (see Figures 3.21 and 3.22) are where you make adjustments on how your camera behaves during your shooting session, as differentiated from the Shooting menus, which adjust how the pictures are actually taken. Your choices include:

- Auto power off
- Auto rotate
- LCD brightness
- LCD auto off
- Date/Time

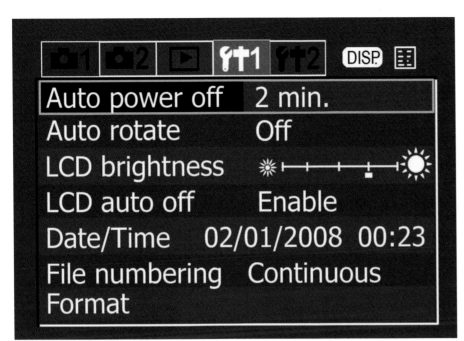

Figure 3.21 Set-Up 1 menu.

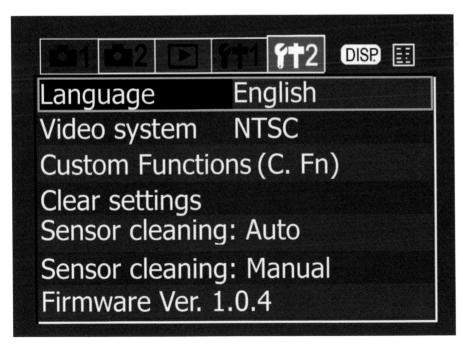

Figure 3.22 Set-Up 2 menu.

- File numbering
- Format
- Language
- Video system
- Custom Functions
- Clear settings
- Sensor cleaning: Auto
- Sensor cleaning: Manual
- Firmware version

Auto Power Off

This setting enables you to determine how long the Digital Rebel XTi remains active before shutting itself off. You can select 1, 2, 4, 8, 15, or 30 minutes, or Off, which leaves the camera turned on indefinitely. However, even if the camera has shut itself off, if the power switch remains in the On position, you can bring the camera back to life by pressing the shutter button.

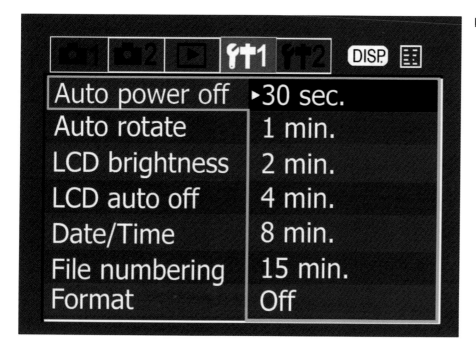

Figure 3.23 Auto Power Off.

SAVING POWER WITH THE Digital Rebel XTi

There are five settings and several techniques you can use to help you stretch the longevity of your XTi's battery. The first setting is the Review Time option described earlier under the Playback menu. The LCD uses a lot of juice, so reducing the amount of time it is used (either for automatic review or for manually playing back your images) can boost the effectiveness of your battery. Auto Power Off turns off most functions (metering and autofocus shut off by themselves about six seconds after you release the shutter button or take a picture) based on the delay you specify. The third setting is the LCD Brightness adjustment described later in this chapter. If you're willing to shade the LCD with your hand, you can often get away with lower brightness settings outdoors, which will further increase the useful life of your battery. The fourth setting is Custom Function 11 (described later in this section), which determines whether or not camera settings are shown on the LCD when the XTi is powered on. The fifth setting is the LCD auto off option, also described in this section, which enables/disables shutting off the LCD when the Display-off sensor detects that you've brought the XTi viewfinder to your eye.

The techniques? Use the internal flash as little as possible; no flash at all or fill flash use less power than a full blast. Turn off image stabilization if your lens has that feature and you feel you don't need it. When transferring pictures from your XTi to your computer, use a card reader instead of the USB cable. Linking your camera to your computer and transferring images using the cable takes longer and uses a lot more power.

Auto Rotate

You can turn this feature On or Off. When activated, the Digital Rebel XTi rotates pictures taken in vertical orientation on the LCD screen so you don't have to turn the camera to view them comfortably. However, this orientation also means that the longest dimension of the image is shown using the shortest dimension of the LCD, so the picture is reduced in size.

LCD Brightness

Choose this menu option and a thumbnail image with a grayscale strip appears on the LCD, as shown in Figure 3.24. Use the left/right cross keys or the Main Dial to adjust the brightness to a comfortable viewing level. Brighter settings use more battery power, but they can allow you to view an image on the LCD outdoors in bright sunlight. When you have the brightness you want, press the Set button to lock it in and return to the menu.

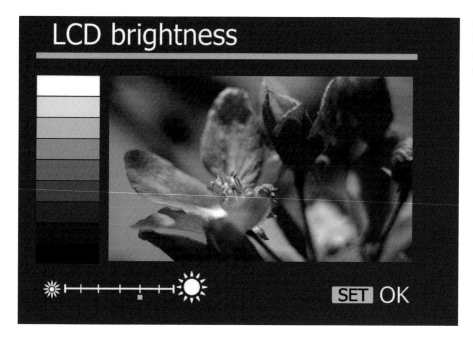

Figure 3.24 Adjust LCD brightness for easier viewing under varying ambient lighting conditions.

LCD Auto Off

When this setting is set to Enable, the LCD will turn off when you bring the viewfinder to your eye. Choose Disable, and the LCD will remain illuminated (although this uses more power). Although the Display-off sensor works well, some people find it annoying to have the LCD blank out when something other than their eye passes near the sensor, so they choose to disable this feature.

Date/Time

Use this option to set the date and time, which will be embedded in the image file along with exposure information and other data.

File Numbering

The Digital Rebel XTi will automatically apply a file number to each picture you take, using consecutive numbering for all your photos over a long period of time, spanning many different memory cards, starting over from scratch when you insert a new card, or when you manually reset the numbers. Numbers are applied from 0001 to 9999, at which time the camera creates a new folder on the card (100, 101, 102, and so forth), so you can have 0001 to 9999 in folder 100, and then numbering will start over in folder 101.

The camera keeps track of the last number used in its internal memory. That can lead to a few quirks you should be aware of. For example, if you insert a memory card that had been used with a different camera, the XTi may start numbering with the next number after the highest number used by the previous camera. (I once had a brand new XTi start numbering files in the 8000 range.) I'll explain how this can happen next.

On the surface, the numbering system seems simple enough: in the menu, you can choose Continuous, Automatic Reset, or Manual Reset. Here is how each works:

- **Continuous.** If you're using a blank/reformatted memory card, the XTi will apply a number that is one greater than the number stored in the camera's internal memory. If the card is not blank and contains images, then the next number will be one greater than the highest number on the card *or* in internal memory. Here are some examples.

  - You've taken 4235 shots with the camera, and you insert a blank/reformatted memory card. The next number assigned will be 4236, based on the value stored in internal memory.

  - You've taken 4235 shots with the camera, and you insert a memory card with a picture numbered 2728. The next picture will be numbered 4236.

  - You've taken 4235 shots with the camera, and you insert a memory card with a picture numbered 8281. The next picture will be numbered 8282, and that value will be stored in the camera's menu as the "high" shot number (and will be applied when you next insert a blank card).

- **Automatic Reset.** If you're using a blank/reformatted memory card, the next photo taken will be numbered 0001. If you use a card that is not blank, the next number will be one greater than the highest number found on the memory card. Each time you insert a memory card, the next number will either be 0001 or one higher than the highest already on the card.

■ **Manual Reset.** The XTi creates a new folder numbered one higher than the last folder created, and restarts the file numbers at 0001. Then, the camera uses the numbering scheme that was previously set, either Continuous or Automatic Reset, each time you subsequently insert a blank or non-blank memory card.

The Rebel XTi assigns a .JPG extension to JPEG files, and .CR2 extension for RAW files. File names for both types begin with IMG_.

Format

Use this item to erase everything on your memory card and set up a fresh file system ready for use. When you select Format, you'll see a display like Figure 3.25, showing the capacity of the card, how much of that space is currently in use, and two choices at the bottom of the screen to Cancel or OK (proceed with the format). A blue-green bar appears on the screen to show the progress of the formatting step.

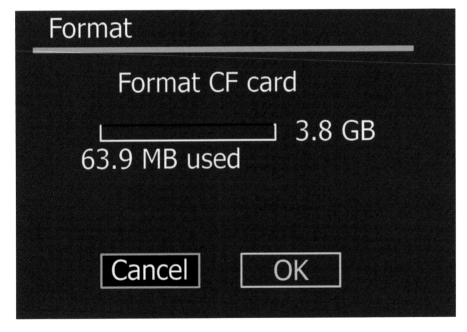

Figure 3.25 Reformatting your memory card removes all the data on it and prepares it for use.

Language

The first entry in the Set-Up 2 menu lets you choose from 15 languages for menu display, using the cross keys to navigate until the language you want to select is highlighted. Press the Set button to activate. Your choices include English, German, French, Dutch, Danish, Finnish, Italian, Norwegian, Swedish, Spanish, Russian, Simplified Chinese, Traditional Chinese, Korean, and Japanese.

If you accidentally set a language you don't read and find yourself with incomprehensible menus, don't panic. Press the Menu button, jump to the Set-Up 2 menu, and then locate the Set-Up menu choice at the top of the list, located immediately above the one displaying either NTSC or PAL in Roman characters (regardless of the language selected), and press the Set button to view the language selection screen.

Video System

This setting controls the output of the XTi through the AV cable when you're displaying images on an external monitor. You can select either NTSC, used in the United States, Canada, Mexico, many Central American, South American, and Caribbean countries, much of Asia, and other countries; or PAL, which is used in the UK, much of Europe, Africa, India, China, and parts of the Middle East.

Custom Functions

Your XTi's 11 Custom Functions features let you customize the behavior of your camera in a variety of ways when using Creative Zone modes. You can find the Custom Function menu in the Set-Up 2 menu.

Canon uses easy Custom Function numbers (C.Fn-01 through C.Fn-11) to represent each of the parameters you can set, and simple numeric values for their individual options. Both the numbers and values are shown on a single screen (see Figure 3.26), so you can access that screen and always tell at a glance which Custom Functions have been set, and, once you've learned a few of the option numbers, exactly what setting has been made. That might sound a little daunting, but, in practice, you won't change many Custom Functions very often, so you'll quickly learn the significance of the settings screen.

For example, if you use the Long Exposure Noise Reduction feature a lot, after you've used the C. Fn-02 function a few times, you'll be able to check the Custom Function screen, glance at the 02 in the top line of functions, and know that if you see a 1 in that spot, noise reduction is turned on. If you see a zero, you'll remember that it is switched off. You'll feel like an expert in no time.

But first, you'll want to take the time to familiarize yourself with the Custom Function menu. Each of the functions is set in exactly the same way, so I'm not going to bog you down with a bunch of illustrations showing how to make this setting or that. One quick run-through using Figure 3.26 should be enough. Here are the key parts of the Custom Function screen:

- **Function name.** A label right under the Custom Function title tells you the name of the function that's currently selected. You don't need to memorize the function numbers.

- **Function number.** The function number appears in two places. In the upper-right corner you'll find a box with the current function clearly designated. In the lower half of the screen is a line of numbers, from 01 to 11. The currently selected function will have an amber underline beneath it.

- **Current setting.** Underneath each Custom Function is a number from 0 to 5 that represents the current setting for that function.

- **Option selection.** When a function is selected, the currently selected option appears in a highlighted box. As you scroll up and down the option list, the setting in the box changes to indicate an alternate value.

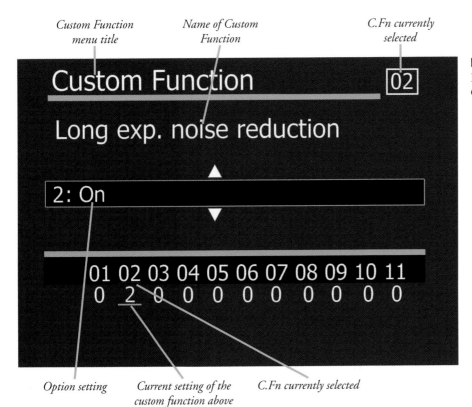

Custom Function menu title *Name of Custom Function* *C.Fn currently selected*

Figure 3.26 The Canon Digital Rebel XTi has 11 Custom Functions.

Option setting *Current setting of the custom function above* *C.Fn currently selected*

In the listings that follow, I'm going to depart from the sometimes-cryptic labels Canon assigns to each Custom Function in the menu, and instead categorize them by what they actually do. I'm also going to provide you with a great deal more information on each option and what it means to your photography.

C.Fn-01: Function of the Set Button and Cross Keys

You already know that the Set button is used to select a choice or option when navigating the menus. However, when you're taking photos, it has no function at all. You can easily remedy that with the C.Fn-01 SET function when shooting. This setting allows you to assign one of four different actions to the Set key. Because the button is within easy reach of your right thumb, that makes it quite convenient for accessing a frequently used function. When C.Fn-01 is set to 0, the Set button has no additional function, and options 1 through 4 assign an action to the button during shooting.

- **0: SET: Picture Style.** During shooting, pressing the Set button produces the Picture Style selection screen.

- **1: SET: Quality.** Pressing the Set button activates the Quality selection menu. You can cycle among the various quality options by rotating the Main Dial or pressing the cross keys.

- **2: SET: Flash exp. comp**. Pressing Set displays the flash exposure compensation screen.

- **3: SET: Playback.** Pressing Set produces the same effect as pressing the Playback button.

- **4: Cross keys: AF frame select.** Allows using the cross keys to choose an autofocus point directly after depressing the shutter release halfway, without pressing the AF/Zoom in button. This choice also changes the Set button's behavior so that pressing it while shooting selects the center autofocus point.

C.Fn-02: Reducing Noise Effects at Shutter Speeds of One Second or Longer

Visual noise is that awful graininess that shows up as multicolored specks in images, and this setting—C.Fn-02 Long exposure noise reduction—helps you manage it. In some ways, noise is like the excessive grain found in some high-speed photographic films. However, while photographic grain is sometimes used as a special effect, it's rarely desirable in a digital photograph.

The visual noise-producing process is something like listening to a CD in your car, and then rolling down all the windows. You're adding sonic noise to the audio signal, and while increasing the CD player's volume may help a bit, you're still contending with an unfavorable signal to noise ratio that probably mutes tones (especially higher treble notes) that you really want to hear.

The same thing happens when the analog signal is amplified: You're increasing the image information in the signal, but boosting the background fuzziness at the same time. Tune in a very faint or distant AM radio station on your car stereo. Then turn up the volume. After a certain point, turning up the volume further no longer helps you hear better. There's a similar point of diminishing returns for digital sensor ISO increases and signal amplification, as well.

These processes create several different kinds of noise. Noise can be produced from high ISO settings. As the captured information is amplified to produce higher ISO sensitivities, some random noise in the signal is amplified along with the photon information. Increasing the ISO setting of your camera raises the threshold of sensitivity so that fewer and fewer photons are needed to register as an exposed pixel. Yet, that also increases the chances of one of those phantom photons being counted among the real-life light particles, too.

Fortunately, the Digital Rebel XTi's sensor and its digital processing chip are optimized to produce the low noise levels, so ratings as high as ISO 800 can be used routinely (although there will be some noise, of course). Use noise reduction to further suppress noise, and at the higher ISO 1600 setting.

A second way noise is created is through longer exposures. Extended exposure times allow more photons to reach the sensor, but increase the likelihood that some photosites will react randomly even though not struck by a particle of light. Moreover, as the sensor remains switched on for the longer exposure, it heats, and this heat can be mistakenly recorded as if it were a barrage of photons. Custom Function 2 can be used to tailor the amount of noise-canceling performed by the digital signal processor.

- **0: Off.** Disables long exposure noise reduction. Use this setting when you want the maximum amount of detail present in your photograph, even though higher noise levels will result. This setting also eliminates the extra time needed to take a picture caused by the noise reduction process. If you plan to use only lower ISO settings (thereby reducing the noise caused by ISO amplification), the noise levels produced by longer exposures may be acceptable. For example, you might be shooting a waterfall at ISO 100 with the camera mounted on a tripod, using a neutral density filter and long exposure to cause the water to blur, as shown in Figure 3.27. To maximize detail in the non-moving portions of your photos, you can switch off long exposure noise reduction.

- **1: Auto.** Applies noise reduction for exposures longer than 1 second if the camera detects long exposure noise.

- **2: On.** When this setting is activated, the XTi applies dark frame subtraction to all exposures longer than 1 second. At this setting, the camera doesn't "decide" whether or not to apply noise reduction. You might want to use this option when you're working with high ISO settings (which will already have noise boosted a bit) and want to make sure that any additional noise from long exposures is eliminated, too.

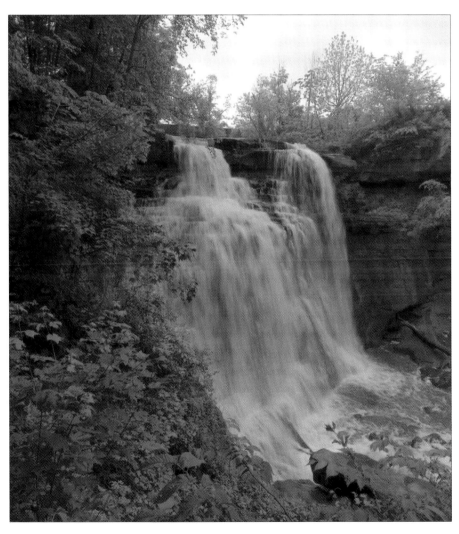

Figure 3.27 When lower ISO settings are used, as in this two-second exposure of a waterfall, long exposure noise reduction might not be needed.

C.Fn-03: Flash Synchronization Speed When Using Aperture Priority

You'll find this setting—C.Fn-03 Flash sync speed in Av mode—useful when using flash. When you're set to aperture priority mode, you select a fixed f/stop and the Digital Rebel XTi chooses an appropriate shutter speed. That works fine when you're shooting by available light. However, when you're using flash, the flash itself provides virtually all of the illumination that makes the main exposure, and the shutter speed determines how much, if any, of the ambient light contributes to a second, non-flash exposure. Indeed, if the camera or subject is moving, you can end up with two distinct exposures in the same frame: the sharply defined flash exposure, and a second, blurry "ghost" picture created by the ambient light.

If you *don't* want that second exposure, you should use the highest shutter speed that will synchronize with your flash (that's 1/200th second with the Digital Rebel XTi). If you do want the ambient light to contribute to the exposure (say, to allow the background to register in night shots, or to use the ghost image as a special effect), use a slower shutter speed. For brighter backgrounds, you'll need to put the camera on a tripod or other support to avoid the blurry ghosts.

- **0: Auto.** The XTi will vary the shutter speed in Av mode from 1/30th to 1/200th second, allowing ambient light to partially illuminate the scene in combination with the flash exposure, as at right in Figure 3.28.

- **1: 1/200th sec. (fixed).** The camera always uses 1/200th second as its shutter speed in Av mode, reducing the effect of ambient light and, probably, rendering the background dark.

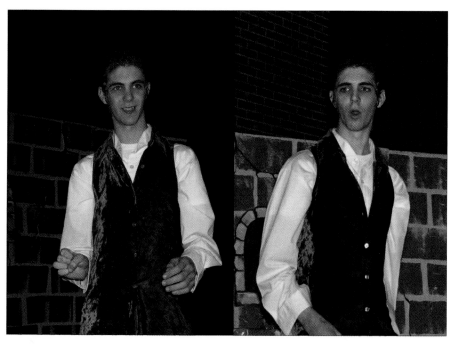

Figure 3.28 At left, a 1/200th second shutter speed eliminated ambient light so only the flash illuminated the scene; at right, a 1/60th second shutter speed let the ambient light supplement the electronic flash.

C.Fn-04: What Happens When You Partially Depress the Shutter Release/Press the AE Lock Button

This setting—C.Fn-04 Shutter button/AE Lock button—controls the behavior of the shutter release and the AE lock button (*). In the option list below, the first action in the pair represents what happens when you press the shutter release; the second action says what happens when the * button is pressed.

- **0: AF/AE lock.** With this option, pressing the shutter release halfway locks in focus; pressing the * button locks exposure. Use this when you want to control each of these actions separately.

- **1: AE lock/AF.** Pressing the shutter release halfway locks exposure; pressing the * button locks autofocus. This setting swaps the action of the two buttons compared to the default 0 option.

- **2: AF/AF lock, no AE lock.** Pressing the AE lock button interrupts the autofocus and locks focus in AI Servo mode. Exposure is not locked at all until the actual moment of exposure when you press the shutter release all the way. This mode is handy when moving objects may pass in front of the camera (say, a tight end crosses your field of view as you focus on the quarterback) and you want to be able to avoid change of focus. Note that you can't lock in exposure using this option.

- **3: AE/AF, no AE lock.** Pressing the shutter release halfway locks in autofocus, except in AI Servo mode, in which you can use the * button to start or stop autofocus. Exposure is always determined at the moment the picture is taken, and cannot be locked.

C.Fn-05: Activation of the Autofocus Assist Lamp

This setting—C.Fn-05 AF-assist beam—determines when the AF assist lamp is activated to emit a pulse of light that helps provide enough contrast for the Digital Rebel XTi to focus on a subject.

- **0: Emits.** The AF assist lamp is lit whenever light levels are too low for accurate focusing using the ambient light.

- **1: Does not emit.** The AF assist lamp is disabled. You might want to use this setting when shooting at concerts, weddings, or darkened locations where the lamp might prove distracting or discourteous.

- **2: Only external flash emits.** The built-in AF assist lamp is disabled, but if a Canon EX dedicated flash unit is attached to the camera, its AF assist beam will be used when needed. Because the flash unit's AF assist is more powerful, you'll find this option useful when you're using flash and are photographing objects in dim light that are more than a few feet away from the camera (and thus not likely to be illuminated usefully by the Digital Rebel XTi's built-in lamp).

C.Fn-06: Exposure Adjustment Increments

This setting—C.Fn-06 Exposure level increments—tells the Digital Rebel XTi the size of the "jumps" it should use when making exposure adjustments—either one-third or one-half stop. The increment you specify here applies to f/stops, shutter speeds, EV changes, and autoexposure bracketing.

- **0: 1/3 stop.** Choose this setting when you want the finest increments between shutter speeds and/or f/stops. For example, the XTi will use shutter speeds such as 1/60th, 1/80th, 1/100th, and 1/125th second, and f/stops such as f/5.6, f/6.3, f/7.1, and f/8, giving you (and the autoexposure system) maximum control.

- **1: 1/2 stop.** Use this setting when you want larger and more noticeable changes between increments. The XTi will apply shutter speeds such as 1/60th, 1/125th, 1/250th, and 1/500th second, and f/stops including f/5.6, f/6.7, f/8, f/9.5, and f/11.

C.Fn-07: Whether It Is Possible to Lock Up the Viewing Mirror Prior to an Exposure

The C.Fn-07 Mirror lockup function determines whether the reflex viewing mirror will be flipped up out of the way in advance of taking a picture, thereby eliminating any residual blurring effects caused by the minuscule amount of camera shake that can be produced if (as is the case normally) the mirror is automatically flipped up an instant before the actual exposure. When shooting telephoto pictures with a very long lens, or close-up photography at extreme magnifications, even this tiny amount of vibration can have an impact.

You'll want to make this adjustment immediately prior to needing the mirror lockup function, because once it has been enabled, the mirror *always* flips up, and picture taking becomes a two-press operation. That is, you press the shutter release once to lock exposure and focus, and to swing the mirror out of the way. Your viewfinder goes blank (of course, the mirror's blocking it). Press the shutter release a second time to actually take the picture. Because the goal of mirror lockup is to produce the sharpest picture possible, and because of the viewfinder blackout, you can see that the camera should be mounted on a tripod prior to taking the picture, and, to avoid accidentally shaking the camera yourself, using an off-camera shutter release mechanism, such as the Canon Remote Switch RS-80N3 or Timer Remote Controller TC-80N3, is a good idea.

- **0: Disable.** Mirror lockup is not possible.

- **1: Enable.** Mirror lockup is activated and will be used for every shot. After 30 seconds, this setting is automatically canceled.

Canon lists some important warnings and techniques related to using mirror lockup in the Digital Rebel XTi manual, and I want to emphasize them here and add a few of my own, even if it means a bit of duplication. Better safe than sorry!

■ **Don't use ML manual for sensor cleaning.** Though locked up, the mirror will flip down again automatically after 30 seconds, which you don't want to happen while you're poking around the sensor with a brush, swab, or air jet. There's a separate menu item—Sensor Cleaning: Manual—for sensor house-keeping. You can find more about this topic later in this chapter and in Chapter 9.

■ **Avoid long exposure to extra-bright scenes.** The shutter curtain, normally shielded from incoming light by the mirror, is fully exposed to the light being focused on the focal plane by the lens mounted on the XTi. When the mirror is locked up, you certainly don't want to point the camera at the sun, and even beach or snow scenes may be unsafe if the shutter curtain is exposed to their illumination for long periods.

■ **ML can't be used in continuous shooting modes.** The Digital Rebel XTi will use single shot mode for mirror lockup exposures, regardless of the sequence mode you've selected.

■ **Use self-timer to eliminate second button press.** If you've activated the self-timer, the mirror will flip up when you press the shutter button down all the way, and then the picture will be taken two seconds later. This technique can help reduce camera shake further if you don't have a remote release available and have to use a finger to press the shutter button.

C.Fn-08: Changing Flash Metering Mode from Evaluative to Averaging

The C.Fn-08 E-TTL II Custom Function allows you to specify the exposure method used to determine flash exposure, and to switch flash exposure compensation on or off. You can find out more about how the Canon Digital Rebel XTi calculates flash exposure in Chapter 7.

■ **0: Evaluative.** The Digital Rebel XTi uses the evaluative metering system to gauge correct flash exposure in all cases, including fill-flash situations.

■ **1: Average.** Flash exposure is measured over the entire flash coverage area, and automatic flash exposure compensation is disabled.

C.Fn-09: When the Flash Is Fired During an Exposure

The C.Fn-09 Shutter curtain sync function tells the XTi whether to trip the flash at the beginning of an exposure or at the end. When a flash picture is taken, the XTi's focal plane shutter opens a curtain to fully expose the sensor and allow the flash to provide illumination for the picture. Then, a second curtain follows the first to cover the sensor again. You can specify whether the flash should be tripped as soon as the first curtain exposes the sensor or whether the flash should be delayed until just before the second curtain closes (which can be anywhere from 1/200th to some seconds later). This timing determines the position of any "ghost" images caused when the subject or camera moves during the exposure. With first-curtain sync, the ghost will appear "ahead" of the subject in the direction of movement (because the flash exposure has already been taken, but the ambient light exposure continues). With second-curtain sync, the ghost image will "trail" the subject, because the flash exposure isn't made until the very end. You'll find a longer explanation and tips for using this effect as well as some examples in Chapter 7.

- **0: 1st-curtain sync.** The flash fires at the beginning of the exposure.

- **1: 2nd-curtain sync.** The flash fires at the end of the exposure, which can produce more natural-looking effects (think streaking superhero) when the ghost image, if any, trails the subject.

C.Fn-10: Magnified View

The C.Fn-10 determines when you can view a magnified image on the LCD by holding down the Print/Share button and pressing the Zoom In button.

- **0: Display.** Can show the magnified view during image playback.

- **1: Image review and playback.** You can activate the magnified view during image review after a shot is taken, or during playback.

C.Fn-11: LCD Display When Power Is Turned On

The C.Fn-11 controls whether the camera settings are shown on the LCD when the camera is powered up.

- **0: Display.** The Digital Rebel XTi always shows settings when the camera is turned on. You can turn the status display off by pressing the Disp. button.

- **1: Retain power OFF status.** The XTi only shows camera settings when powered up if these settings were on display when the camera was turned off. If you turned off the status display (with the Disp. button) just before the camera is turned off, the display will not be shown the next time the camera is switched on.

Clear Settings

This choice can be used to either clear all camera settings or clear all Custom Functions. You can also choose Cancel if you change your mind, as shown in Figure 3.29. When you choose to clear camera settings, both shooting parameters and image recording parameters will be returned to their default values. Exposure and flash compensation values will be set to zero, white balance/color correction and bracketing features will be turned off, and the XTi will be set to shoot Large JPEG photos using evaluative metering, the standard Picture Style, and ISO 100. However, any Custom Functions you've made will be retained.

Select Clear All Custom Functions, and any C.Fn. settings that don't have zero values will be changed back to the default zero. To reset both camera settings and Custom Functions, you must perform both steps. Custom Functions are covered earlier in this chapter.

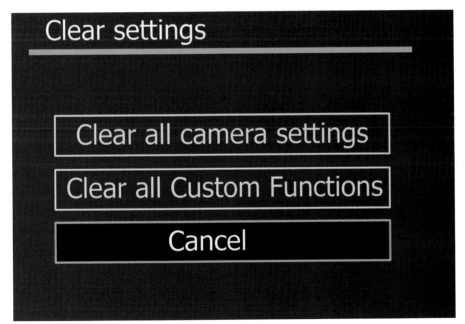

Figure 3.29 Reset your camera to its default values for both shooting and recording settings, and Custom Functions.

Sensor Cleaning: Auto

One of the Rebel XTi's best new features is the automatic sensor cleaning system that reduces or eliminates the need to clean your camera's sensor manually using brushes, swabs, or bulb blowers (you'll find instructions on how to do that in Chapter 9). Canon has applied anti-static coatings to the sensor and other portions of the camera body interior to counter charge build-ups that attract dust. A separate filter over the sensor vibrates ultrasonically each time the XTi is powered on or off, shaking loose any dust.

Use this menu entry (shown in Figure 3.30) to enable or disable automatic sensor cleaning on power up (select Set Up to choose), or to activate automatic cleaning during a shooting session (select Clean Now).

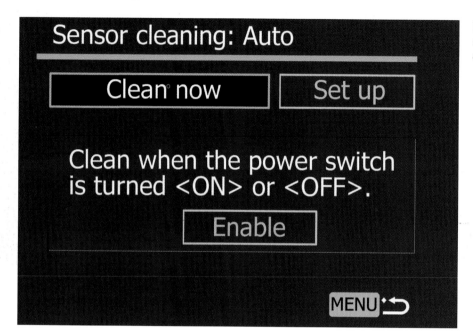

Figure 3.30 You can activate automatic sensor cleaning, or enable/disable it on power up.

Sensor Cleaning: Manual

Use this to flip up the mirror and open the shutter for sensor cleaning. If the battery level is too low to safely carry out the cleaning operation, the XTi will let you know and refuse to proceed, unless you use the optional AC Adapter Kit ACK-E2. You can read more about sensor cleaning in Chapter 9.

Firmware Version

You can see the current firmware release in use in the menu listing. If you want to update to a new firmware version, insert a memory card containing the binary file, and press the Set button to begin the process. You can read more about firmware updates in Chapter 9.

4

Getting the Right Exposure

The Canon EOS Digital Rebel XTi gives you complete control over many of the basic functions of the camera. These include exposure, sensitivity (ISO settings), color balance, focus, and image parameters like sharpness and contrast. You can choose to let the camera set any or all of these for you automatically. Or, you can opt to fine-tune how the XTi applies its automatic settings. If you want absolute creative control over any of these functions, you can set them manually, too. That's why the Digital Rebel XTi is such a versatile tool for creating images.

This chapter explains the shooting basics of exposure, either as an introduction or as a refresher course, depending on your current level of expertise. When you finish this chapter, you'll understand most of what you need to know to take photographs in a broad range of situations.

Getting a Handle on Exposure

Exposure can make or break your photo. Correct exposure brings out the detail in the areas you want to picture, providing the range of tones and colors you need to create the desired image. Poor exposure can cloak important details in shadow, or wash them out in glare-filled featureless expanses of white. However, getting the perfect exposure can be tricky, because digital sensors can't capture all the tones we are able to see. If the range of tones in an image is extensive, embracing both inky black shadows and bright highlights, we often must settle for an exposure that renders most of those tones—but not all—in a way that best suits the photo we want to produce.

There are four things within our control that affect exposure, listed in "chronological" order (that is, as the light moves from the subject to the sensor):

- **Reflected, transmitted, or emitted light.** We see and photograph objects by light that is reflected from our subjects, transmitted (say, from translucent objects that are lit from behind), or emitted (by a candle or television screen). When more or less light reaches the lens from the subject, we need to adjust the exposure. This part of the equation is under our control to the extent we can increase the amount of light falling on or passing through the subject (by adding extra light sources or using reflectors), or by pumping up the light that's emitted (by increasing the brightness of the glowing object).

- **Light transmitted by the lens.** Not all the illumination that reaches the front of the lens makes it all the way through. Filters can remove some of the light before it enters the lens. Inside the lens barrel is a variable-sized diaphragm called an *aperture* that dilates and contracts to admit more or less of the light that enters the lens. You, or the XTi's autoexposure system, can control exposure by varying the size of the aperture. The relative size of the aperture is called the *f/stop*.

- **Light passing through the shutter.** Once light passes through the lens, the amount of time the sensor is exposed to that light is determined by the XTi's shutter, which can remain open for as long as 30 seconds (or even longer if you use the Bulb setting) or as briefly as 1/4000th second.

- **Light captured by the sensor.** All the light falling onto the sensor is captured. If the number of photons reaching a particular photosite doesn't pass a set threshold, no information is recorded. Similarly, if too much light illuminates a pixel in the sensor, then the excess isn't recorded or, worse, spills over to contaminate adjacent pixels. We can modify the minimum and maximum number of pixels that contribute to image detail by adjusting the ISO setting. At higher ISOs, the incoming light is amplified to boost the effective sensitivity of the sensor.

These four factors—quantity of light, light passed by the lens, the amount of time the shutter is open, and the sensitivity of the sensor—all work proportionately and reciprocally to produce an exposure. That is, if you double the amount of light, increase the aperture by one stop, make the shutter speed twice as long, or boost the ISO setting 2X, you'll get twice as much exposure. Similarly, you can increase any of these factors while decreasing one of the others by a similar amount to keep the same exposure.

F/STOPS AND SHUTTER SPEEDS

If you're *really* new to more advanced cameras you might need to know that the lens aperture, or f/stop, is a ratio, much like a fraction, which is why f/2 is larger than f/4, just as 1/2 is larger than 1/4. However, f/2 is actually *four times* as large as f/4. (If you remember your high school geometry, you'll know that to double the area of a circle, you multiply its diameter by the square root of two: 1.4.)

Lenses are usually marked with intermediate f/stops that represent a size that's twice as much/half as much as the previous aperture. So, a lens might be marked:

f/2, f/2.8, f/4, f/5.6, f/8, f/11, f/16, f/22

with each larger number representing an aperture that admits half as much light as the one before, as shown in Figure 4.1.

Shutter speeds are actual fractions (of a second), but the numerator is omitted in displays, so that 60, 125, 250, 500, 1000, and so forth represent 1/60th, 1/125th, 1/250th, 1/500th, and 1/1000th second.

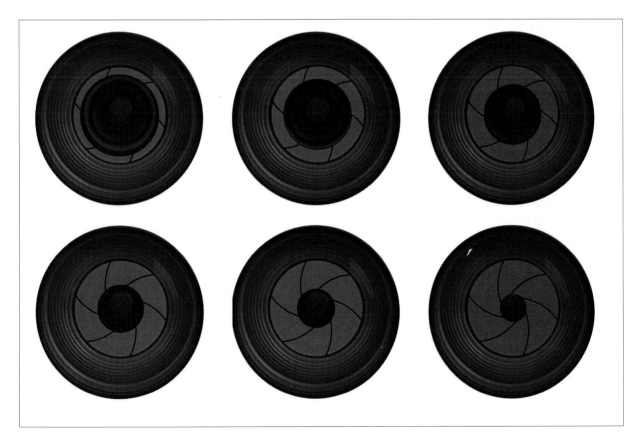

Figure 4.1 Top row (left to right): f/2, f/2.8, f/4; bottom row: f/5.6, f/8, f/11.

Most commonly, exposure settings are made using the aperture and shutter speed, followed by adjusting the ISO sensitivity if it's not possible to get the preferred exposure (that is, the one that uses the "best" f/stop or shutter speed for the depth-of-field or action stopping we want). Table 4.1 shows equivalent (same) exposure settings using various shutter speeds and f/stops.

Table 4.1 Equivalent Exposures

Shutter Speed	f/stop
1/30th second	f/22
1/60th second	f/16
1/125th second	f/11
1/250th second	f/8
1/500th second	f/5.6
1/1000th second	f/4
1/2000th second	f/2.8
1/4000th second	f/2

When the XTi is set for P mode, the metering system selects the correct exposure for you automatically, but you can change quickly to an equivalent exposure by pressing the shutter-release button ("locking" the current exposure), and then spinning the Main Dial until the desired equivalent exposure combination is displayed. This Program Shift mode does not work when you're using flash, and only applies to the next exposure you take; if you want to shift again for your next shot, you'll need to repeat the adjustment process.

In Aperture Priority (Av) and Shutter Priority (Tv) modes, you can change to an equivalent exposure, but only by adjusting either the aperture (the camera chooses the shutter speed) or shutter speed (the camera selects the aperture). I'll cover all these exposure modes later in the chapter.

How the Digital Rebel XTi Calculates Exposure

Your Canon Digital Rebel XTi calculates exposure by measuring the light that passes through the lens and bounces up by the mirror to sensors located in the focusing screen, using a pattern you can select (more on that later) and based on the assumption that each area being measured reflects about the same amount of light as a neutral gray card with 18 percent reflectance. That assumption is necessary, because different subjects reflect different amounts of light. In a photo containing a white cat and a dark gray cat, the white cat might reflect five times as much light as the gray cat. An exposure based on the white cat will cause the gray cat to appear to be black, while an exposure based only on the gray cat will make the white cat washed out. Light-measuring devices handle this by assuming that the areas measured average a standard value of 18 percent gray, a figure that's long been used as a rough standard (not all vendors calibrate their metering for exactly 18 percent gray) for many years.

You could, in many cases, arrive at a reasonable exposure by pointing your XTi at an evenly lit object, such as an actual gray card or the palm of your hand (but increase the exposure by one stop in the latter case, because the human palm—of any ethnic group—reflects about twice as much light as a gray card). It's more practical, though, to use your XTi's system to meter the actual scene, using the options available to you when using one of the Creative Zone modes (P, Tv, Av, M, and A-DEP). (In Basic Zone modes, the metering decisions are handled entirely by the camera's programming.) (See Figure 4.2.)

F/STOPS VERSUS STOPS

In photography parlance, f/stop always means the aperture or lens opening. However, for lack of a current commonly used word for one exposure increment, the term *stop* is often used. (In the past, EV served this purpose, but Exposure Value and its abbreviation has been inextricably intertwined with its use in describing Exposure Compensation.) In this book, when I say "stop" by itself (no *f*) I mean one whole unit of exposure, and I am not necessarily referring to an actual f/stop or lens aperture. So, adjusting the exposure by "one stop" can mean changing to the next shutter speed increment (say, from 1/125th second to 1/250th second) or the next aperture (such as f/4 to f/5.6). Similarly, 1/3 stop or 1/2 stop increments can mean either shutter speed or aperture changes, depending on the context. Be forewarned.

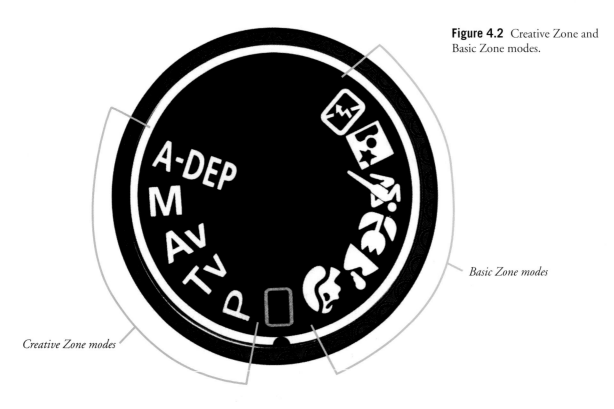

Figure 4.2 Creative Zone and Basic Zone modes.

Basic Zone modes

Creative Zone modes

In most cases, your camera's light meter will do a good job of calculating the right exposure, especially if you use the exposure tips in the next section. But if you want to double-check, or feel that exposure is especially critical, take the light reading off an object of known reflectance. Photographers sometimes carry around an 18 percent gray card (available from any camera store) and, for critical exposures, actually use that card, placed in the subject area, to measure exposure. If the card is present in at least one final picture, it can be used to zero in on color balance in an image editor.

To meter properly in the Creative Zone, you'll want to choose both the *metering method* (how light is evaluated) and *exposure method* (how the appropriate shutter speeds and apertures are chosen). I'll describe both in the following sections.

Choosing a Metering Method

The XTi has three different schemes used in Creative Zone modes for evaluating the light received by its exposure sensors. You can choose among them while the camera's exposure system is active (tap the shutter release to wake it up) by pressing the left cross key to produce the selection screen shown in Figure 4.3, and then pressing the left/right cross keys until the mode you want is selected. Press the Set button to confirm your choice.

- **Evaluative.** The XTi slices up the frame into 35 different zones, shown in Figure 4.4. The zones used are linked to the autofocus system. The camera evaluates the measurements, giving extra emphasis to the metering zones that indicate sharp focus, to make an educated guess about what kind of picture you're taking, based on examination of thousands of different real-world photos. For example, if the top sections of a picture are much lighter than the bottom portions, the algorithm can assume that the scene is a landscape photo with lots of sky. This mode is the best all-purpose metering method for most pictures. I'll explain how to choose an autofocus/exposure zone in the section on autofocus operation later in this chapter.

- **Partial.** This is a *faux* spot mode, using roughly nine percent of the image area to calculate exposure, which, as you can see by Figure 4.5, is a rather large spot. Use this mode if the background is much brighter or darker than the subject.

- **Center-weighted.** In this mode, the exposure meter emphasizes a zone in the center of the frame to calculate exposure, as roughly shown in Figure 4.5, on the theory that, for most pictures, the main subject will be located in the center. Center-weighting works best for portraits, architectural photos, and other pictures in which the most important subject is located in the middle of the frame. As the name suggests, the light reading is *weighted* toward the central portion, but information is also used from the rest of the frame. If your main subject is surrounded by very bright or very dark areas, the exposure might not be exactly right. However, this scheme works well in many situations if you don't want to use one of the other modes.

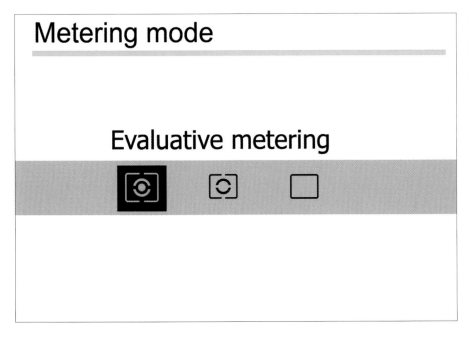

Figure 4.3 Press the Metering Mode button (the left cross key) and then choose from Evaluative, Partial, or Center-weighted averaging modes.

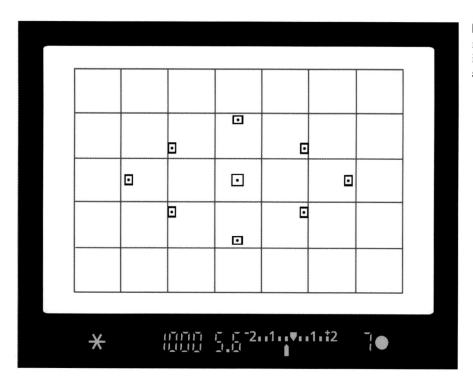

Figure 4.4 Evaluative metering divides the frame into 35 zones linked to the active autofocus point.

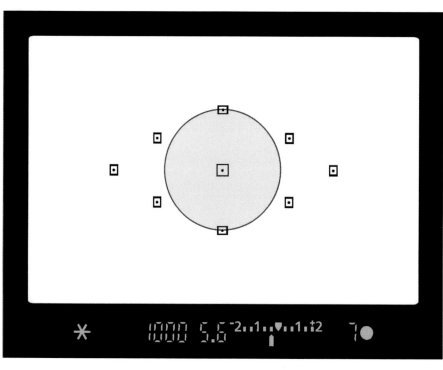

Figure 4.5 Partial metering collects exposure data from a center spot representing about nine percent of the image.

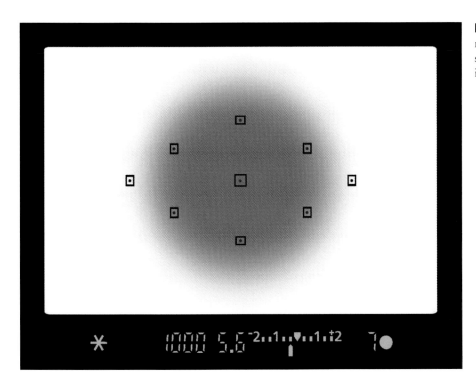

Figure 4.6 Center-weighted metering measures the entire scene, but emphasizes the area in the center of the frame.

Choosing a Creative Zone Exposure Method

You'll find five methods for choosing the appropriate shutter speed and aperture within the Creative Zone settings. Your choice of which is best for a given shooting situation will depend on things like your need for lots of (or less) depth-of-field, a desire to freeze action or allow motion blur, or how much noise you find acceptable in an image. Each of the Digital Rebel XTi's exposure methods emphasizes one aspect of image capture or another. This section introduces you to all five available on the Mode Dial.

A-DEP

The Automatic Depth-of-Field exposure mode is a handy method to use when you want to maximize the range of sharpness in your image. The camera actually selects an f/stop that will allow as much of the subject matter you've framed as possible to be in sharp focus, and then it applies the shutter speed necessary to provide a good exposure at that aperture. The disadvantage of this mode is that you relinquish control over shutter speed, f/stop, and focus distance (which makes A-DEP a bit more like a Basic Zone scene mode than a true Creative Zone mode). You might end up with the required depth-of-field (DOF), but you might get a blurry photo because the XTi has selected a shutter speed that's too slow for hand-holding!

A-DEP performs its magic by examining the nine autofocus points in the viewfinder to discover the nearest and farthest objects in the frame. Then, it chooses an aperture and focus point that supplies the required DOF (if possible) and sets the appropriate shutter speed. Obviously, you must have the lens set to autofocus for this mode to work (if not, the XTi switches to P exposure mode). The focus zones that can be rendered in sharp focus will flash red; other zones that can't be included in the focus range remain black, as shown in Figure 4.7. Press the DOF button on the front of the camera while holding the shutter release down halfway to check the range of focus. This mode won't work under all conditions, for example, with flash or if you're using manual focus. The viewfinder provides you with status information:

- **Flashing red AF points.** Shows the subjects covered by the DOF range set.

- **Blinking aperture indicator in viewfinder.** The desired DOF range cannot be set, because the subjects are separated too widely for sufficient depth-of-field at the smallest available aperture.

- **Blinking 30 shutter speed in viewfinder.** Illumination is too dim to provide requested DOF at the current ISO setting.

- **Blinking 4000 shutter speed in viewfinder.** Illumination is too bright to provide requested DOF at the current ISO setting.

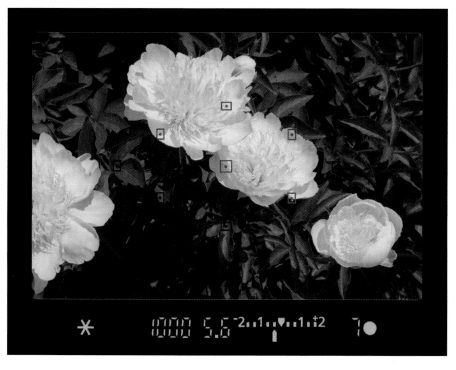

Figure 4.7 A-DEP mode can provide automatic depth-of-field for many types of subjects.

Because of the limitations of A-DEP mode, I don't favor it. However, it's fun to play with and may come in handy in certain situations, especially when you're shooting quickly and don't have time to manipulate depth-of-field manually.

Aperture Priority

In Av mode, you specify the lens opening used, and the XTi selects the shutter speed. Aperture priority is especially good when you want to use a particular lens opening to achieve a desired effect. Perhaps you'd like to use the smallest f/stop possible to maximize depth-of-field in a close-up picture. Or, you might want to use a large f/stop to throw everything except your main subject out of focus. Maybe you'd just like to "lock in" a particular f/stop because it's the sharpest available aperture with that lens. Or, you might prefer to use, say, f/2.8 on a lens with a maximum aperture of f/1.4, because you want the best compromise between speed and sharpness.

Aperture priority can even be used to specify a *range* of shutter speeds you want to use under varying lighting conditions, which seems almost contradictory. But think about it. You're shooting a soccer game outdoors with a telephoto lens and want a relatively high shutter speed, but you don't care if the speed changes a little should the sun duck behind a cloud. Set your XTi to Av, and adjust the aperture until a shutter speed of, say, 1/1000th second is selected at your current ISO setting. (In bright sunlight at ISO 400, that aperture is likely to be around f/11.) Then, go ahead and shoot, knowing that your XTi will maintain that f/11 aperture (for sufficient DOF as the soccer players move about the field), but will drop down to 1/750th or 1/500th second if necessary should the lighting change a little.

A blinking 30 or 4000 shutter speed in the viewfinder and status LCD indicates that the XTi is unable to select an appropriate shutter speed at the selected aperture and that over- and underexposure will occur at the current ISO setting. That's the major pitfall of using Av: you might select an f/stop that is too small or too large to allow an optimal exposure with the available shutter speeds. For example, if you choose f/2.8 as your aperture and the illumination is quite bright (say, at the beach or in snow), even your camera's fastest shutter speed might not be able to cut down the amount of light reaching the sensor to provide the right exposure. Or, if you select f/8 in a dimly lit room, you might find yourself shooting with a very slow shutter speed that can cause blurring from subject movement or camera shake. Aperture priority is best used by those with a bit of experience in choosing settings. Many seasoned photographers leave their XTi set on Av all the time.

Shutter Priority

Shutter priority (Tv) is the inverse of aperture priority: you choose the shutter speed you'd like to use, and the camera's metering system selects the appropriate f/stop. Perhaps you're shooting action photos and you want to use the absolute fastest shutter speed available with your camera, or you might want to use a slow shutter speed to add some blur to an otherwise static photograph.

Shutter priority mode gives you some control over how much action-freezing capability your digital camera brings to bear in a particular situation. For the action photo shown in Figure 4.8, I set the shutter speed to 1/1000th second to freeze the pole vaulter as he passed over the bar, and let the Rebel XTi choose the right aperture.

However, you'll need to keep the amount of existing light in mind when choosing your preferred shutter speed. Otherwise, you'll also encounter the same problem as with aperture priority when you select a shutter speed that's too long or too short for correct exposure. I've shot outdoor soccer games on sunny Fall evenings and used shutter priority mode to lock in a 1/1000th second shutter speed, only to find my XTi refused to shoot when the sun dipped behind some trees and there was no longer enough light to shoot at that speed, even with the lens wide open.

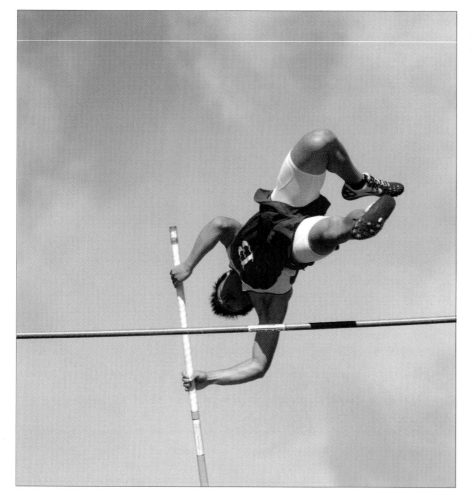

Figure 4.8 Select a fast shutter speed to stop action, and let the Rebel XTi choose the aperture in shutter priority mode.

Like Av mode, it's possible to choose an inappropriate shutter speed. If that's the case, the maximum aperture of your lens (to indicate underexposure) or the minimum aperture (to indicate overexposure) will blink.

Program Mode

Program mode (P) uses the XTi's built-in smarts to select the correct f/stop and shutter speed using a database of picture information that tells it which combination of shutter speed and aperture will work best for a particular photo. If the correct exposure cannot be achieved at the current ISO setting, the shutter speed indicator in the viewfinder will blink 30 or 4000, indicating under- or overexposure (respectively). You can then boost or reduce the ISO to increase or decrease sensitivity.

The XTi's recommended exposure can be overridden if you want. Use the EV setting feature (described later, because it also applies to Tv and Av modes) to add or subtract exposure from the metered value. And, as I mentioned earlier in this chapter, you can change from the recommended setting to an equivalent setting (as shown in Table 4.1) that produces the same exposure, but using a different combination of f/stop and shutter speed. To accomplish this:

1. Press the shutter release down halfway to lock in the current base exposure, or press the AE Lock button on the back of the camera. (The latter method actually makes the next step easier for me.)

2. Spin the Main Dial to change the shutter speed (the XTi will adjust the f/stop to match).

Your adjustment remains in force for a single exposure; if you want to change from the recommended settings for the next exposure, you'll need to repeat those steps.

MAKING EV CHANGES

Sometimes you'll want more or less exposure than indicated by the Digital Rebel XTi's metering system. Perhaps you want to underexpose to create a silhouette effect, or overexpose to produce a high-key look. It's easy to use the XTi's Exposure Compensation system to override the exposure recommendations. Press the shutter release halfway, then press and hold the Aperture/Exposure Compensation button (to the upper right of the LCD panel), and rotate the Main Dial to add or subtract exposure. The exposure scale in the viewfinder and on the status LCD indicates the EV change you've made. The EV change you've made remains for the exposures that follow, until you manually zero out the EV setting with the Main Dial. EV changes are ignored when using M (manual exposure) or any of the Basic Zone modes.

Manual Exposure

Part of being an experienced photographer comes from knowing when to rely on your Digital Rebel XTi's automation (including P mode and Basic Zone settings), when to go semiautomatic (with Tv or Av), and when to set exposure manually (using M). Some photographers actually prefer to set their exposure manually, as the XTi will be happy to provide a viewfinder indication of when its metering system agrees that the settings provide the proper exposure.

Manual exposure can come in handy in some situations. You might be taking a silhouette photo and find that none of the exposure modes or EV correction features give you exactly the effect you want. Set the exposure manually to use the exact shutter speed and f/stop you need. Or, you might be working in a studio environment using multiple flash units. The additional flashes are triggered by slave devices (gadgets that set off the flash when they sense the light from another flash, or, perhaps from a radio or infrared remote control). Your camera's exposure meter doesn't compensate for the extra illumination, so you need to set the aperture manually.

Even though, depending on your proclivities, you might not need to set exposure manually very often, you should still make sure you understand how it works. Fortunately, the Digital Rebel XTi makes setting exposure manually very easy. Just set the Mode Dial to M, turn the Main Dial to set the shutter speed, and hold down the Aperture/Exposure Compensation button while spinning the Main Dial to adjust the aperture. Press the shutter-release button halfway or press the AE Lock button, and the exposure scale in the viewfinder shows you how far your chosen setting diverges from the metered exposure.

Selecting an Autofocus/Exposure Zone Manually

If you're using P, Av, Tv, or M shooting modes and Evaluative metering, you can select the autofocus zone manually (and thus the zone linked to the metering system). As I mentioned in Chapter 1, the Digital Rebel XTi uses seven different focus points to calculate correct focus. In A-DEP, or any of the Basic Zone shooting modes, the focus point is selected automatically by the camera. In the other Creative Zone modes, you can allow the camera to select the focus point automatically, or you can specify which focus point should be used.

To set the focus point manually, look through the viewfinder and then press the AF point selection button on the extreme upper-right corner of the back of the camera, and use either the cross keys (which move highlighting directly to a point) or the Main Dial (which rotates through all the points in turn) to select the zone you want to use. As you cycle among the focus points, each will be illuminated in turn, and will be highlighted on the status LCD. Press the Set button to switch back and forth between the center autofocus point and automatic selection. In Evaluative metering mode, the focus point you select will be emphasized in calculating exposure, as shown in Figure 4.9.

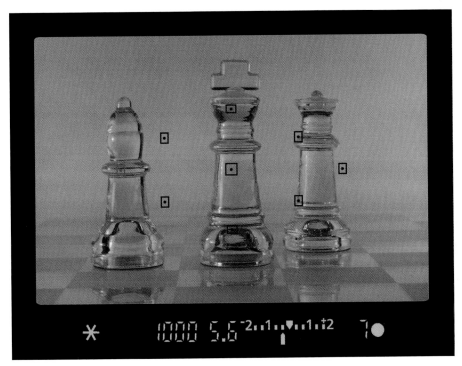

Figure 4.9 Select an autofocus point manually, and the XTi's exposure meter will link to that point in Evaluative metering mode.

Adjusting Exposure with ISO Settings

Another way of adjusting exposures is by changing the ISO sensitivity setting when you're using one of the Creative Zone modes. Sometimes photographers forget about this option, because the common practice is to set the ISO once for a particular shooting session (say, at ISO 100 or 200 for bright sunlight outdoors, or ISO 800 when shooting indoors) and then forget about ISO. The reason for that is that ISOs higher than 100 or 200 are seen as "bad" or "necessary evils." However, changing the ISO is a valid way of adjusting exposure settings, particularly with the Canon Digital Rebel XTi, which produces good results at ISO settings that create grainy, unusable pictures with some other camera models.

Indeed, I find myself using ISO adjustment as a convenient alternate way of adding or subtracting EV when shooting in manual mode, and as a quick way of choosing equivalent exposures when in automatic or semiautomatic modes. For example, I've selected a manual exposure with both f/stop and shutter speed suitable for my image using, say, ISO 200. I can change the exposure in 1/3 stop increments by tapping the ISO key (the up cross key). The menu on the LCD, shown in Figure 4.10, will display a list of ISO settings, which you can then choose using the up/down cross keys or by rotating the Main Dial and pressing the Set button to lock in your choice. Only one-stop increments are available: ISO 100, 200, 400, 800, and 1600. I can keep my preferred f/stop and shutter speed, but still adjust the exposure in manual mode by varying the ISO setting.

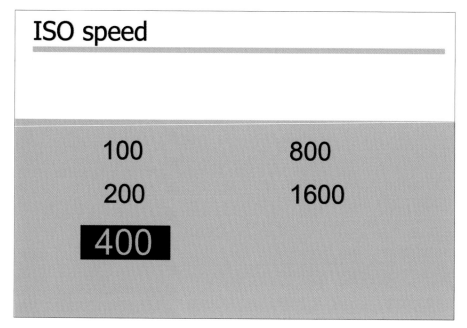

Figure 4.10 Choose from ISO 100 through ISO 1600 in the ISO Speed menu.

Or, perhaps I am using Tv mode and the metered exposure at ISO 200 is 1/500th second at f/11. If I decide on the spur of the moment I'd rather use 1/500th second at f/8, I can tap the ISO button and switch quickly to ISO 100. Of course, it's a good idea to monitor your ISO changes, so you don't end up at ISO 1600 accidentally. ISO settings can, of course, also be used to boost or reduce sensitivity in particular shooting situations.

Bracketing

Bracketing is a method for shooting several consecutive exposures using different settings, as a way of improving the odds that one will be exactly right. Before digital cameras took over the universe, it was common to bracket exposures, shooting, say, a series of three photos at 1/125th second, but varying the f/stop from f/8 to f/11 to f/16. In practice, smaller than whole-stop increments were used for greater precision. Plus, it was just as common to keep the same aperture and vary the shutter speed, although in the days before electronic shutters, film cameras often had only whole increment shutter speeds available.

Today, cameras like the XTi can bracket exposures much more precisely using auto exposure bracketing (AEB). When this feature is activated, the XTi takes three consecutive photos: one at the metered "correct" exposure, one with less exposure, and one with more exposure, using an increment of your choice up to +2/-2 stops. Choose between increments by setting Custom Function 06 to 0 (1/3 stop) or 1 (1/2 stop). In Av mode, the shutter speed will change, while in Tv mode, the aperture will change.

Bracketing can also be used with image editor features like Photoshop's Merge to HDR capability, which allows combining multiple images taken at different exposures to incorporate the shadow, midtone, and highlight detail from each into one photo with a longer tonal range. Your camera needs to be placed on a tripod, of course, to ensure that each of the three images will differ only in exposure.

Using AEB is trickier than it needs to be, but you can follow these steps:

1. Press Menu button and press the Jump button to skip to the Shooting 2 menu. Scroll to the AEB position and press the Set button. A green dot appears on the plus/minus scale.

2. Use the left/right cross keys or Main Dial to spread the three dots to the range you want for your bracketed set. For example, with the dots clustered tightly together, the three bracketed exposures will be spread out over a single stop. Separating the cluster produces a wider range and larger exposure change between the three shots in the bracket set, as shown in Figure 4.11.

3. Press the Set button to enter the settings and the Menu button to exit the menu system. The bracketing icon appears on the LCD display.

4. Take your three photos. You can use single shooting mode to take the trio of pictures yourself, use the self-timer (which will expose all three pictures after the delay), or switch to continuous shooting mode to take the three pictures in a burst.

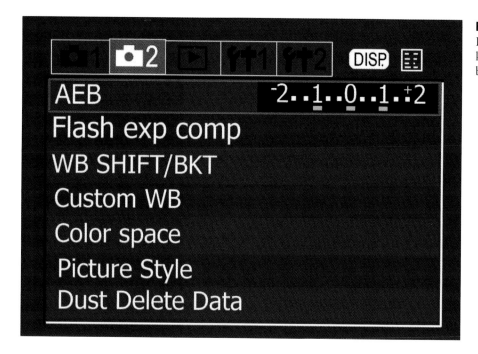

AEB   ⁻2..1..0..1.⁺2
Flash exp comp
WB SHIFT/BKT
Custom WB
Color space
Picture Style
Dust Delete Data

Figure 4.11 Rotate the Main Dial or use the left/right cross keys to set the increment between bracketed shots.

5. As the shots are taken, three indicators will appear on the exposure scale in the viewfinder, with one of them flashing for each bracketed photo, showing when the base exposure, underexposure, and overexposure are taken.

6. Bracketing remains in effect when the set is taken so you can continue shooting bracketed exposures until you use the electronic flash, or return to the menu to cancel bracketing.

Figure 4.12 shows a bracketed series of shots.

Dealing with Noise

Image noise is that random grainy effect that some like to use as a visual effect, but which, most of the time, is objectionable because it robs your image of detail even as it adds that "interesting" texture. Noise is caused by two different phenomena: high ISO settings and long exposures.

High ISO noise commonly appears when you raise your camera's sensitivity setting above ISO 400. With Canon cameras, which are renowned for their good ISO noise characteristics, noise may become visible at ISO 800, and is usually fairly noticeable at ISO 1600. This kind of noise appears as a result of the amplification needed to increase the sensitivity of the sensor. While higher ISOs do pull details out of dark areas, they also amplify non-signal information randomly, creating noise.

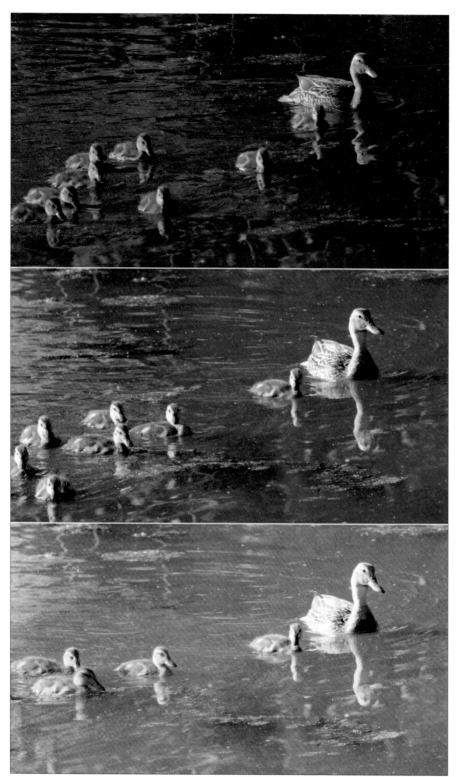

Figure 4.12 Bracketing allows shooting a series of shots at different exposures automatically.

A similar noisy phenomenon occurs during long time exposures, which allow more photons to reach the sensor, increasing your ability to capture a picture under low-light conditions. However, the longer exposures also increase the likelihood that some pixels will register random phantom photons, often because the longer an imager is "hot" the warmer it gets, and that heat can be mistaken for photons.

There's also a special kind of noise that CMOS sensors like the one used in the XTi are potentially susceptible to. With a CCD, the entire signal is conveyed off the chip and funneled through a single amplifier and analog to digital conversion circuit. Any noise introduced there is, at least, consistent. CMOS imagers, on the other hand, contain millions of individual amplifiers and A/D converters, all working in unison. Because all these circuits don't necessarily all process in precisely the same way all the time, they can introduce something called fixed-pattern noise into the image data.

Fortunately, Canon's electronics geniuses have done an exceptional job minimizing noise from all causes in the XTi. Even so, you might still want to apply the optional long exposure noise reduction that can be activated using Custom Function 02. This type of noise reduction involves the XTi taking a second, blank exposure, and comparing the random pixels in that image with the photograph you just took. Pixels that coincide in the two represent noise and can safely be suppressed. This noise reduction system, called *dark frame subtraction*, effectively doubles the amount of time required to take a picture, and it is used only for exposures longer than one second. Noise reduction can reduce the amount of detail in your picture, as some image information may be removed along with the noise. So, you might want to use this feature with moderation.

To activate your XTi's long exposure noise reduction feature, go to the Custom Function Menu, choose C.Fn-02, shown in Figure 4.13, and press the Set button. You can then use the up/down cross keys to scroll among the three options (0 through 2), originally described in Chapter 3, but recapped here:

- **0: Off.** Disables long exposure noise reduction.
- **1: Auto.** Applies noise reduction for exposures longer than 1 second if the camera detects long exposure noise.
- **2: On.** When this setting is activated, the XTi applies noise reduction to all exposures longer than 1 second.

You can also apply noise reduction to a lesser extent using Photoshop, and when converting RAW files to some other format, using your favorite RAW converter or an industrial-strength product like Noise Ninja (www.picturecode.com) to wipe out noise after you've already taken the picture.

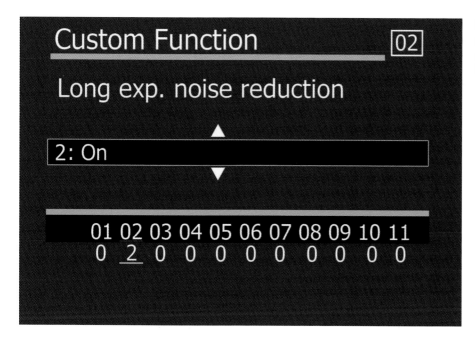

Figure 4.13 Long exposure noise reduction can reduce random pixels produced at longer shutter speeds.

Fixing Exposures with Histograms

While you can often recover poorly exposed photos in your image editor, your best bet is to arrive at the correct exposure in the camera, minimizing the tweaks that you have to make in post-processing. However, you can't always judge exposure just by viewing the image on your XTi's LCD after the shot is made. Ambient light may make the LCD difficult to see, and the brightness level you've set can affect the appearance of the playback image.

Instead, you can use a histogram, which is a chart displayed on the Digital Rebel's LCD that shows the number of tones being captured at each brightness level. You can use the information to provide correction for the next shot you take. The XTi offers two histogram variations: one that shows overall brightness levels for an image, and an alternate version that separates the red, green, and blue channels of your image into separate histograms.

Both types are charts that include up to 256 vertical lines on a horizontal axis that show the number of pixels in the image at each brightness level, from 0 (black) on the left side to 255 (white) on the right. The more pixels at a given level, the taller the bar at that position. If no bar appears at a particular position on the scale from left to right, there are no pixels at that particular brightness level.

A typical histogram produces a mountain-like shape, with most of the pixels bunched in the middle tones, with fewer pixels at the dark and light ends of the scale. Ideally, though, there will be at least some pixels at either extreme, so that your image has both a true black and a true white representing some details. Learn to spot histograms that represent over- and underexposure, and add or subtract exposure using an EV modification to compensate.

For example, Figure 4.15 shows the histogram for an image that is badly underexposed. You can guess from the shape of the histogram that many of the dark tones to the left of the graph have been clipped off. There's plenty of room on the right side for additional pixels to reside without having them become overexposed.

DISPLAYING HISTOGRAMS

To view histograms on your screen, press the Disp. button while an image is shown on the LCD. Keep pressing the button until the histogram(s) are shown. The display will cycle between basic information, advanced information (with histogram display), and no information (a screen with only the image shown). You'll also see a thumbnail at the left side of the screen with your image displayed. Overexposed areas will blink, as shown by the dark (but non-blinking on the printed page) area in Figure 4.14, which is your prompt to reduce the exposure using exposure compensation. (See the "Making EV Changes" sidebar earlier in this chapter.) To change your histogram type from Brightness to RGB, use the Histogram setting in the Playback menu, as discussed in Chapter 3.

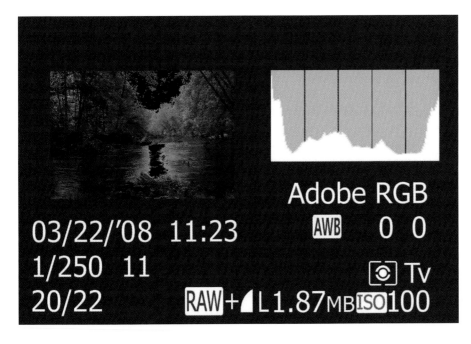

Figure 4.14 A histogram shows the relationship of tones in an image.

Or, a histogram might look like Figure 4.16, which is overexposed. In either case, you can increase or decrease the exposure (either by changing the f/stop or shutter speed in manual mode or by adding or subtracting an EV value in autoexposure mode) to produce the corrected histogram shown in Figure 4.17, in which the tones "hug" the right side of the histogram to produce as many highlight details as possible. See "Making EV Changes" earlier in this chapter, for information on dialing in exposure compensation.

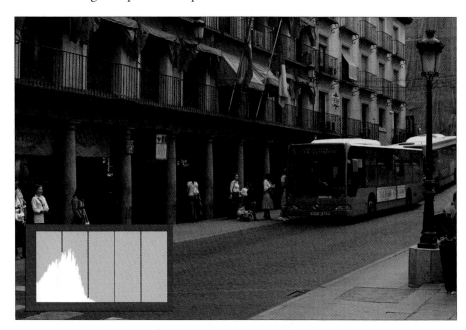

Figure 4.15 The histogram shows that this image is underexposed.

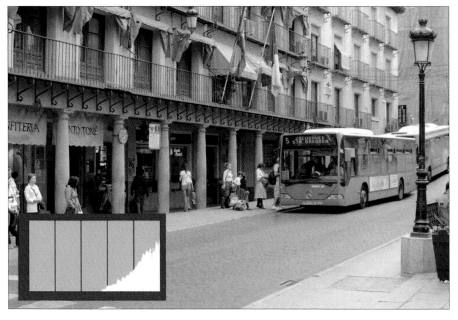

Figure 4.16 This histogram shows that the image is significantly overexposed.

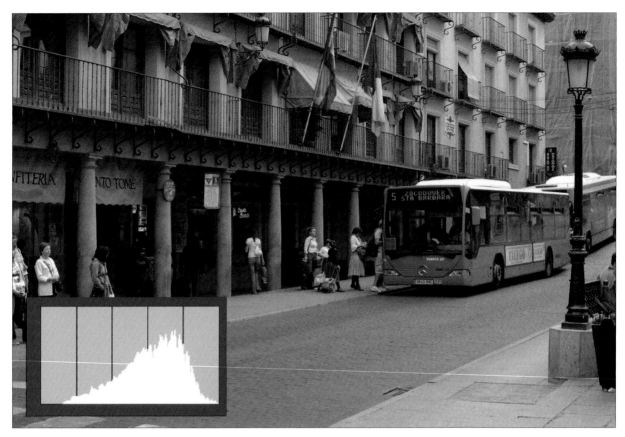

Figure 4.17 A properly exposed image will have a histogram resembling this one.

The histogram can also be used to aid in fixing the contrast of an image, although gauging incorrect contrast is more difficult. For example, if the histogram shows all the tones bunched up in one place in the image, the photo will be low in contrast. If the tones are spread out more or less evenly, the image is probably high in contrast. In either case, your best bet may be to switch to RAW (if you're not already using that format) so you can adjust contrast in post processing. However, you can also change to a user-defined Picture Style (User Def. 1, User Def. 2, or User Def. 3) in the Picture Style menu, with contrast set lower (-2 to 0) or higher (0 to +2) as required. You'll find more about using Picture Styles in Chapter 5.

Basic Zone Modes

Your Canon Digital Rebel XTi includes seven Basic Zone shooting modes that can automatically make all the basic settings needed for certain types of shooting situations, such as portraits, landscapes, close-ups, sports, night portraits, and "no-flash zone" pictures. They are especially useful when you suddenly encounter a picture-taking opportunity and don't have time to decide exactly which Creative Zone mode you want to use. Instead, you can spin the Mode Dial to the appropriate Basic Zone mode and fire away, knowing that, at least you have a fighting chance of getting a good or usable photo.

Basic Zone modes are also helpful when you're just learning to use your XTi. After you've learned how to operate your camera, you'll probably prefer one of the Creative Zone modes that provide more control over shooting options. The Basic Zone scene modes may give you few options or none at all. Here are the modes available:

- **Full Auto.** This is the mode to use when you hand your camera to a total stranger and ask him or her to take your picture posing in front of the Leaning Tower of Pisa. All the photographer has to do is press the shutter-release button. Every other decision is made by the camera's electronics.

- **Portrait.** This mode tends to use wider f/stops and faster shutter speeds, providing blurred backgrounds and images with no camera shake. If you hold down the shutter release, the XTi will take a continuous sequence of photos, which can be useful in capturing fleeting expressions in portrait situations.

- **Landscape.** The XTi tries to use smaller f/stops for more depth-of-field, and boosts saturation slightly for richer colors.

- **Close-Up.** This mode is similar to the Portrait setting, with wider f/stops to isolate your close-up subjects and high shutter speeds to eliminate the camera shake that's accentuated at close focusing distances. However, if you have your camera mounted on a tripod or you are using an image-stabilized (IS) lens, you might want to use the Creative Zone aperture priority (Av) mode instead, so you can specify a smaller f/stop with additional depth-of-field.

- **Sports.** In this mode, the XTi tries to use high shutter speeds to freeze action, switches to High Speed Continuous drive to allow taking a quick sequence of pictures with one press of the shutter release, and uses AI Servo AF to continually refocus as your subject moves around in the frame. You can find more information on autofocus options in Chapter 5.

■ **Night Portrait.** Combines flash with ambient light to produce an image that is mainly illuminated by the flash, but the background is exposed by the available light. This mode uses longer exposures, so a tripod, monopod, or IS lens is a must.

■ **Flash Off.** Absolutely prevents the built-in or external flash from firing, which you might want in some situations, such as religious ceremonies, museums, classical music concerts, and your double-naught spy activities.

5

Advanced Shooting with Your Canon EOS Digital Rebel XTi

Now that you have a good understanding of exposure under your belt, you'll want to master some of the other techniques that can contribute to great images. In this chapter, I'm going to show you how to work with some additional exposure options, use the automatic and manual focusing controls available with the Canon EOS Digital Rebel XTi, and explain some of the many ways you can fine-tune your images with optimized white balance, sharpening, tonal values, and color.

More Exposure Options

In Chapter 4, you learned techniques for getting the *right* exposure, but I haven't explained all your exposure options just yet. You'll want to know about the *kind* of exposure settings that are available to you with the Canon Digital Rebel XTi. There are options that let you control when the exposure is made, or even how to make an exposure that's out of the ordinary in terms of length (time or bulb exposures). The sections that follow explain your camera's special exposure features, and even discuss a few it does not have (and why it doesn't).

Very Short Exposures

Exposures that seem impossibly brief can reveal a world we didn't know existed. In the 1930s, Dr. Harold Edgerton, a professor of electrical engineering at MIT, pioneered high-speed photography using a repeating electronic flash unit he patented called the *stroboscope*. As the inventor of the electronic flash, he popularized its use to freeze objects in motion, and you've probably seen his photographs of bullets piercing balloons and drops of milk forming a coronet-shaped splash.

Electronic flash freezes action by virtue of its extremely short duration—as brief as 1/50,000th second or less. Although the Rebel XTi's built-in flash unit can give you these ultra-quick glimpses of moving subjects, an external flash, such as one of the Canon Speedlites, offers even more versatility. You can read more about using electronic flash to freeze action in Chapter 7.

Of course, the XTi is fully capable of stopping all but the fastest movement using only its shutter speeds, which range all the way up to an astonishing 1/4000th second. Indeed, you'll rarely have need for such a brief shutter speed in ordinary shooting. If you wanted to use an aperture of f/1.8 at ISO 100 outdoors in bright sunlight, for some reason, a shutter speed of 1/4000th second would more than do the job. You'd need a faster shutter speed only if you moved the ISO setting to a higher sensitivity (for some unknown reason). Under less than full sunlight, 1/4000th second is more than fast enough for any conditions you're likely to encounter.

Most sports action can be frozen at 1/2000th second or slower, and for many sports a slower shutter speed is actually preferable, for example, to allow the wheels of a racing automobile or motorcycle, or the propeller on a classic aircraft to blur realistically. Figure 5.1 is another example. The 1/2000th second shutter speed effectively stopped the batter in mid-stroke, but allowed the 90-mph fastball to blur. If the fastball were perfectly sharp, it might look as if it had been glued to the bat. The blur tells us that this shot wasn't faked.

But if you want to do some exotic action-freezing photography without resorting to electronic flash, the XTi's top shutter speed is at your disposal. Here are some things to think about when exploring this type of high-speed photography:

■ **You'll need a lot of light.** High shutter speeds cut very fine slices of time and sharply reduce the amount of illumination that reaches your sensor. To use 1/4000th second at an aperture of f/8 you'd need an ISO setting of 1600—even in full daylight. To use an f/stop smaller than f/8 or an ISO setting lower than 1600, you'd need *more* light than full daylight provides. (That's why electronic flash units work so well for high-speed photography under the right conditions; they provide both the brief shutter speed and the high levels of illumination needed.)

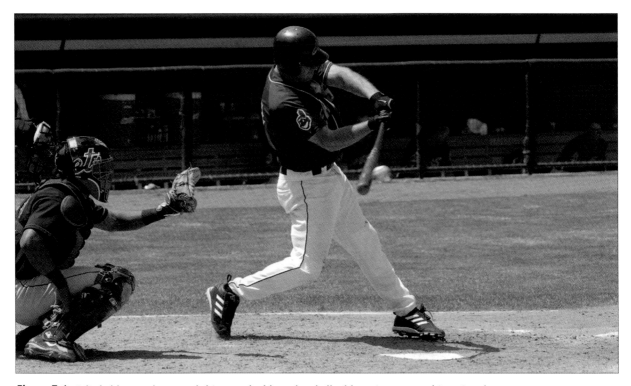

Figure 5.1 A little blur can be a good thing, as the blurry baseball adds excitement to this action shot.

■ **Forget about reciprocity failure.** If you're an old-time film shooter, you might recall that very brief shutter speeds (as well as very high light levels and very *long* exposures) produced an effect called *reciprocity failure*, in which given exposures ended up providing less than the calculated value because of the way film responded to very short, very intense, or very long exposures of light. The consensus today is that sensors don't suffer from this defect, so you don't need to make an adjustment when using high shutter speeds or brief flash bursts (nor for very long exposures, either).

■ **No elongation effect.** This is another old bugaboo that has largely been solved through modern technology, but I wanted to bring it to your attention anyway. In olden times, cameras used shutters that traveled horizontally. To achieve faster shutter speeds, focal plane shutters (located just in front of the plane of the sensor), open only a smaller-than-frame-sized slit so that, even though the shutter is already traveling at its highest rate of speed, the film/sensor is exposed for a briefer period of time as the slit moves across the surface. At very short shutter speeds, and with subjects moving horizontally at very fast velocities, it was possible for the subject to partially "keep up" with the shutter if it were traveling in the same direction as the slit, producing an elongated effect. Conversely, subjects moving in the opposite direction of shutter motion could be compressed. Today, shutters like those in the XTi move vertically and at a higher maximum rate of speed. So, unless you're photographing a rocket blasting into space, and holding the camera horizontally, to boot (or shooting a racing car in vertical orientation), it's almost impossible to produce unwanted elongation/compression.

- **Don't combine high shutter speeds with electronic flash.** You might be tempted to use an electronic flash with a high shutter speed. Perhaps you want to stop some action in daylight with a brief shutter speed, and use electronic flash only as supplemental illumination to fill in the shadows. Unfortunately, under most conditions you can't use flash with your XTi at any shutter speed faster than 1/200th second. That's the fastest speed at which the camera's focal plane shutter is fully open: at shorter speeds, the "slit" described above comes into play, so that the flash will expose only the small portion of the sensor exposed by the slit during its duration. (Check out "High-Speed Sync" in Chapter 7 if you want to see how you *can* use shutter speeds faster than 1/200th second with certain Canon Speedlites, albeit at much-reduced effective power levels.)

Working with Short Exposures

You can have a lot of fun exploring the kinds of pictures you can take using very brief exposure times, whether you decide to take advantage of the action-stopping capabilities of your electronic flash, or work with the Canon Digital Rebel XTi's faster shutter speeds. Here are a few ideas to get you started:

- **Revealing images.** Fast shutter speeds can help you reveal the real subject behind the façade, by freezing constant motion to capture an enlightening moment in time. Legendary fashion/portrait photographer Philippe Halsman used leaping photos of famous people, such as the Duke and Duchess of Windsor, Richard Nixon, and Salvador Dali to illuminate their real selves. Halsman said, "*When you ask a person to jump, his attention is mostly directed toward the act of jumping and the mask falls so that the real person appears.*" Try some high-speed portraits of people you know in motion to see how they appear when concentrating on something other than the portrait.

- **Create unreal images.** High-speed photography can also produce photographs that show your subjects in ways that are quite unreal. A helicopter in mid-air with its rotors frozen, or a motorcyclist banking into a turn, but with all motion stopped so that the rider and machine look as if they were standing still at an odd angle, make for an unusual picture. When we're accustomed to seeing subjects in motion, seeing them stopped in time can verge on the surreal.

■ **Capture unseen perspectives.** Some things are *never* seen in real life, except when viewed in a stop-action photograph. Edgerton's balloon bursts were only a starting point. Freeze a hummingbird in flight for a view of wings that never seem to stop. Or, capture the splashes as liquid falls into a bowl, as shown in Figure 5.2. No electronic flash was required for this image (and wouldn't have illuminated the water in the bowl as evenly). Instead, a clutch of high intensity lamps and an ISO setting of 1600 allowed the Rebel XTi to capture this image at 1/2000th second.

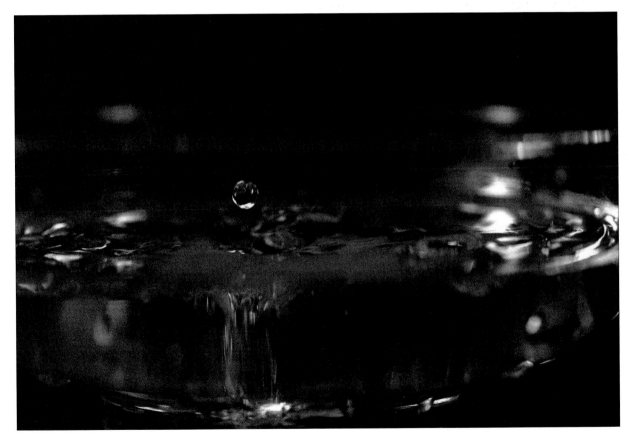

Figure 5.2 A large amount of artificial illumination and an ISO 1600 sensitivity setting allowed capturing this shot at 1/2000th second without use of an electronic flash.

- **Vanquish camera shake and gain new angles.** Here's an idea that's so obvious it isn't always explored to its fullest extent. A high enough shutter speed can free you from the tyranny of a tripod, making it easier to capture new angles, or to shoot quickly while moving around, especially with longer lenses. I tend to use a monopod or tripod for almost everything when I'm not using an image-stabilized lens and end up missing some shots because of a reluctance to adjust my camera support to get a higher, lower, or different angle. If you have enough light and can use an f/stop wide enough to permit a high shutter speed, you'll find a new freedom to choose your shots. I have a favored 170mm-500mm lens that I use for sports and wildlife photography, almost invariably with a tripod, as I don't find the "reciprocal of the focal length" rule particularly helpful in most cases. (I would *not* handhold this hefty lens at its 500mm setting with a 1/500th second shutter speed under most circumstances.) However, at 1/2000th second or faster, it's entirely possible for a steady hand to use this lens without a tripod or monopod's extra support, and I've found that my whole approach to shooting animals and other elusive subjects changes in high-speed mode. Selective focus allows dramatically isolating my prey wide open at f/6.3, too.

Long Exposures

Longer exposures are an additional doorway into another world, showing us how even familiar scenes can look much different when photographed over periods measured in seconds. At night, long exposures produce streaks of light from moving, illuminated subjects like automobiles or amusement park rides. Concerts take on a new look when performers are photographed using exposures of a second or two, as you can see in Figure 5.3. Extra-long exposures of seemingly pitch-dark subjects can reveal interesting views using light levels barely enough to see by. At any time of day, including daytime (in which case you'll often need the help of neutral density filters to make the long exposure practical), a slow shutter speed can cause moving objects to vanish entirely, because they don't remain stationary long enough to register in a photograph.

Three Ways to Take Long Exposures

There are actually three common types of lengthy exposures: *timed exposures, bulb exposures, and time exposures.* The Rebel XTi offers only the first two, but once you understand all three, you'll see why Canon made the choices it did.

- **Timed exposures.** These are long exposures from 1 second to 30 seconds, measured by the camera itself. To take a picture in this range, simply use Manual or Tv modes and use the Main Dial to set the shutter speed to the length of time you want, choosing from preset speeds of 1.0, 1.5, 2.0, 3.0, 4.0, 6.0, 8.0, 10.0, 15.0, 20.0, or 30.0 seconds (if you've specified 1/2 stop increments for exposure adjustments), or 1.0, 1.3, 1.6, 2.0, 2.5, 3.2, 4.0, 5.0, 6.0, 8.0, 10.0, 13.0, 15.0, 20.0, 25.0, and 30.0 seconds (if you're using 1/3 stop increments). The advantage of timed exposures is that the camera does all the calculating for you. There's no need for a stop-watch. If you review your image on the LCD and decide to try again with the exposure doubled or halved, you can dial in the correct exposure with precision. The disadvantage of timed exposures is that you can't take a photo for longer than 30 seconds.

■ **Bulb exposures.** This type of exposure is so-called because in the olden days the photographer squeezed and held an air bulb attached to a tube that provided the force necessary to keep the shutter open. Traditionally, a bulb exposure is one that lasts as long as the shutter-release button is pressed; when you release the button, the exposure ends. To make a bulb exposure with the XTi, set the camera on Manual mode and use the Main Dial to select the shutter speed immediately after 30 seconds—buLB. Then, press the shutter to start the exposure, and release it again to close the shutter. If you'd like to simulate a time exposure (described above), you can use the Canon RS-60E3 that attaches to the terminal on the left side of the camera under the rubber cover. You can also use the infrared wireless controllers RC-1 and RC-5.

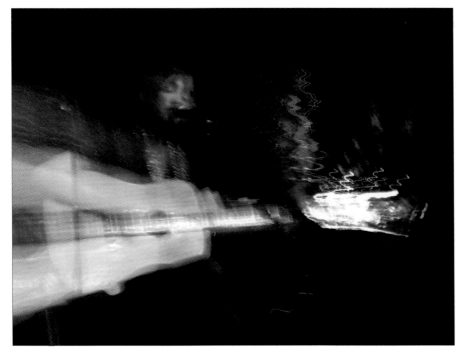

Figure 5.3 Although the camera was mounted on a monopod for this concert photo, the Rebel XTi was deliberately jiggled during the two-second exposure to produce an interesting pattern of streaks.

■ **Time exposures.** This is a setting found on some cameras to produce longer exposures. With cameras that implement this option, the shutter opens when you press the shutter-release button, and remains open until you press the button again. Usually, you'll be able to close the shutter using a mechanical cable release or, more commonly, an electronic release cable. The advantage of this approach is that you can take an exposure of virtually any duration without the need for special equipment (the tethered release is optional). You can press the shutter-release button, go off for a few minutes, and come back to close the shutter (assuming your camera is still there). The disadvantages of this mode are exposures must be timed manually, and with shorter exposures it's possible for the vibration of manually opening and closing the shutter to register in the photo. For longer exposures, the period of vibration is relatively brief and not usually a problem—and there is always the release cable option to eliminate photographer-caused camera shake entirely. While the XTi does not have a built-in time exposure capability, you can simulate it with the bulb exposure technique, described previously.

Working with Long Exposures

Because the Rebel XTi produces such good images at longer exposures, and there are so many creative things you can do with long-exposure techniques, you'll want to do some experimenting. Get yourself a tripod or another firm support, and take some test shots with long exposure noise reduction both enabled and disabled (to see whether you prefer low noise or high detail) and get started. Here are some things to try:

■ **Make people invisible.** One very cool thing about long exposures is that objects that move rapidly enough won't register at all in a photograph, while the subjects that remain stationary are portrayed in the normal way. That makes it easy to produce people-free landscape photos and architectural photos at night or, even, in full daylight if you use a neutral density filter (or two or three) to allow an exposure of at least a few seconds. At ISO 100, f/22, and a pair of 8X (three-stop) neutral density filters, you can use exposures of nearly two seconds; overcast days and/or even more neutral density filtration would work even better if daylight people-vanishing is your goal. They'll have to be walking *very* briskly, and across the field of view (rather than directly toward the camera) for this to work. At night, it's much easier to achieve this effect with the 20- to 30-second exposures that are possible, as you can see in Figures 5.4 and 5.5.

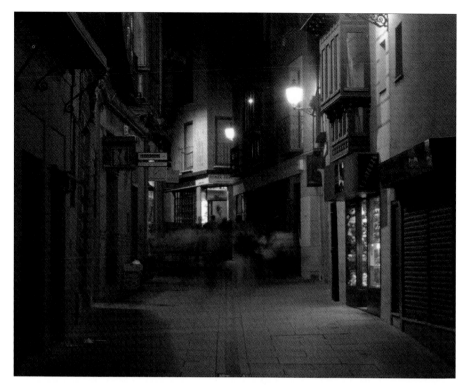

Figure 5.4 This alleyway thronged with people, as you can see in this two-second exposure using only the available illumination.

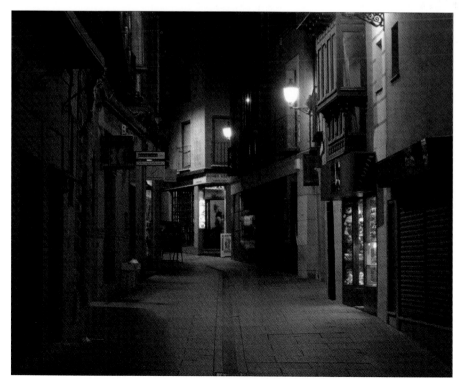

Figure 5.5 With the camera still on a tripod, a 30-second exposure rendered the passersby invisible.

- **Create streaks.** If you aren't shooting for total invisibility, long exposures with the camera on a tripod can produce some interesting streaky effects. Even a single 8X ND filter will let you shoot at f/22 and 1/6th second in daylight, giving you results as shown in Figure 5.6.

- **Produce light trails.** At night, car headlights and taillights and other moving sources of illumination can generate interesting light trails, as shown in Figure 5.7. Your camera doesn't even need to be mounted on a tripod; hand-holding the XTi for longer exposures adds movement and patterns to your trails. You can produce light trails using a tripod, too: when shooting fireworks, a longer exposure may allow you to combine several bursts into one picture.

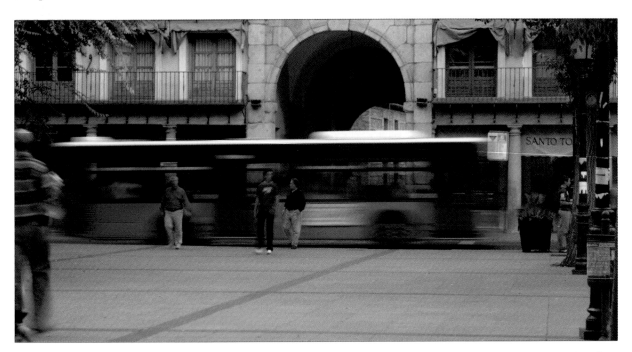

Figure 5.6 The busses passing by this public square moved quickly enough to be shown only as a blur at 1/6th second in this tripod-mounted shot in full daylight, with an 8X neutral density filter allowing the long exposure.

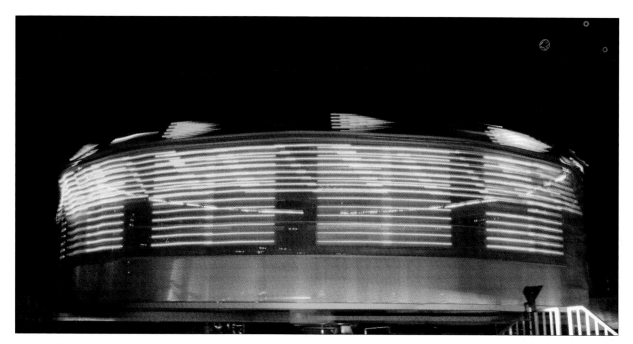

Figure 5.7 Long exposures can transform the most mundane nighttime subjects, such as this amusement park ride, into an interesting light-trails display.

- **Blur waterfalls, etc.** You'll find that waterfalls and other sources of moving liquid produce a special type of long-exposure blur, because the water merges into a fantasy-like veil that looks different at different exposure times, and with different waterfalls. Cascades with turbulent flow produce a rougher look at a given longer exposure than falls that flow smoothly. Although blurred waterfalls have become almost a cliché, there are still plenty of variations for a creative photographer to explore.

- **Show total darkness in new ways.** Even on the darkest, moonless nights, there is enough starlight or glow from distant illumination sources to see by, and, if you use a long exposure, there is enough light to take a picture, too. I was visiting a park after dark, and I saw that the dim light from the lamps in the parking lot provided sufficient light to see a distant stand of trees. A 30-second exposure with the lens of the tripod-mounted camera almost wide open revealed the scene shown in Figure 5.8, even though in real life there was barely enough light to make out the closest tree.

Figure 5.8 A 30-second exposure on a dark night revealed this park setting, illuminated only with spill light from an adjacent parking lot.

Delayed Exposures

Sometimes it's desirable to have a delay of some sort before a picture is actually taken. Perhaps you'd like to get in the picture yourself, and would appreciate it if the camera waited 10 seconds after you press the shutter release to actually take the picture. Maybe you want to give a tripod-mounted camera time to settle down and damp any residual vibration after the release is pressed, to improve sharpness for an exposure with a relatively slow shutter speed. It's possible you want to explore the world of time-lapse photography. The next sections present your delayed exposure options.

Self-Timer

The Rebel XTi has a built-in self-timer with a semi-fixed 10-second delay. Activate the timer by pressing the Drive mode selection button continually until the self-timer icon appears on the LCD status panel. Press the shutter-release button halfway to lock in focus on your subjects (if you're taking a self-portrait, focus on an object at a similar distance). When you're ready to take the photo, continue pressing the shutter release the rest of the way. The lamp on the front of the camera will blink slowly for eight seconds and the beeper will chirp (if you haven't disabled it in the Shooting 1 menu as described in Chapter 3). During the final two seconds the beeper sounds more rapidly and the lamp remains on until the picture is taken. The status LCD displays a countdown clock icon while all this is going on.

The only way to vary the delay time is to enable the mirror lockup feature (C.Fn-07), which sets the delay to a mere two seconds. This is something you might want to do if you're shooting close-ups, landscapes, or other types of pictures using the self-timer only to trip the shutter in the most vibration-free way possible. Forget to bring along your tripod, but still want to take a close-up picture with a precise focus setting? Set your digital camera to the self-timer function, and then put the camera on any reasonably steady support, such as a fence post or a rock. When you're ready to take the picture, press the shutter release. The camera might rock back and forth for a second or two, but it will settle back to its original position before the self-timer activates the shutter. The self-timer remains active until you turn it off—even if you power down the XTi.

Getting into Focus

Learning to use the Canon Digital Rebel XTi's autofocus system is easy, but you do need to fully understand how the system works to get the most benefit from it. Once you're comfortable with autofocus, you'll know when it's appropriate to use the manual focus option, too. The important thing to remember is that focus isn't absolute. For example, some things that look in sharp focus at a given viewing size and distance might not be in focus at a larger size and/or closer distance. In addition, the goal of optimum focus isn't always to make things look sharp. Not all of an image will be or should be sharp. Controlling exactly what is sharp and what is not is part of your creative palette. Use of depth-of-field characteristics to throw part of an image out of focus while other parts are sharply focused is one of the most valuable tools available to a photographer. But selective focus works only when the desired areas of an image are in focus properly. For the digital SLR photographer, correct focus can be one of the trickiest parts of the technical and creative process.

To make your job easier, the Rebel XTi has a precision nine-point autofocus system that uses a separate CMOS sensor in the viewing system to measure the contrast of the image. When the contrast is highest at the active autofocus point(s), that part of the image is in sharp focus. These points can be selected automatically by the camera, or manually by you, the photographer. They're represented by the nine boxes visible in the viewfinder (see Figure 5.9, in which the active illuminated AF point can be seen).

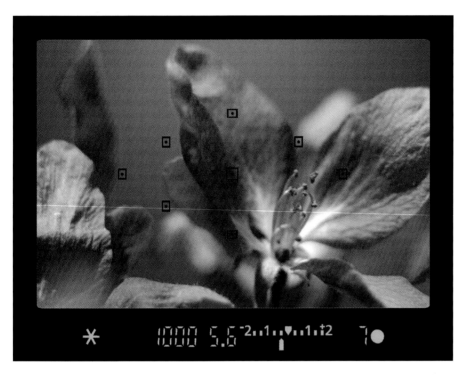

Figure 5.9 Any of the nine autofocus points can be selected by the photographer manually, or by the camera automatically.

Your camera's autofocus sensors require a minimum amount of light to operate, which is why autofocus capabilities are possible only with lenses having an f/5.6 or larger maximum aperture. If necessary, the AF assist preflash from the XTi's built-in flash and the autofocus assist provided by Canon's dedicated flash units offer additional light that helps assure enough illumination for autofocus. (The Digital Rebel XTi's front panel lamp does not serve as an autofocus assist lamp, as it does on some other Canon cameras, including the EOS 30D.)

The XTi has three AF modes: One Shot AF (also known as single autofocus), AI Servo (continuous autofocus), and AI Focus AF (which switches between the two as appropriate). I'll explain all of these in more detail later in this section.

MANUAL FOCUS

With manual focus activated by sliding the switch on the lens, your XTi lets you set the focus yourself. There are some advantages and disadvantages to this approach. While your batteries will last longer in manual focus mode, it will take you longer to focus the camera for each photo, a process that can be difficult. Modern digital cameras, even dSLRs, depend so much on autofocus that the viewfinders of models that have less than full-frame-sized sensors are no longer designed for optimum manual focus. Pick up any film camera and you'll see a bigger, brighter viewfinder with a focusing screen that's a joy to focus on manually. Today, you'd need a full-frame digital camera, like the Canon EOS 5D, to get such a bright view and easy focus.

Focus Pocus

Although Canon introduced its autofocus system in the 1980s, back in the day of film cameras, prior to that focusing was always done manually. Honest. Even though viewfinders were bigger and brighter than they are today, special focusing screens, magnifiers, and other gadgets were often used to help the photographer achieve correct focus. Imagine what it must have been like to focus manually under demanding, fast-moving conditions such as sports photography.

Focusing was problematic because our eyes and brains have poor memory for correct focus, which is why your eye doctor must shift back and forth between sets of lenses and ask "Does that look sharper, or was it sharper before?" in determining your correct prescription. Similarly, manual focusing involves jogging the focus ring back and forth as you go from almost in focus to sharp focus to almost focused again. The little clockwise and counterclockwise arcs decrease in size until you've zeroed in on the point of correct focus. What you're looking for is the image with the most contrast between the edges of elements in the image.

The XTi's autofocus mechanism, like all such systems found in SLR cameras, also evaluates increases and decreases in sharpness, but is able to remember the progression perfectly, so that autofocus can lock in much more quickly and, with an image that has sufficient contrast, more precisely. Unfortunately, while the XTi's focus system finds it easy to measure degrees of apparent focus at each of the focus points in the viewfinder, it doesn't really know with any certainty *which* object should be in sharpest focus. Is it the closest object? The subject in the center? Something lurking *behind* the closest subject? A person standing over at the side of the picture? Figure 5.10 illustrates the dilemma. Many of the techniques for using autofocus effectively involve telling the Rebel XTi exactly what it should be focusing on.

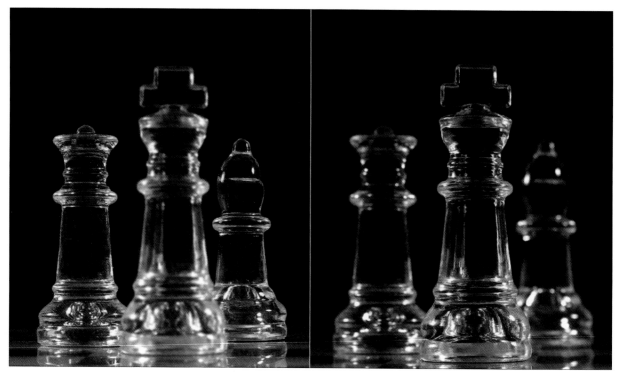

Figure 5.10 Only you can decide whether the focus point should be the chess pieces in back (left), or the one in front (right).

Adding Circles of Confusion

But there are other factors in play, as well. You know that increased depth-of-field brings more of your subject into focus. But more DOF also makes autofocusing (or manual focusing) more difficult because the contrast is lower between objects at different distances. So, autofocus with a 200mm lens (or zoom setting) may be easier than at a 28mm focal length (or zoom setting) because the longer lens has less apparent depth-of-field. By the same token, a lens with a maximum aperture of f/1.8 will be easier to autofocus (or manually focus) than one of the same focal length with an f/4 maximum aperture, because the f/4 lens has more depth-of-field *and* a dimmer view.

To make things even more complicated, many subjects aren't polite enough to remain still. They move around in the frame, so that even if the XTi is sharply focused on your main subject, it may change position and require refocusing. An intervening subject may pop into the frame and pass between you and the subject you meant to photograph. You (or the XTi) have to decide whether to lock focus on this new subject or remain focused on the original subject. Finally, there are some kinds of subjects that are difficult to bring into sharp focus because they lack enough contrast to allow the XTi's AF system (or our eyes) to lock in. Blank walls, a clear blue sky, or other subject matter may make focusing difficult.

If you find all these focus factors confusing, you're on the right track. Focus is, in fact, measured using something called a *circle of confusion*. An ideal image consists of zillions of tiny little points, which, like all points, theoretically have no height or width. There is perfect contrast between the point and its surroundings. You can think of each point as a pinpoint of light in a darkened room. When a given point is out of focus, its edges decrease in contrast and it changes from a perfect point to a tiny disc with blurry edges (remember, blur is the lack of contrast between boundaries in an image). (See Figure 5.11.)

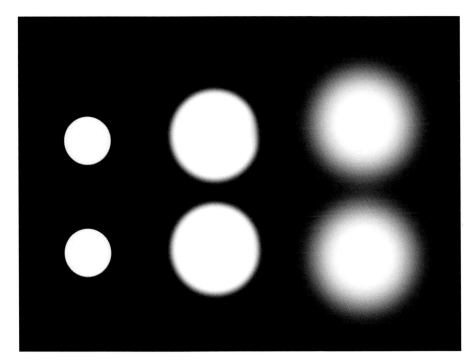

Figure 5.11 When a pinpoint of light (left) goes out of focus, its blurry edges form a circle of confusion (center and right).

If this blurry disc is small enough, our eye still perceives it as a point. It's only when the disc grows large enough that we can see it as a blur rather than a sharp point that a given point is viewed as out of focus. You can see, then, that enlarging an image, either by displaying it larger on your computer monitor or by making a large print, also enlarges the size of each circle of confusion. Moving closer to the image does the same thing. So, parts of an image that may look perfectly sharp in a 5 × 7-inch print viewed at arm's length might appear blurry when blown up to 11 × 14 and examined at the same distance. Take a few steps back, however, and it may look sharp again.

To a lesser extent, the viewer also affects the apparent size of these circles of confusion. Some people see details better at a given distance, and they may perceive smaller circles of confusion than someone standing next to them. For the most part, however, such differences are small. Truly blurry images will look blurry to just about everyone under the same conditions.

Technically, there is just one plane within your picture area, parallel to the back of the camera (or sensor, in the case of a digital camera), that is in sharp focus. That's the plane in which the points of the image are rendered as precise points. At every other plane in front of or behind the focus plane, the points show up as discs that range from slightly blurry to extremely blurry (see Figure 5.12). In practice, the discs in many of these planes will still be so small that we see them as points, and that's where we get *depth-of-field*. DOF is just the range of planes that include discs that we perceive as points rather than blurred splotches. The size of this range increases as the aperture is reduced in size, and is allocated roughly one-third in front of the plane of sharpest focus and two-thirds behind it.

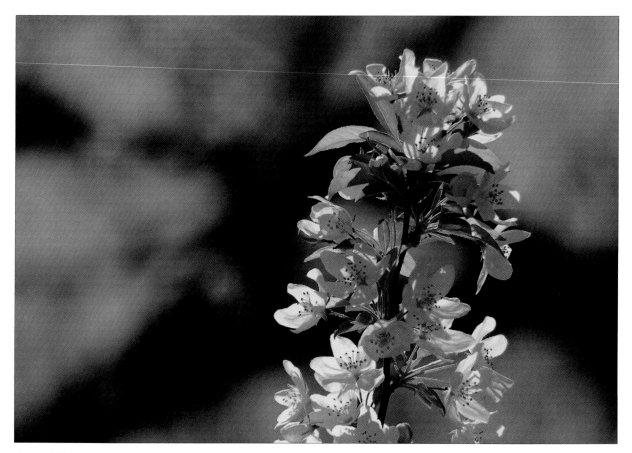

Figure 5.12 Only the blossoms in the foreground are in focus; the area behind them appears blurry because the depth-of-field is limited.

Making Sense of Sensors

The number and type of autofocus sensors can affect how well the system operates. The new Digital Rebel XTi and the EOS 30D have nine focus points, while the Canon EOS-1Ds Mark II and Canon EOS-1D Mark III have a whopping 45 autofocus focus points. These focus sensors can consist of vertical or horizontal lines of pixels, cross-shapes, and often a mixture of these types within a single camera. The more AF points available, the more easily the camera can differentiate among areas of the frame, and the more precisely you can specify the area you want to be in focus if you're manually choosing a focus spot.

As the camera collects contrast information from the sensors, it then evaluates it to determine whether the desired sharp focus has been achieved. The calculations may include whether the subject is moving, and whether the camera needs to "predict" where the subject will be when the shutter-release button is fully depressed and the picture is taken. The speed with which the camera is able to evaluate focus and then move the lens elements into the proper position to achieve the sharpest focus determines how fast the autofocus mechanism is. Although your XTi will almost always focus more quickly than a human, there are types of shooting situations where that's not fast enough.

For example, if you're having problems shooting sports because the XTi's autofocus system manically follows each moving subject, a better choice might be to switch autofocus modes or shift into manual and prefocus on a spot where you anticipate the action will be, such as a goal line or soccer net. At night football games, for example, when I am shooting with a telephoto lens almost wide open, I often focus manually on one of the referees who happens to be standing where I expect the action to be taking place (say, a halfback run or a pass reception). When I am less sure about what is going to happen, I may switch to AI Servo autofocus and let the camera decide.

Your Autofocus Mode Options

Choosing the right autofocus mode when using Creative Zone modes, and the way in which focus points are selected is your key to success. Using the wrong mode for a particular type of photography can lead to a series of pictures that are all sharply focused—on the wrong subject. When I first started shooting sports with an autofocus SLR (back in the film camera days), I covered one game alternating between shots of base runners and outfielders with pictures of a promising young pitcher, all from a position next to the third-base dugout. The base runner and outfielder photos were great, because their backgrounds didn't distract the autofocus mechanism. But all my photos of the pitcher had the focus tightly zeroed in on the fans in the stands behind him. Because I was shooting film instead of a digital camera, I didn't know about my gaffe until the film was developed.

A simple change, such as locking in focus or focus zone manually, or even manually focusing, would have done the trick.

To save battery power, your XTi doesn't start to focus the lens until you partially depress the shutter release. But, autofocus isn't some mindless beast out there snapping your pictures in and out of focus with no feedback from you after you press that button. There are several settings you can modify that return at least a modicum of control to you. Your first decision should be whether you set the XTi to One Shot, AI Servo AF, or AI Focus AF. As I mentioned in Chapter 1, to choose autofocus mode press the AF button (the right cross key) and spin the Main Dial or press the up/down cross keys to choose from the three modes that appear on the camera setting display (shown again in Figure 5.13). Press Set to lock in your choice. (The AF/M switch on the lens must be set to AF before you can change autofocus mode.)

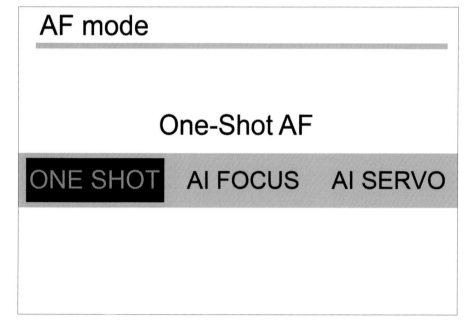

Figure 5.13 Rotate the Main Dial until the AF choice you want is shown on the LCD.

One Shot AF

In this mode, also called *single autofocus*, focus is set once when the release button is pressed halfway, and remains at that setting until the button is fully depressed, taking the picture, or until you release the shutter button without taking a shot. For non-action photography, this setting is usually your best choice, because it minimizes out-of-focus pictures (at the expense of spontaneity). The drawback here is that you might not be able to take a picture at all while the camera is seeking focus; you're locked out until the autofocus mechanism is happy with the current setting. One Shot AF/single autofocus is sometimes referred to as *focus priority* for that reason. Because of the small delay while the camera zeroes in on correct focus, you might experience slightly more shutter lag. This mode uses less battery power.

When sharp focus is achieved, the selected focus point will flash red in the viewfinder, and the focus confirmation light at the lower right will flash green. Press the AE/FE lock button simultaneously and the exposure will be locked at the same time. By keeping the shutter button depressed halfway, you'll find you can reframe the image while retaining the focus (and exposure) that's been set.

AI Focus AF

This setting is actually a combination of the first two. When selected, the camera focuses using One Shot AF and locks in the focus setting. But, if the subject begins moving, it will switch automatically to AI Servo AF and change the focus to keep the subject sharp. AI Focus AF is a good choice when you're shooting a mixture of action pictures and less dynamic shots and want to use One Shot AF when possible without losing the advantages of AI Servo AF when it would be useful.

AI Servo AF

This mode, also known as *continuous autofocus* is the mode to use for sports and other fast-moving subjects. In this mode, once the shutter release is partially depressed, the camera sets the focus but continues to monitor the subject, so that if it moves or you move, the lens will be refocused to suit. Focus and exposure aren't really locked until you press the shutter release down all the way to take the picture. You'll often see continuous autofocus referred to as *release priority*. If you press the shutter release down all the way while the system is refining focus, the camera will go ahead and take a picture, even if the image is slightly out of focus. You'll find that AI Servo AF produces the least amount of shutter lag of any auto-focus mode: press the button, and the camera fires. It also uses the most battery power, because the autofocus system operates as long as the shutter-release button is partially depressed.

AI Servo AF uses a technology called *predictive AF*, which allows the XTi to calculate the correct focus if the subject is moving toward or away from the camera at a constant rate. It uses either the automatically selected AF point or the point you select manually to set focus.

Setting AF Point

You can change which of the nine focus points the Canon Digital Rebel XTi uses to calculate correct focus, or allow the camera to select the point for you. As I mentioned in Chapter 1, in A-DEP, or any of the Basic Zone shooting modes, the focus point is always selected automatically by the camera. In the other Creative

Zone modes, you can allow the camera to select the focus point automatically, or you can specify which focus point should be used.

To set the focus point manually, look through the viewfinder and then press the AF point selection button on the upper-right corner of the back of the camera, and use either the cross keys (which move highlighting directly to a point) or the Main Dial (which rotates through all the points in turn) to select the zone you want to use (see Figure 5.14). As you cycle among the focus points, each will be illuminated in turn. Press the Set button to switch back and forth between the center autofocus point and automatic selection.

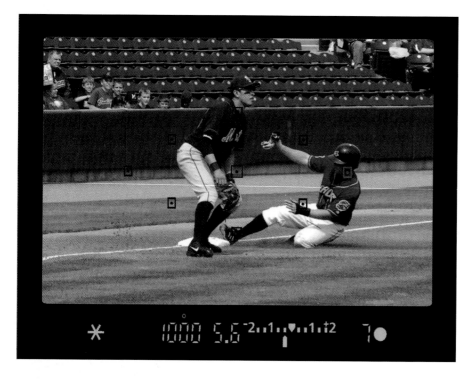

Figure 5.14 When selecting focus points manually, use the cross keys or rotate the Main Dial to select specific points.

Continuous Shooting

The Canon Digital Rebel XTi has a single continuous shooting mode that grabs shots at a speedy three frames per second rate. This capability reminds me how far digital photography has brought us. The first accessory I purchased when I worked as a sports photographer some years ago was a motor drive for my film SLR. It enabled me to snap off a series of shots in rapid succession, which came in very handy when a fullback broke through the line and headed for the end zone. Even a seasoned action photographer can miss the decisive instant when a crucial block is made, or a baseball superstar's bat shatters and pieces of cork fly out. Continuous shooting simplifies taking a series of pictures, either to ensure that one has more or less the exact moment you want to capture or to capture a sequence that is interesting as a collection of successive images.

The XTi's "motor drive" capabilities are, in many ways, much superior to what you get with a film camera. For one thing, a motor-driven film camera can eat up film at an incredible pace, which is why many of them are used with cassettes that hold hundreds of feet of film stock. At three frames per second (typical of film cameras), a short burst of a few seconds can burn up as much as half of an ordinary 36-exposure roll of film. Digital cameras, in contrast, have reusable "film," so if you waste a few dozen shots on non-decisive moments, you can erase them and shoot more.

The increased capacity of digital film cards gives you a prodigious number of frames to work with. At a baseball game I covered earlier this year, I took more than 1000 images in a couple hours. Yet, even shooting RAW+JPEG Fine I could fit more than 212 images on a single 4 GB Compact Flash card. If I'd switched to JPEG, I could have taken about 913 images without switching cards. Even at the top speed of three frames per second that the XTi is capable of, that's a lot of shooting. Given an average burst of about eight frames per sequence (nobody really takes 15-20 shots or more of one play in a baseball game), I was able to capture 32 different sequences before I needed to swap cards.

On the other hand, at a football game I covered later in the same month (there are some weird sports overlaps in early September!), the longer bursts came in handy, because running and passing plays often lasted 5 to 10 seconds, and changed in character as the action switched from the quarterback dropping back to pass or hand off the ball, to the receiver or running back trying to gain as much yardage as possible. Even simple plays, like a punt, seemed more exciting when captured in a sequence of shots, as in Figure 5.15.

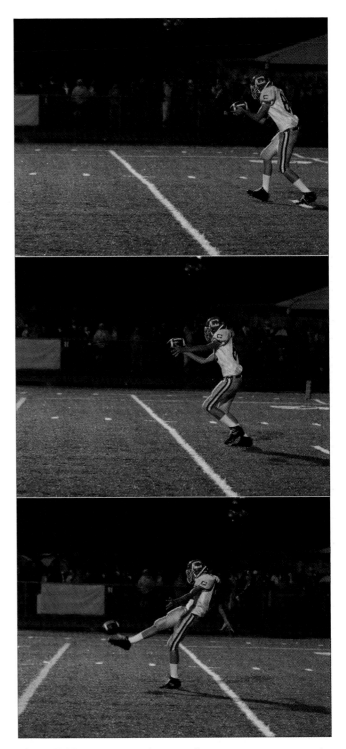

Figure 5.15 Continuous shooting allows you to capture an entire sequence of exciting moments as they unfold.

To use the XTi's continuous shooting mode, press the Drive button and choose from cycle among Single Shot, Continuous, and Self-Timer in the menu that pops up on the LCD (see Figure 5.16). When you partially depress the shutter button, the viewfinder will display a number representing the maximum number of shots you can take at the current quality settings. (If your battery is low, this figure will be lower.) The XTi will generally allow you to take as many as 27 JPEG shots in a single burst, or 10 RAW photos.

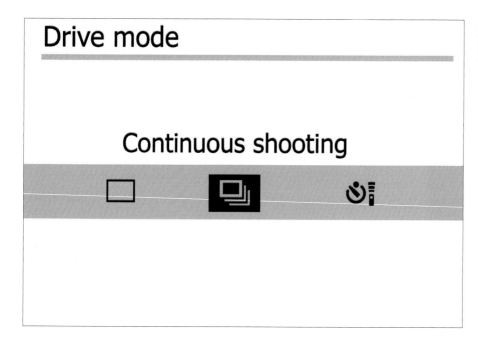

Figure 5.16 Press Drive button until the Continuous icon appears.

To increase this number, reduce the image quality setting by switching to JPEG only (from JPEG+RAW), to a lower JPEG quality setting, or by reducing the XTi's resolution from L to M or S. The reason the size of your bursts is limited is that continuous images are first shuttled into the XTi's internal memory buffer, and then doled out to the Compact Flash card as quickly as they can be written to the card. Technically, the XTi takes the RAW data received from the digital image processor and converts it to the output format you've selected—either .jpg or .cr2 (RAW)—and deposits it in the buffer ready to store on the card.

This internal "smart" buffer can suck up photos much more quickly than the CF card and, indeed, some memory cards are significantly faster or slower than others. When the buffer fills, you can't take any more continuous shots (a buSY indicator appears in the viewfinder and LCD status panel) until the XTi has written some of them to the card, making more room in the buffer.

Setting Image Parameters

You can fine-tune the images that you take in several different ways. For example, if you don't want to choose a predefined white balance or use white balance bracketing (both discussed earlier in this book), you can set a custom white balance based on the illumination of the site where you'll be taking photos, or choose a white balance based on color temperature. With the Picture Styles options, you can set up customized sharpening, tone, color, saturation, and hue for various types of pictures, plus three personal sets of settings that you can recall at any time. This section shows you how to use the available image parameters.

Customizing White Balance

Back in the film days, color films were standardized, or balanced, for a particular "color" of light. Digital cameras like the Rebel XTi use a particular "white balance" matched to the color of light used to expose your photograph. The right white balance is measured using a scale called *color temperature*. Color temperatures were assigned by heating a mythical "black body radiator" and recording the spectrum of light it emitted at a given temperature in degrees Kelvin. So, daylight at noon has a color temperature in the 5500 to 6000 degree range. Indoor illumination is around 3400 degrees. Hotter temperatures produce bluer images (think blue-white hot) while cooler temperatures produce redder images (think of a dull-red glowing ember). Because of human nature, though, bluer images are actually called "cool" (think wintry day) and redder images are called "warm," (think ruddy sunset) even though their color temperatures are reversed.

If a photograph is exposed indoors under warm illumination with a digital camera sensor balanced for cooler daylight, the image will appear much too reddish (see Figure 5.17). An image

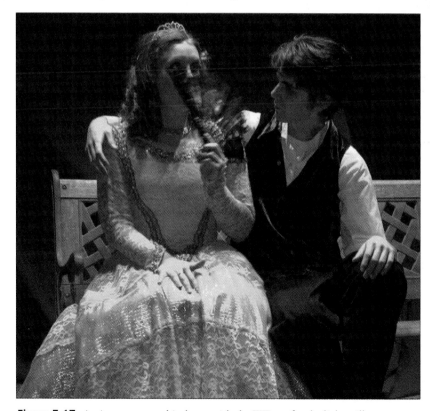

Figure 5.17 An image exposed indoors with the WB set for daylight will appear too reddish.

exposed outdoors with the white balance set for incandescent illumination will seem much too blue (see Figure 5.18). These color casts may be too strong to remove in an image editor from JPEG files, although if you shoot RAW you can change the WB setting to the correct value when you import the image into your editor.

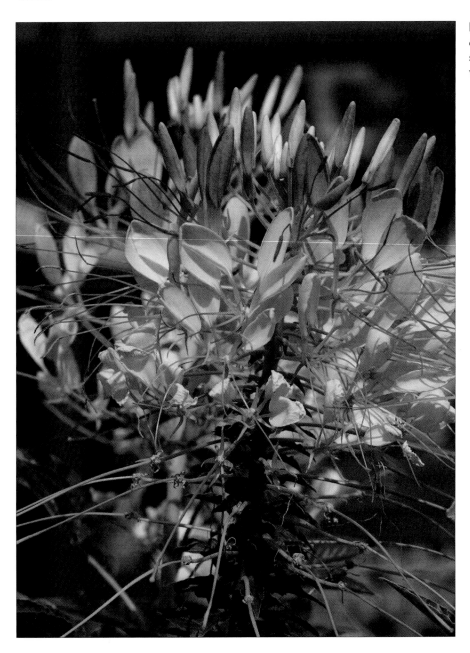

Figure 5.18 An image exposed outdoors with the WB set for tungsten illumination will appear too blue.

The Auto White Balance (AWB) examines your scene and chooses an appropriate value. However, the XTi's selection process is far from foolproof. Under bright lighting conditions it may assume that the light source is daylight and balance the picture accordingly, even though, in fact, you may be shooting under extremely bright incandescent illumination. In dimmer light, the camera's electronics may assume that the illumination is tungsten, and color balance for that.

To access the Digital Rebel XTi's white balance options, press the WB button (the down cross key) to produce a list of choices, shown in Figure 5.19. Use the cross keys and Set button to choose the white balance setting you want. The presets in the WB list apply specific color temperatures. For example, the Daylight setting sets WB to 5200K, while the Shade setting uses a much bluer 7000K. The chief difference between direct daylight and shade or even tungsten light sources is nothing more than the proportion of red and blue light. The spectrum of colors is continuous, but it is biased toward one end or the other.

However, some types of fluorescent lights produce illumination that has a severe deficit in certain colors, such as only *particular* shades of red. If you looked at the spectrum or rainbow of colors encompassed by such a light source, it would have black bands in it, representing particular wavelengths of light that are absent. You can't compensate for this deficiency by adding all tones of red. That's why the White Fluorescent Light setting of your XTi may provide less than satisfactory results with other kinds of fluorescent bulbs. If you take many photographs under

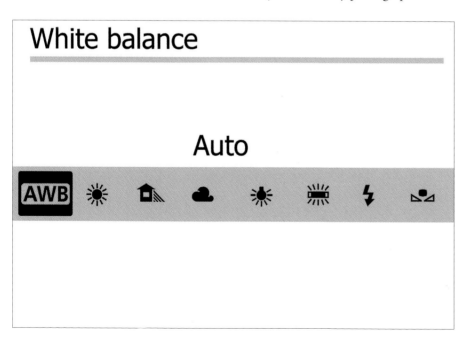

Figure 5.19 Press the WB button and choose a white balance preset value from the menu.

a particular kind of non-compatible fluorescent light, you might want to investigate specialized fluorescent light filters for your lenses, available from camera stores.

However, you might also get acceptable results using the final choice on the WB list. Custom allows you to use specific white balances you've set yourself using the Custom WB choice in the Shooting Menu 2. As I described in Chapter 3, to set a custom white balance you'll need to focus manually (with the lens set on MF) on a plain white or gray object, such as a card or wall, making sure the object fills the center of the viewfinder. Then, take a photo under the lighting conditions you want to use as your custom white balance.

Then, press the Menu button and select Custom WB. Use the cross keys (if necessary) to scroll among the available pictures until the reference image you just took appears and press the Set button to store the white balance of the image as your Custom setting. The setting will remain in your XTi's memory.

Finally, as I described in Chapter 3, you can *shift* the XTi's standard color temperature that is used as a basis for all its corrections, changing the default temperature to a new value with a bias toward the green, magenta, blue, or amber directions, which correspond to movements along the central axes of the chart shown in Figure 5.20 in the up (green), down (magenta), left (blue), or right (amber/yellow) directions. You can also combine biases of adjacent hues by moving the cursor diagonally toward the upper left (more blue and more green), upper right (more green and more amber), lower right (more amber and more magenta), and lower left (more magenta and more blue).

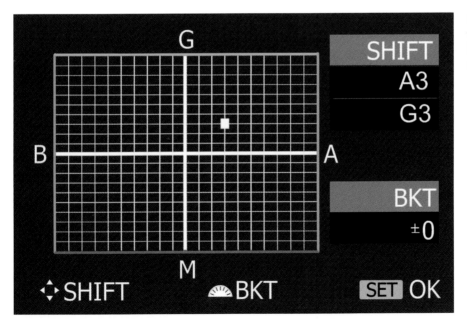

Figure 5.20 The standard white balance setting can be biased in a direction of your choosing.

Picture Style Parameters

As I outlined in detail in Chapter 3, you can redefine the amount of sharpening, contrast, color saturation, and color tone for any of the five user-definable Picture Styles (Standard, Portrait, Landscape, Neutral, and Faithful) and create your own styles in User Def. 1, User Def. 2, and User Def. 3. In addition, you can modify the sharpening, contrast, filter effect, and toning effect options in the Monochrome parameter set. You can learn how to make these changes in Chapter 3, but here is a summary of how the key parameters affect your images.

- **Sharpness**. Increases or decreases the contrast of the edge outlines in your image, making the photo appear more or less sharp. You can select sharpening from 0 to +2 or 0 to −2. Remember that boosting sharpness also increases the overall contrast of an image, so you'll want to use this parameter in conjunction with the contrast parameter with caution.

- **Contrast**. Compresses the range of tones in an image (increase contrast from 0 to +2) or expands the range of tones (from 0 to −2) to decrease contrast. Higher contrast images tend to lose detail in both shadows and highlights, while lower contrast images retain the detail but appear more flat and have less snap.

- **Color saturation**. You can adjust the richness of the color from low saturation (0 to −2) to high saturation (0 to +2). Lower saturation produces a muted look that can be more realistic for certain kinds of subjects, such as humans. Higher saturation produces a more vibrant appearance, but can be garish and unrealistic if carried too far. Boost your saturation if you want a vivid image, or to brighten up pictures taken on overcast days.

- **Color tone**. This parameter changes the bias of the image toward the red or yellow ends of the scale, with settings from 0 to −2 producing ruddier skin tones, and 0 to +2 creating more yellowish skin tones.

- **Filter effect** (Monochrome only). Choose from Yellow, Orange, Red, or Green filters, or None.

- **Toning effect** (Monochrome only). Select from Sepia, Blue, Purple, or Green toning, or None.

6

Working with Lenses

One of the best things about owning a Canon Digital Rebel XTi is the extensive collection of compatible lenses available to enhance its capabilities. Thousands of current and older lenses introduced by Canon and third-party vendors since 1987 can be used to give you a wider view, bring distant subjects closer, let you focus closer, shoot under lower-light conditions, or provide a more detailed, sharper image for critical work. Other than the sensor itself, the lens you choose for your dSLR is the most important component in determining image quality and perspective of your images.

This chapter explains how to select the best lenses for the kinds of photography you want to do.

But First, a Word from Our Sensor

One pervasive consideration that will trip us up in this chapter (and throughout this book) is the omnipresent *lens crop factor*. If the sensor is smaller than the standard 35mm film frame (24mm × 36mm), then any given lens will produce a field of view that's *cropped* from that full frame. To express the "real" field of view in 35mm terms, you must multiply a lens's focal length by the crop factor, which in the case of the XTi is 1.6X. Canon also sells dSLRs with 1.3X and 1X (full frame) sensors, which provide the fields of view shown in Figure 6.1. At this writing, Canon's camera line includes the Canon EOS-1Ds Mark II and Canon EOS 5D,

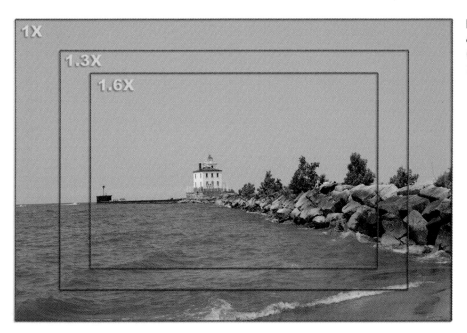

Figure 6.1 Canon offers digital SLRs with full-frame (1X) crops, as well as 1.3X and 1.6X crops.

which both provide a full-frame, 1X crop (or non-crop) of the image, compared to a film camera. The Canon EOS-1D Mark III offers a 1.3X crop, while the Canon EOS 30D and all the Digital Rebel models offer a 1.6X crop of the full-frame sensor area.

If you're accustomed to using full-frame film or digital cameras, you might find it helpful to use the crop factor as a multiplier to translate a lens's real focal length into the full-frame equivalent. If you've worked with full-frame film cameras for many years, and you have come to think of an 85mm lens as a short telephoto, multiplying that focal length by 1.6 to arrive at the lens's 136mm medium tele-photo field-of-view can be useful. However, as time passes, fewer and fewer pho-tographers buying the Rebel XTi will have compiled experience with full-frame cameras, and so it makes more sense to just refer to the lens's "real" focal length rather than make a conversion that might not be necessary. It's like driving in Canada or Europe at 60 kph. If your destination is 120 kilometers distant, you don't need to translate that into 73 miles and your traveling speed into 36.6 mph to figure out you'll be there in two hours. So, throughout most of this book I've been using actual focal lengths and not equivalents, except when referring to spe-cific wide angle or telephoto focal length ranges and their fields of view.

Your First Lens

Some Canon dSLRs are almost always purchased with a lens. The Digital Rebel, Digital Rebel XT, and Digital Rebel XTi, for example, are often bought as entry-level cameras, frequently by first-time SLR or dSLR owners who find the Canon EF-S 18-55mm f/3.5-5.6 autofocus lens an irresistible bargain at about $100 over the cost of the camera body alone. Other, more advanced, Canon models, including the EOS-1D Mark III, EOS-1Ds Mark II, and EOS 5D, are generally purchased without a lens by veteran Canon photographers who already have a complement of optics to use with their cameras.

The Canon Digital Rebel XTi is an excellent first Canon camera for photographers experienced with another camera line, or for ambitious beginners, so an economical "kit" lens can be very attractive. However, you'll also find many purchasers who are upgrading from the original Digital Rebel model, from a Canon film camera, or who are buying the XTi as a second camera body to complement another Canon camera. These owners, too, generally have lenses they can use with their new XTi.

So, depending on which category you fall into, you'll need to make a decision about what kit lens to buy, or decide what other kind of lenses you need to fill out your complement of Canon optics. This section will cover "first lens" concerns, while later in the chapter we'll look at "add-on lens" considerations.

When deciding on a first lens, you'll want to consider several factors:

- **Cost.** Even at its modest price, you might have stretched your budget a bit to purchase your Digital Rebel XTi, so you might want to keep the cost of your first lens fairly low. Fortunately, excellent lenses are available that will add from $100 to $300 to the price of your camera if purchased at the same time.

- **Zoom range.** If you have only one lens, you'll want a fairly long zoom range to provide as much flexibility as possible. Fortunately, the two most popular basic lenses for the XTi (see the next section) have 3X to 5X zoom ranges, extending from moderate wide angle/normal out to medium telephoto. Either is fine for everyday shooting, portraits, and some types of sports.

- **Adequate maximum aperture.** You'll want an f/stop of at least f/3.5 to f/4 for shooting under fairly low light conditions. The thing to watch for is the maximum aperture when the lens is zoomed to its telephoto end. You may end up with no better than an f/5.6 maximum aperture. That's not great, but you can often live with it.

- **Image quality.** Your starter lens should have good image quality, because that's one of the primary factors that will be used to judge your photos. Even at its low price, the 18-55mm kit lens includes extra-low dispersion glass and aspherical elements that minimize distortion and chromatic aberration; it's sharp enough for most applications. If you read the user evaluations in the online photography forums, you know that owners of the kit lens have been very pleased with its image quality.

- **Size matters.** A good walking around lens is compact in size and light in weight.

- **Fast/close focusing.** Your first lens should have a speedy autofocus system (which is where the ultrasonic motor/USM found in all but the bargain-basement lenses is an advantage; you'll find USM in the name of the lens if it's present). Close focusing (to 12 inches or closer) will let you use your basic lens for some types of macro photography.

You can find comparisons of the lenses discussed in the next section, as well as third-party lenses from Sigma, Tokina, Tamron, and other vendors, in online groups and websites. I'll provide my recommendations, but more information is always helpful.

Buy Now, Expand Later

The XTi is commonly available with several good, basic lenses that can serve you well as a "walk around" lens (one you keep on the camera most of the time, especially when you're out and about without your camera bag). The number of options available to you is actually quite amazing, even if your budget is limited to about $100-$350 for your first lens. One other vendor, for example, offers only 18mm-70mm and 18mm-55mm kit lenses in that price range, plus a 24mm-85mm zoom. Two of the most popular starter lenses Canon offers are shown in Figure 6.2. Canon's best-bet first lenses are:

- **Canon EF-S 18-55mm f/3.5-5.6 USM Autofocus Lens.** This is the least expensive option, which, depending on where you buy your camera, may add only about $100 to the purchase price of the body alone. This medium-wide to short telephoto lens (29mm-88mm full frame equivalent) is the standard lens sold as the basic kit lens for the Digital Rebel XTi for those on a budget. It is designed exclusively for Canon dSLRs with a 1.6X crop factor, and shouldn't be used on full-frame cameras (more on this later). A maximum aperture of f/5.6 at 55mm makes this a relatively slow lens that's not great for low-light shooting. You can often find the 18-55mm lens available separately for $100-$140.

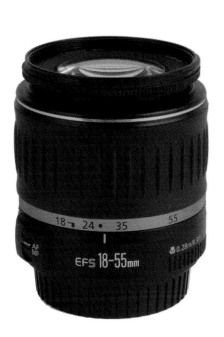
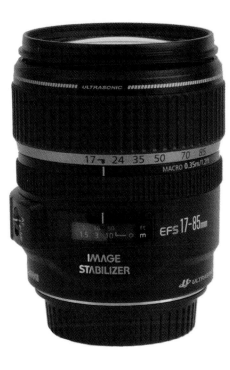

Figure 6.2 The Canon EF-S 18-55mm f/3.5-5.6 USM Autofocus lens (left) and Canon EF-S 17-85mm f/4-5.6 IS USM Autofocus lens (right) are two of the most popular starter lenses for the Digital Rebel XTi.

- **Canon EF-S 17-85mm f/4-5.6 IS USM Autofocus Lens.** This lens smashes through the arbitrary $350 price barrier I set earlier, but I'm making an exception because the 17-85mm lens is probably the most popular "basic" lens sold with the XTi, despite its $500-plus price tag. The allure here is the built-in image stabilization, which allows you to shoot rock-solid photos at shutter speeds that are at least two or three notches slower than you'd need normally (say, 1/8th second instead of 1/30th or 1/60th second), as long as your subject isn't moving. It also has a quiet, fast, reliable ultrasonic motor (more on that later, too). This is another lens designed for the 1.6X crop factor; all the remaining lenses in this list can also be used on full-frame cameras (I'll tell you why later in this chapter).

- **Canon EF 55-200mm f/4.5-5.6 II USM Autofocus Lightweight Compact Telephoto Zoom Lens.** If you bought the 18-55mm kit lens, this one picks up where that one leaves off, going from short telephoto to medium long (88mm-320mm full-frame equivalent). It's actually faster at 55mm than the basic kit lens, and it features a desirable ultrasonic motor. Best of all, it's very affordable at around $225. If you can afford only two lenses, the 18-55mm and this one make a good basic set.

- **Canon EF 24-85mm f/3.5-4.5 USM Autofocus Wide-Angle Telephoto Zoom Lens.** If you can get by with normal focal length to medium telephoto range, Canon offers four affordable lenses, plus one more expensive killer lens that's worth the extra expenditure. All of them can be used on full-frame or cropped-frame digital Canons, which is why they include "wide angle" in their product names. They're really wide-angle lenses only when mounted on a full-frame camera. This one, priced in the $300 range offers a useful range of focal lengths, extending from the equivalent of 38mm to 136mm.

- **Canon EF 28-105mm f/3.5-4.5 II USM Autofocus Wide-Angle Telephoto Zoom Lens.** If you want to save about $100 and gain a little reach, this 45mm-168mm (equivalent) lens might be what you are looking for.

- **Canon EF 28-135mm f/3.5-5.6 IS USM Image-Stabilized Autofocus Wide-Angle Telephoto Zoom Lens.** Image stabilization is especially useful at longer focal lengths, which makes this 45mm-216mm (equivalent) lens worth its $400-plus price tag.

- **Canon EF 28-200mm f/3.5-5.6 USM Autofocus Wide-Angle Telephoto Zoom Lens.** If you want one lens to do everything except wide-angle photography, this 7X zoom lens costs less than $400 and takes you from the equivalent of 45mm out to a long 320mm.

- **Canon Zoom Wide-Angle Telephoto EF 24-70mm f/2.8L USM Autofocus Lens.** I couldn't leave this premium lens out of the mix, even though it costs well over $1,000. (You can probably find it used in excellent condition at www.keh.com or www.bhphotovideo.com.) As part of Canon's L-series (Luxury) lens line, it offers the best sharpness over its focal range when compared with any of the other lenses in this list. Best of all, it's fast (for a zoom) with an f/2.8 maximum aperture that *doesn't change* as you zoom out. Unlike the other lenses, which may offer only an f/5.6 maximum f/stop at their longest zoom setting, this is a *constant aperture* lens, which retains its maximum f/stop. The added sharpness, constant aperture, and ultra-smooth USM motor is what you're paying for with this lens.

What Lenses Can You Use?

The previous section helped you sort out what lens you need to buy with your XTi (assuming you already didn't own any Canon lenses). Now, you're probably wondering what lenses can be added to your growing collection. (Trust me, it will grow.) You need to know which lenses are suitable and, most importantly, which lenses are fully compatible with your Digital Rebel XTi.

With the Rebel XTi, the compatibility issue is a simple one: it accepts any lens with the EF or EF-S designation, with full availability of all autoaperture, auto-focus, autoexposure, and image-stabilization features (if present). It's comforting to know that any EF (for full-frame or cropped sensors) or EF-S (for cropped sensor cameras only) will work as designed with your camera.

In addition to EF and EF-S lenses, you can also attach Nikon F mount, Olympus OM, Leica R, and M42 ("Pentax screw mount") and some older Canon lenses using the previous lens mounting system with a simple adapter, if you don't mind losing automatic focus and aperture control. If you use one of these lenses, you'll need to focus manually (even if the lens operates in autofocus mode on the camera it was designed for), and adjust the f/stop to the aperture you want to use to take the picture (because you lose the autoaperture feature, as well).

YOU AUTO KNOW

With so many automatic features available in lenses, it's easy to get confused. They've been available for Canon cameras for so long that we tend to take them for granted. Even so, you need to have a clear understanding of these capabilities, because some lenses and accessories don't have them. Here's a quick refresher.

■ **Auto aperture.** The lens remains set to its maximum (wide open) aperture while you are viewing and composing the image. When the shutter release is pressed, the aperture automatically changes (*stops down*) to the f/stop used to expose the image (the *taking aperture*). This enables you to compose your image using the brightest possible view, and also at the f/stop that provides the least amount of depth-of-field, so you can better estimate whether or not the sharply focused (and out-of-focus) parts of the image are what you want. You can also stop down the lens to the taking aperture by pressing the depth-of-field button. If you use older lenses (with an adapter) that have aperture rings, or so-called *preset* lenses, which were a type of lens with a manual aperture that you always had to stop down manually to the preset taking aperture, you don't get the benefit of auto aperture operation.

■ **Autoexposure.** When the Rebel XTi is set to a Basic Zone or Creative Zone exposure mode other than Manual, the camera can tell the lens which f/stop to use for automatic exposure. Usually the aperture is selected by the camera, but it can be chosen by you in Aperture Priority mode.

■ **Autofocus.** Autofocus is the ability of the Rebel XTi to set sharp focus for you, although you can also manually focus when the lens is set to the M position, or you are using a lens that does not have autofocus capabilities (with an adapter; all EF and EF-S lenses have electronic focus).

That means that lenses that don't have an aperture ring (such as Nikon G-series lenses) must be used only at their maximum aperture. Because of these limitations, you probably won't want to make extensive use of "foreign" lenses on your XTi, but an adapter can help you when you really, really need to use a particular focal length but don't have a suitable Canon-compatible lens. For example, I occasionally use an older 400mm lens that was originally designed for the Nikon line on my XTi. The lens needs to be mounted on a tripod for steadiness anyway, so its slower operation isn't a major pain. Another good match for me is the 105mm Micro-Nikkor that I sometimes use with my Rebel XTi (see Figure 6.3). Macro photos, too, are most often taken with the camera mounted on a tripod, and manual focus makes a lot of sense for fine-tuning focus and depth-of-field. Because of the contemplative nature of close-up photography, it's not much of an inconvenience to stop down to the taking aperture just before exposure.

The limitations on use of lenses within Canon's own product line (as well as lenses produced for earlier Canon SLRs by third-party vendors) is fairly clear-cut. The Digital Rebel XTi cannot be used with any of Canon's earlier lens mounting schemes for its film cameras, including the immediate predecessor to the EF mount, the FD mount (introduced with the Canon F1 in 1964 and used until the Canon T60 in 1990), FL (1964–1971), or the original Canon R mount (1959–1964). That's really all you need to know. While you'll find FD-to-EF adapters for about $40, you'll lose so many functions that it's rarely worth the bother.

In retrospect, the switch to the EF mount seems like a very good idea, because the initial EOS film cameras can now be seen as the beginning of Canon's rise to eventually become the leader in film and (later) digital SLR cameras. By completely revamping its lens mounting system, the company was able to take advantage of the latest advances in technology without compromise.

For example, when the original EF bayonet mount was introduced in 1987, the system incorporated new autofocus technology (EF actually stands for "electro focus") in a more rugged and less complicated form. A tiny motor was built into the lens itself, eliminating the need for mechanical linkages with the camera. Instead, electrical contacts are used to send power and the required focusing information to the motor. That's a much more robust and resilient system that made it easier for Canon to design faster and more accurate autofocus mechanisms just by redesigning the lenses.

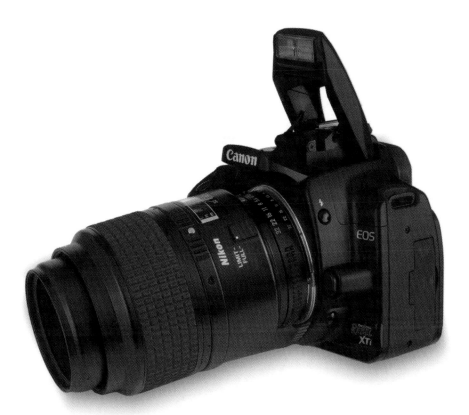

Figure 6.3 Is a Nikon lens mounted on a Canon camera sacrilege? In this case, it's just a good use of available resources.

WHY SO MANY LENS MOUNTS?

Four different lens mounts in 40-plus years might seem like a lot of different mounting systems, especially when compared to the Nikon F mount of 1959, which retained quite a bit of compatibility with that company's digital camera bodies during that same span. However, in digital photography terms, the EF mount itself is positively ancient, having remained reasonably stable for almost two decades. Lenses designed for the EF system work reliably with every EOS film and digital camera ever produced.

However, at the time, yet another lens mount switch, especially a change from the traditional breech system to a more conventional bayonet-type mount, was indeed a daring move by Canon. One of the reasons for staying with a particular lens type is to "lock" current users into a specific camera system. By introducing the EF mount, Canon in effect cut loose every photographer in its existing user base. If they chose to upgrade, they were free to choose another vendor's products and lenses. Only satisfaction with the previous Canon product line and the promise of the new system would keep them in the fold.

EF vs. EF-S

Today, in addition to its EF lenses, Canon offers lenses that use the EF-S (the S stands for "short back focus") mount, with the chief difference being (as you might expect) lens components that extend farther back into the camera body of some of Canon's latest digital cameras (specifically those with smaller than full-frame sensors), such as the XT and XTi. As I'll explain next, this refinement allows designing more compact, less-expensive lenses especially for those cameras, but which don't fit models like the EOS 5D, 1Ds Mark II, or 1D Mark III and 1D Mark II N (even though the latter two cameras do have a sensor that is smaller than full frame).

Canon's EF-S lens mount variation was born in 2003, when the company virtually invented the consumer-oriented digital SLR category by introducing the original EOS 300D/Digital Rebel, a dSLR that cost less than $1,000 *with lens* at a time when all other interchangeable lens digital cameras (including the XTi's "grandparent," the original EOS 10D) were priced closer to $2,000 with a basic lens. Like the EOS 10D introduced earlier that same year, the Digital Rebel featured a smaller than full-frame sensor with a 1.6X crop factor (Canon calls this format APS-C). But the Digital Rebel accepted lenses that took advantage of the shorter mirror found in APS-C cameras, with elements of shorter focal length lenses (wide angles), that extended *into* the camera, space that was off limits in other models because the mirror passed through that territory as it flipped up to expose the shutter and sensor.

In short (so to speak), the EF-S mount made it easier to design less-expensive, wide-angle lenses that could be used *only* with 1.6X-crop cameras (they can't be mounted on other Canon cameras), and featured a simpler design and reduced coverage area suitable for those non-full-frame models. The new mount made it possible to produce lenses like the ultra-wide EF-S 10-22mm f/3.5-4.5 USM lens, which has the equivalent field of view as a 16mm-35mm zoom on a full-frame camera.

Suitable cameras for EF-S lenses include the original Digital Rebel/300D, the Digital Rebel XT/350D, the Canon EOS 20D/30D, and, of course, the Digital Rebel XTi/400D. The EF-S lenses cannot be used on the EOS 10D, the 1D Mark II N (which has a 28.7mm × 19.1mm APS-H sensor with a 1.3X crop factor), or any of the full-frame digital or film EOS models. It's easy to tell an EF lens from an EF-S lens: the latter incorporate EF-S into their name! Plus, EF lenses have a raised red dot on the barrel that is used to align the lens with a matching dot on the camera when attaching the lens. EF-S lenses and compatible bodies use a white square instead. EF-S lenses also have a rubber ring at the attachment end that provides a bit of weather/dust sealing and protects the back components of the lens if a user attempts to mount it on a camera that is not EF-S compatible.

Ingredients of Canon's Alphanumeric Soup

The actual product names of individual Canon lenses are fairly easy to decipher; they'll include either the EF or EF-S designation, the focal length or focal length range of the lens, its maximum aperture, and some other information. Additional data may be engraved on the barrel or ring surrounding the front element of the lens, as shown in Figure 6.4. Here's a decoding of what the individual designations mean:

- **EF/EF-S.** If the lens is marked EF, it can safely be used on any Canon EOS camera, film or digital. If it is an EF-S lens, it should be used only on an EF-S compatible camera, such as the Digital Rebels, EOS 20D/30D/XT/XTi, and any newer APS-C cameras introduced after the publication of this book.

- **Focal length.** Given in millimeters or a millimeter range, such as 60mm in the case of a popular Canon macro lens, or 17-55mm, used to describe a medium-wide to short telephoto zoom.

- **Maximum aperture.** The largest f/stop available with a particular lens is given in a string of numbers that might seem confusing at first glance. For example, you might see *1:1.8* for a fixed-focal length (prime) lens, and *1:4.5-5.6* for a zoom. The initial 1: signifies that the f/stop given is actually a ratio or fraction (in regular notation, f/ replaces the 1:), which is why a 1:2 (or f/2) aperture is larger than a 1:4 (or f/4) aperture—just as 1/2 is larger than 1/4. With most zoom lenses, the maximum aperture changes as the lens is zoomed toward the telephoto position, so a range is given instead: 1:3.5-5.6. (Some zooms, called *constant aperture* lenses, keep the same maximum aperture throughout their range.)

- **Autofocus type.** Most newer Canon lenses that aren't of the bargain-basement type use Canon's *ultrasonic motor* autofocus system (more on that later), and they are given the USM designation. If USM does not appear on the lens or its model name, the lens uses the less-sophisticated AFD (arc-form drive) autofocus system or the micromotor (MM) drive mechanism.

- **Series.** Canon adds a Roman number to many of its products to represent an updated model with the same focal length or focal length range, so some lenses will have a II or III added to their name.

- **Pro quality.** Canon's more expensive lenses with more rugged construction and higher optical quality, intended for professional use, include the letter L (for "luxury") in their product name. You can further differentiate these lenses visually by a red ring around the lens barrel and the off-white color of the metal barrel itself in virtually all telephoto L-series lenses. (Some L-series lenses have shiny or textured black plastic exterior barrels.) Internally, every L lens includes at least one lens element that is built of ultra-low dispersion glass, constructed of expensive fluorite crystal, or uses an expensive ground (not molded) aspheric (non-spherical) lens component.

- **Filter size.** You'll find the front lens filter thread diameter in millimeters included on the lens, preceded by a Ø symbol, as in Ø58 or Ø72.

- **Special purpose lenses.** Some Canon lenses are designed for specific types of work, and they include appropriate designations in their names. For example, close-focusing lenses such as the Canon EF-S 60mm f/2.8 Macro USM lens incorporate the word *Macro* into their name. Lenses with perspective control features preface the lens name with T-S (for tilt-shift). Lenses with built-in image stabilization features, such as the nifty EF 28-300mm f/3.5-5.6L IS USM telephoto zoom include *IS* in their product names.

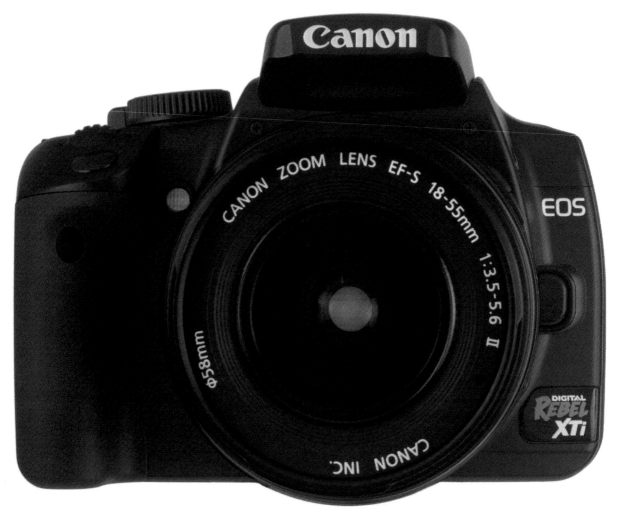

Figure 6.4 Most of the key specifications of the lens are engraved in the ring around the front element.

SORTING THE LENS MOTOR DRIVES

Incorporating the autofocus motor inside the lens was an innovative move by Canon, and it allowed the company to produce better and more sophisticated lenses as technology became available to upgrade the focusing system. As a result, you'll find four different types of motors in Canon-designed lenses, each with cost and practical considerations.

- **AFD (Arc-form drive) and Micromotor (MM) drives** are built around tiny versions of electromagnetic motors, which generally use gear trains to produce the motion needed to adjust the focus of the lens. Both are slow, noisy, and not particularly effective with larger lenses. Manual focus adjustments are possible only when the motor drive is disengaged.

- **Micromotor ultrasonic motor (USM) drives** use high-frequency vibration to produce the motion used to drive the gear train, resulting in a quieter operating system at a cost that's not much more than that of electromagnetic motor drives. With the exception of a couple lenses that have a slipping clutch mechanism, manual focus with this kind of system is possible only when the motor drive is switched off and the lens set in manual mode. This is the kind of USM system you'll find in lower cost lenses.

- **Ring ultrasonic motor (USM) drives**, available in two different types (*electronic focus ring USM* and *ring USM*), also use high-frequency movement, but generate motion using a pair of vibrating metal rings to adjust focus. Both variations allow a feature called Full Time Manual (FTM) focus, which lets you make manual adjustments to the lens's focus even when the autofocus mechanism is engaged. With electronic focus ring USM, manual focus is possible only when the lens is mounted on the camera and the camera is turned on; the focus ring of lenses with ring USM can be turned at any time.

Your Second (and Third...) Lens

There are really only two advantages to owning just a single lens. One of them is creative. Keeping one set of optics mounted on your XTi all the time forces you to be especially imaginative in your approach to your subjects. I once visited Europe with only a single camera body and 35mm f/2 lens. The experience was actually quite exciting, because I had to use a variety of techniques to allow that one lens to serve for landscapes, available light photos, action, close-ups, portraits, and other kinds of images. Canon makes an excellent 35mm f/2 lens (which focuses down to 9.6 inches) that's perfect for that kind of experiment, although, today my personal choice would be the sublime Canon Wide-Angle EF 35mm f/1.4L USM Autofocus lens.

Of course, it's more likely that your "single" lens is actually a zoom, which is, in truth, many lenses in one, taking you from, say, 17mm to 85mm (or some other range) with a rapid twist of the zoom lever. You'll still find some creative challenges when you stick to a single zoom lens's focal lengths.

The second advantage of the unilens camera is a marginal technical benefit. If you don't exchange lenses, the chances of dust and dirt getting inside your XTi and settling on the sensor is reduced (but *not* eliminated entirely). Although I've known some photographers who minimized the number of lens changes they made for this very reason, reducing the number of lenses you work with is not a productive or rewarding approach for most of us, especially when you consider that the XTi has a built-in dust "eliminator" feature.

It's more likely that you'll succumb to the malady known as *Lens Lust*, which is defined as an incurable disease marked by a significant yen for newer, better, longer, faster, sharper, anything-er optics for your camera. In its worst manifestations, sufferers find themselves with lenses that have overlapping zoom ranges or capabilities, because one or the other offers a slight margin in performance or suitability for specific tasks. When you find yourself already lusting after a new lens before you've really had a chance to put your latest purchase to the test, you'll know the disease has reached the terminal phase.

What Lenses Can Do for You

A saner approach to expanding your lens collection is to consider what each of your options can do for you, and then choose the type of lens that will really boost your creative opportunities. Here's a general guide to the sort of capabilities you can gain by adding a lens to your repertoire.

- **Wider perspective.** Your 18-55mm f/3.5-5.6 or 17-85mm f/4-5.6 lens has served you well for moderate wide-angle shots. Now you find your back is up against a wall and you *can't* take a step backward to take in more subject matter. Perhaps you're standing on the rim of the Grand Canyon, and you want to take in as much of the breathtaking view as you can. You might find yourself just behind the baseline at a high school basketball game and want an interesting shot with a little perspective distortion tossed in the mix. There's a lens out there that will provide you with what you need, such as the EF-S 10-22mm f/3.5-4.5 USM zoom. If you want to stay in the sub-$600 price category, you'll need something like the Sigma Super Wide-Angle 10-20mm f/4-5.6 EX DC HSM Autofocus lens. The two lenses provide the equivalent of a 16mm to 32/35mm wide-angle view. Also available is the Canon Fisheye EF 15mm f/2.8 Autofocus lens. A similar lens is available from Sigma, which offers an extra-wide circular fisheye, the Sigma Fisheye 8mm f/3.5 EX DG Circular Fisheye. One of my personal favorites is Tokina's 10-17mm fisheye zoom, which gives you a choice of super-wide perspectives. Your extra-wide choices may not be abundant, but they are there. Figure 6.5 shows the perspective you get from an ultra wide-angle lens. You can compare that with Figure 6.6, which shows the field of view of the approximately 35mm focal length that is considered "normal" for a camera with a 1.6X crop factor.

- **Bring objects closer.** A long lens brings distant subjects closer to you, offers better control over depth-of-field, and avoids the perspective distortion that wide-angle lenses provide. They compress the apparent distance between objects in your frame. In the telephoto realm, Canon is second to none, with a dozen or more offerings in the sub-$600 range, including the Canon EF 100-300mm f/4.5-5.6 USM Autofocus and Canon EF 70-300mm f/4-5.6 IS USM Autofocus Telephoto zoom lenses, and a broad array of zooms and fixed-focal length optics if you're willing to spend up to $1,000 or a bit more. Don't forget that the Digital Rebel XTi's crop factor narrows the field of view of all these lenses, so your 70-300mm lens looks more like a 112mm-480mm zoom through the viewfinder. Figure 6.7 was taken from the same position as Figure 6.6, but with a 500mm lens.

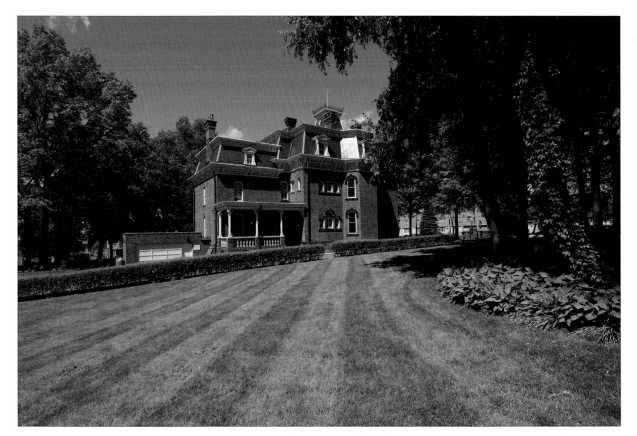

Figure 6.5 An ultra wide-angle lens provided this view of an Italianate mansion.

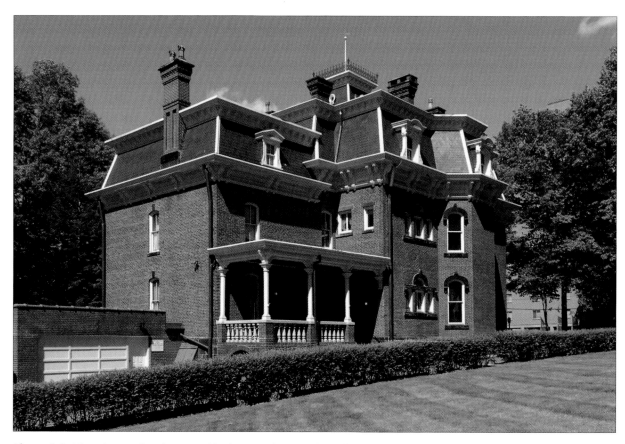

Figure 6.6 This photo, taken from roughly the same distance (but off to the left side), shows the view of what is considered a "normal" focal length for the Rebel XTi.

- **Bring your camera closer.** Macro lenses allow you to focus to within an inch or two of your subject. Canon's best close-up lenses are all fixed focal length optics in the 50mm to 180mm range (including the well-regarded Canon EF-S 60mm f/2.8 Compact and Canon EF 100mm f/2.8 USM Macro Autofocus lenses). But you'll find macro zooms available from Sigma and others. They don't tend to focus quite as close, but they do provide a bit of flexibility when you want to vary your subject distance (say, to avoid spooking a skittish creature).

- **Look sharp.** Many lenses, particularly Canon's luxury "L" line, are prized for their sharpness and overall image quality. While your run-of-the-mill lens is likely to be plenty sharp for most applications, the very best optics are even better over their entire field of view (which means no fuzzy corners), are sharper at a wider range of focal lengths (in the case of zooms), and have better correction for various types of distortion. That's why the Canon EF 28-105mm f/3.5-4.5 II USM zoom lens costs a couple hundred dollars, while

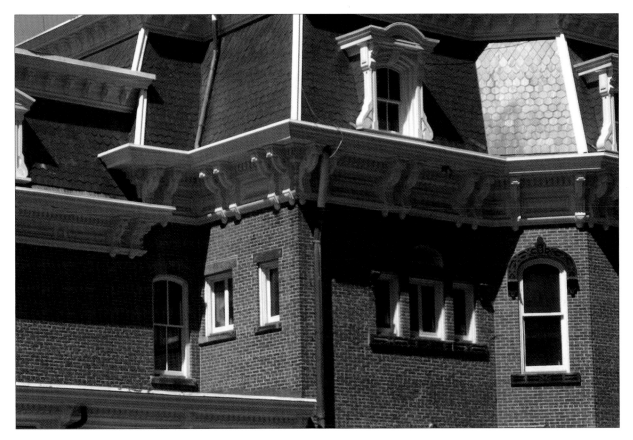

Figure 6.7 A telephoto lens captured this close-up view of the mansion from approximately the same shooting position.

the "similar" (in zoom range only) Canon EF 24-105mm f/4L IS USM zoom is priced $1,000 higher.

- **More speed.** Your Canon EF 100-300mm f/4.5-5.6 Telephoto zoom lens might have the perfect focal length and sharpness for sports photography, but the maximum aperture won't cut it for night baseball or football games, or, even, any sports shooting in daylight if the weather is cloudy or you need to use some ungodly fast shutter speed, such as 1/4000th second. You might be happier with the Canon EF 100mm f/2 medium telephoto for close-range stuff, or even the pricier Canon EF 135mm f/2 L. If money is no object, you can spring for Canon's 400mm f/2.8 and 600mm f/4 L-series lenses (both with image stabilization, and priced in the $6,500-and-up stratosphere). Or, maybe you just need the speed, and you can benefit from an f/1.8 or f/1.4 lens in the 20mm-85mm range. They're all available in Canon mounts (there's even an 85mm f/1.2 for the real speed demons). With any of these lenses you may be able to continue photographing under all but the dimmest of lighting conditions.

- **Special features.** Accessory lenses give you special features, such as tilt/shift capabilities to correct for perspective distortion in architectural shots. Canon offers three of these TS-E lenses in 24mm, 45mm, and 90mm focal lengths, at a little over $1,000 each. You'll also find macro lenses, including the MP-E 65mm f/2.8 1-5X macro photo lens which shoots *only* in the 1X to 5X life-size range. If you want diffused images, check out the EF 135mm f/2.8 with two soft-focus settings. The fisheye lenses mentioned earlier, and all IS (image-stabilized) lenses also count as special-feature optics.

Zoom or Prime?

Zoom lenses have changed the way serious photographers take pictures. One of the reasons that I own 12 SLR film bodies is that in ancient times it was common to mount a different fixed focal-length prime lens on various cameras and walk around with two or three cameras around your neck (or tucked in a camera case) so you'd be ready to take a long shot or an intimate close-up or wide-angle view on a moment's notice, without the need to switch lenses. It made sense (at the time) to have a half-dozen or so bodies (two to use, one in the shop, one in transit, and a couple backups). Zoom lenses of the time had a limited zoom range, were heavy, and not very sharp (especially when you tried to wield one of those monsters handheld).

That's all changed today. Lenses like the razor-sharp Canon EF 28-300mm f/3.5-5.6L IS USM can boast 10X or longer zoom ranges, in a package that's about 7 inches long, and while not petite at 3.7 pounds, quite usable handheld (especially with IS switched on). Although such a lens might seem expensive at $2,200-plus, it's actually much less costly than the six or so lenses it replaces.

When selecting between zoom and prime lenses, there are several considerations to ponder. Here's a checklist of the most important factors. I already mentioned image quality and maximum aperture earlier, but those aspects take on additional meaning when comparing zooms and primes.

- **Logistics.** As prime lenses offer just a single focal length, you'll need more of them to encompass the full range offered by a single zoom. More lenses mean additional slots in your camera bag and extra weight to carry. Just within Canon's line alone you can select from about a dozen general-purpose prime lenses in 28mm, 35mm, 50mm, 85mm, 100mm, 135mm, 200mm, and 300mm focal lengths, all of which are overlapped by the 28-300mm zoom I mentioned earlier. Even so, you might be willing to carry an extra prime lens or two in order to gain the speed or image quality that the lens offers.

■ **Image quality.** Prime lenses usually produce better image quality at their focal length than even the most sophisticated zoom lenses at the same magnification. Zoom lenses, with their shifting elements and f/stops that can vary from zoom position to zoom position, are in general more complex to design than fixed focal-length lenses. That's not to say that the very best prime lenses can't be complicated as well. However, the exotic designs, aspheric elements, low-dispersion glass, and Canon's new diffraction optics (DO) technology can be applied to improving the quality of the lens rather than wasting a lot of it on compensating for problems caused by the zoom process itself.

■ **Maximum aperture.** Because of the same design constraints, zoom lenses usually have smaller maximum apertures than prime lenses, and the most affordable zooms have a lens opening that grows effectively smaller as you zoom in. The difference in lens speed verges on the ridiculous at some focal lengths. For example, the 18mm-55mm basic zoom gives you a 55mm f/5.6 lens when zoomed all the way out, while prime lenses in that focal length commonly have f/1.8 or faster maximum apertures. Indeed, the fastest f/2, f/1.8, f/1.4, and f/1.2 lenses are all primes, and if you require speed, a fixed focal length lens is what you should rely on. Figure 6.8 shows an image taken with a Canon 85mm f/1.8 Series EF USM Telephoto lens.

■ **Speed.** Using prime lenses takes time and slows you down. It takes a few seconds to remove your current lens and mount a new one, and the more often you need to do that, the more time is wasted. If you choose not to swap lenses, when using a fixed focal-length lens you'll still have to move closer or farther away from your subject to get the field of view you want. A zoom lens allows you to change magnifications and focal lengths with the twist of a ring and generally saves you a great deal of time.

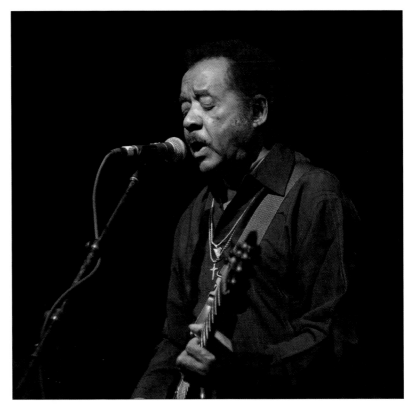

Figure 6.8 An 85mm f/1.8 lens was perfect for this handheld photo of bluesman Jimmy Johnson.

Categories of Lenses

Lenses can be categorized by their intended purpose—general photography, macro photography, and so forth—or by their focal length. The range of available focal lengths is usually divided into three main groups: wide-angle, normal, and telephoto. Prime lenses fall neatly into one of these classifications. Zooms can overlap designations, with a significant number falling into the catchall wide-to-telephoto zoom range. This section provides more information about focal length ranges, and how they are used.

Any lens with an equivalent focal length of 10mm to 20mm is said to be an ultrawide-angle lens; from about 20mm to 40mm (equivalent) is said to be a wide-angle lens. Normal lenses have a focal length roughly equivalent to the diagonal of the film or sensor, in millimeters, and so fall into the range of about 45mm to 60mm (on a full-frame camera). Telephoto lenses usually fall into the 75mm and longer focal lengths, while those from about 300mm-400mm and longer are often referred to as super-telephotos.

Using Wide-Angle and Wide-Zoom Lenses

To use wide-angle prime lenses and wide zooms, you need to understand how they affect your photography. Here's a quick summary of the things you need to know.

- **More depth-of-field.** Practically speaking, wide-angle lenses offer more depth-of-field at a particular subject distance and aperture. (But see the next sidebar for an important note.) You'll find that helpful when you want to maximize sharpness of a large zone, but not very useful when you'd rather isolate your subject using selective focus (telephoto lenses are better for that).

- **Stepping back.** Wide-angle lenses have the effect of making it seem that you are standing farther from your subject than you really are. They're helpful when you don't want to back up, or can't because there are impediments in your way.

- **Wider field of view.** While making your subject seem farther away, as implied previously, a wide-angle lens also provides a larger field of view, including more of the subject in your photos. Table 6.1 shows the diagonal field of view offered by an assortment of lenses, taking into account the crop factor introduced by the Digital Rebel XTi's smaller-than-full-frame sensor.

Table 6.1 Field of View at Various Focal Lengths

Diagonal Field of View	Focal Length at 1X Crop	Focal Length at 1.6X Crop
107 degrees	16mm	10mm
94 degrees	20mm	12mm
84 degrees	24mm	15mm
75 degrees	28mm	18mm
63 degrees	35mm	22mm
47 degrees	50mm	31mm
28 degrees	85mm	53mm
18 degrees	135mm	85mm
12 degrees	200mm	125mm
8.2 degrees	300mm	188mm

- **More foreground.** As background objects retreat, more of the foreground is brought into view by a wide-angle lens. That gives you extra emphasis on the area that's closest to the camera. Photograph your home with a normal lens/normal zoom setting, and the front yard probably looks fairly conventional in your photo (that's why they're called "normal" lenses). Switch to a wider lens and you'll discover that your lawn now makes up much more of the photo. So, wide-angle lenses are great when you want to emphasize that lake in the foreground, but problematic when your intended subject is located farther in the distance.

- **Super-sized subjects.** The tendency of a wide-angle lens to emphasize objects in the foreground, while de-emphasizing objects in the background can lead to a kind of size distortion that may be more objectionable for some types of subjects than others. Shoot a bed of flowers up close with a wide angle, and you might like the distorted effect of the larger blossoms nearer the lens. Take a photo of a family member with the same lens from the same distance, and you're likely to get some complaints about that gigantic nose in the foreground.

- **Perspective distortion.** When you tilt the camera so that the plane of the sensor is no longer perpendicular to the vertical plane of your subject, some parts of the subject are now closer to the sensor than they were before, while other parts are farther away. So, buildings, flagpoles, or NBA players appear to be falling backward, as you can see in Figure 6.9. While this kind of apparent distortion (it's not caused by a defect in the lens) can happen with any lens, it's most apparent when a wide-angle is used.

- **Steady cam.** You'll find that you can handhold a wide-angle lens at slower shutter speeds, without need for image stabilization, more easily than you can handhold a telephoto lens. The reduced magnification of the wide lens or wide-zoom setting doesn't emphasize camera shake like a telephoto lens does.

- **Interesting angles.** Many of the factors already listed combine to produce more interesting angles when shooting with wide-angle lenses. Raising or lowering a telephoto lens a few feet probably will have little effect on the appearance of the distant subjects you're shooting. The same change in elevation can produce a dramatic effect for the much-closer subjects typically captured with a wide-angle lens or wide-zoom setting.

The crop factor strikes again! You can see from this table that wide-angle lenses provide a broader field of view, and that, because of the XTi's 1.6 crop factor, lenses must have a shorter focal length to provide the same field of view. If you like working with a 28mm lens with your full-frame camera, you'll need an 18mm lens for your Digital Rebel XTi to get the same field of view. (Some focal lengths have been rounded slightly for simplification.)

DOF IN DEPTH

The DOF advantage of wide-angle lenses is diminished when you enlarge your picture; believe it or not, a wide-angle image enlarged and cropped to provide the same subject size as a telephoto shot would have the *same* depth-of-field. Try it: take a wide-angle photo of a friend, and then zoom in to duplicate the picture in a telephoto image. Then, enlarge the wide shot so your friend is the same size in both. The wide photo will have the same depth-of-field (and will have much less detail, too).

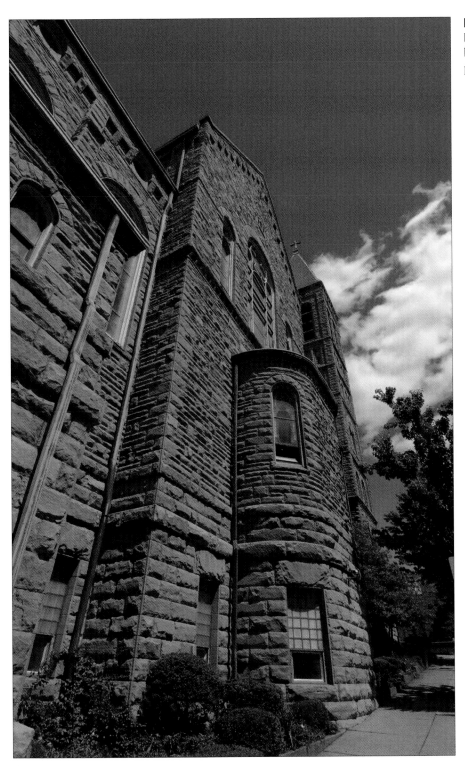

Figure 6.9 Tilting the camera back produces this "falling back" look in architectural photos.

Avoiding Potential Wide-Angle Problems

Wide-angle lenses have a few quirks that you'll want to keep in mind when shooting, so you can avoid falling into some common traps. Here's a checklist of tips for avoiding common problems:

- **Symptom: converging lines.** Unless you want to use wildly diverging lines as a creative effect, it's a good idea to keep horizontal and vertical lines in landscapes, architecture, and other subjects carefully aligned with the sides, top, and bottom of the frame. That will help you avoid undesired perspective distortion. Sometimes it helps to shoot from a slightly elevated position so you don't have to tilt the camera up or down.

- **Symptom: color fringes around objects.** Lenses are often plagued with fringes of color around backlit objects, produced by *chromatic aberration*, which comes in two forms: *longitudinal/axial*, in which all the colors of light don't focus in the same plane, and *lateral/transverse*, in which the colors are shifted to one side, as you can see in Figure 6.10. Axial chromatic aberration can be reduced by stopping down the lens, but transverse CA cannot. Both can be reduced by using lenses with the use of low diffraction index glass (or UD elements, in Canon nomenclature) and by incorporating elements that cancel the chromatic aberration of other glass in the lens. For example, a strong positive lens made of low dispersion crown glass (made of a soda-lime-silica composite) may be mated with a weaker negative lens made of high-dispersion flint glass, which contains lead.

- **Symptom: lines that bow outward.** Some wide-angle lenses cause straight lines to bow outward, with the strongest effect at the edges. In fisheye (or *curvilinear*) lenses, this defect is a feature. When distortion is not desired, you'll need to use a lens that has corrected barrel distortion. Manufacturers like Canon do their best to minimize or eliminate it (producing a *rectilinear* lens), often using *aspherical* lens elements (which are not cross-sections of a sphere). You can also minimize barrel distortion simply by framing your photo so that the edges where the defect is most obvious can be cropped out of the picture.

- **Symptom: dark corners and shadows in flash photos.** The Canon Digital Rebel XTi's built-in electronic flash is designed to provide even coverage for lenses as wide as 17mm. If you use a wider lens, you can expect darkening, or *vignetting* in the corners of the frame. At wider focal lengths, the lens hood of some lenses (my 17mm-85mm lens is a prime offender) can cast a semi-circular shadow in the lower portion of the frame when using the built-in flash. Sometimes removing the lens hood or zooming in a bit can eliminate the shadow. Mounting an external flash unit, such as the mighty Canon

580EX can solve both problems, as the 580EX Speedlite has zoomable coverage up to 114 degrees with the included adapter, sufficient for a 9mm rectilinear lens (14mm equivalent). Its higher vantage point eliminates the problem of lens-hood shadow (and, probably, red-eye effects), too.

■ **Symptom: light and dark areas when using polarizing filter.** If you know that polarizers work best when the camera is pointed 90 degrees away from the sun, and have the least effect when the camera is oriented 180 degrees from the sun, you know only half the story. With lenses having a focal length of 10mm to 18mm (the equivalent of 16mm-28mm), the angle of view (107 to 75 degrees diagonally, or 97 to 44 degrees horizontally) is extensive enough to cause problems. Think about it: when a 10mm lens is pointed at the proper 90-degree angle from the sun, objects at the edges of the frame will be oriented at 135 to 41 degrees, with only the center at exactly 90 degrees. Either edge will have much less of a polarized effect. The solution is to avoid using a polarizing filter with lenses having an actual focal length of less than 18mm (or 28mm equivalent).

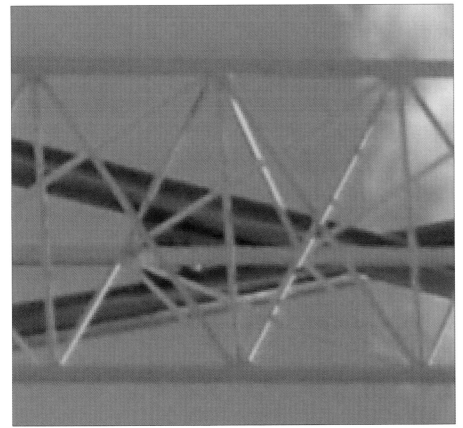

Figure 6.10 Chromatic aberration produces color fringing, which can be seen as both cyan and magenta fringes in the crossbars of this flagpole. Canon lenses with low-dispersion UD glass elements minimize this effect.

Using Telephoto and Tele-Zoom Lenses

Telephoto lenses also can have a dramatic effect on your photography, and Canon is especially strong in the long-lens arena, with lots of choices in many focal lengths and zoom ranges. You should be able to find an affordable telephoto or tele-zoom to enhance your photography in several different ways. Here are the most important things you need to know about. In the next section, I'll concentrate on telephoto considerations that can be problematic—and how to avoid those problems.

- **Selective focus.** Long lenses have reduced depth-of-field within the frame, allowing you to use selective focus to isolate your subject. You can open the lens up wide to create shallow depth-of-field, or close it down a bit to allow more to be in focus. The flip side of the coin is that when you *want* to make a range of objects sharp, you'll need to use a smaller f/stop to get the DOF you need. Like fire, the depth-of-field of a telephoto lens can be friend or foe. Figure 6.11 shows a photo of a red panda, with the telephoto lens and wider f/stop used to de-emphasize the background, which happened to include a distracting glass barrier.

- **Getting closer.** Telephoto lenses bring you closer to wildlife, sports action, and candid subjects. No one wants to get a reputation as a surreptitious or "sneaky" photographer (except for paparazzi), but when applied to candids in an open and honest way, a long lens can help you capture memorable moments while retaining enough distance to stay out of the way of events as they transpire.

- **Reduced foreground/increased compression.** Telephoto lenses have the opposite effect of wide-angles: they reduce the importance of things in the foreground by squeezing everything together. This compression even makes distant objects appear to be closer to subjects in the foreground and middle ranges. You can use this effect as a creative tool.

- **Accentuates camera shakiness.** Telephoto focal lengths hit you with a double-whammy in terms of camera/photographer shake. The lenses themselves are bulkier, more difficult to hold steady, and may even produce a barely perceptible seesaw rocking effect when you support them with one hand halfway down the lens barrel. Telephotos also magnify any camera shake. It's no wonder that image stabilization is popular in longer lenses.

- **Interesting angles require creativity.** Telephoto lenses require more imagination in selecting interesting angles, because the "angle" you do get on your subjects is so narrow. Moving from side to side or a bit higher or lower can make a dramatic difference in a wide-angle shot, but raising or lowering a telephoto lens a few feet probably will have little effect on the appearance of the distant subjects you're shooting.

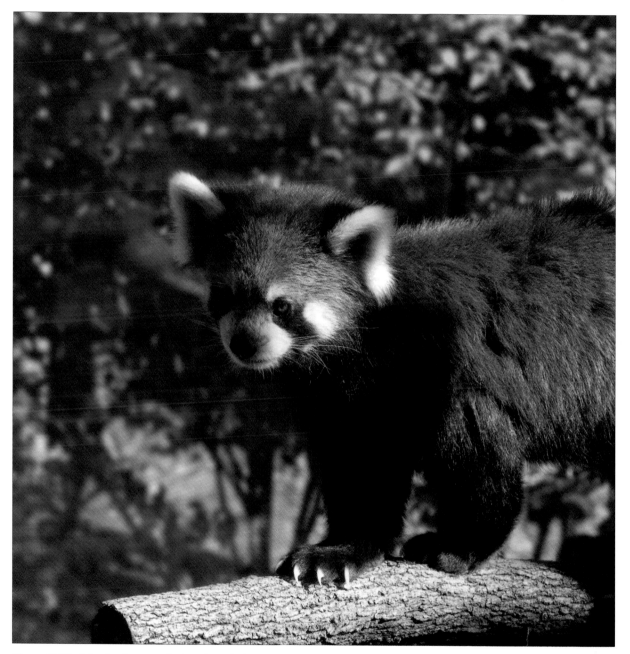

Figure 6.11 Selective focus applied in this telephoto shot helped minimize the distracting glass barrier in the background.

Avoiding Telephoto Lens Problems

Many of the "problems" that telephoto lenses pose are really just challenges, and not that difficult to overcome. Here is a list of the seven most common picture maladies, and suggested solutions.

- **Symptom: flat faces in portraits.** Head-and-shoulders portraits of humans tend to be more flattering when a focal length of 50mm to 85mm is used. Longer focal lengths compress the distance between features like noses and ears, making the face look wider and flat. A wide angle might make noses look huge and ears tiny when you fill the frame with a face. So stick with 50mm to 85mm focal lengths, going longer only when you're forced to shoot from a greater distance; and wider only when shooting three-quarters/full-length portraits, or group shots.

- **Symptom: blur due to camera shake.** Use a higher shutter speed (boosting ISO if necessary), consider an image-stabilized lens, or mount your camera on a tripod, monopod, or brace it with some other support. Of those three solutions, only the first will reduce blur caused by *subject* motion; an IS lens or tripod won't help you freeze a racecar in mid-lap.

- **Symptom: color fringes.** Chromatic aberration is the most pernicious optical problem found in telephoto lenses. There are others, including spherical aberration, astigmatism, coma, curvature of field, and similarly scary-sounding phenomena. The best solution for any of these is to use a better lens that offers the proper degree of correction. But that's not always possible. Your second-best choice may be to correct the fringing in your favorite RAW conversion tool or image editor. Photoshop's Lens Correction filter (found in the Distort menu) offers sliders that minimize both red/cyan and blue/yellow fringing.

- **Symptom: lines that curve inward.** Pincushion distortion is found in many telephoto lenses. You might find after a bit of testing that it is worse at certain focal lengths with your particular zoom lens. Like chromatic aberration, it can be partially corrected using tools like Photoshop's Lens Correction filter.

- **Symptom: low contrast from haze or fog.** When you're photographing distant objects, a long lens shoots through a lot more atmosphere, which generally is muddied up with extra haze and fog. That dirt or moisture in the atmosphere can reduce contrast and mute colors. Some feel that a skylight or UV filter can help, but this practice is mostly a holdover from the film days. Digital sensors are not sensitive enough to UV light for a UV filter to have much effect. So you should be prepared to boost contrast and color saturation in your Picture Styles menu or image editor if necessary.

- **Symptom: low contrast from flare.** Lenses are furnished with lens hoods for a good reason: to reduce flare from bright light sources at the periphery of the picture area, or completely outside it. Because telephoto lenses often create images that are lower in contrast in the first place, you'll want to be especially careful to use a lens hood to prevent further effects on your image (or shade the front of the lens with your hand).

- **Symptom: dark flash photos.** Edge-to-edge flash coverage isn't a problem with telephoto lenses as it is with wide angles. The shooting distance is. A long lens might make a subject that's 50 feet away look as if it's right next to you, but your camera's flash isn't fooled. You'll need extra power of distant flash shots, and probably more power than your XTi's built-in flash provides. The shoe-mount Canon 580EX Speedlite, for example, can automatically zoom its coverage down to that of a medium telephoto lens, providing a theoretical full-power shooting aperture of about f/8 at 50 feet and ISO 400. (Try *that* with the built in flash!)

Telephotos and Bokeh

Bokeh describes the aesthetic qualities of the out-of-focus parts of an image, and whether out-of-focus points of light—circles of confusion—are rendered as distracting fuzzy discs, or whether they smoothly fade into the background. *Boke* is a Japanese word for "blur," and the h was added to keep English speakers from rendering it monosyllabically to rhyme with *broke*. Although bokeh is visible in blurry portions of any image, it's of particular concern with telephoto lenses, which, thanks to the magic of reduced depth-of-field, produce more obviously out-of-focus areas.

Bokeh can vary from lens to lens, or even within a given lens depending on the f/stop in use. Bokeh becomes objectionable when the circles of confusion are evenly illuminated, making them stand out as distinct discs, or, worse, when these circles are darker in the center, producing an ugly "doughnut" effect. A lens defect called spherical aberration may produce out-of-focus discs that are brighter on the edges and darker in the center, because the lens doesn't focus light passing through the edges of the lens exactly as it does light going through the center. (Mirror or *catadioptric* lenses also produce this effect.)

Other kinds of spherical aberration generate circles of confusion that are brightest in the center and fade out at the edges, producing a smooth blending effect, as you can see at bottom in Figure 6.12. Ironically, when no spherical aberration is present at all, the discs are a uniform shade, which, while better than the doughnut effect, is not as pleasing as the bright center/dark edge rendition. The shape of the disc also comes into play, with round smooth circles considered the best, and nonagonal or some other polygon (determined by the shape of the lens diaphragm) less desirable.

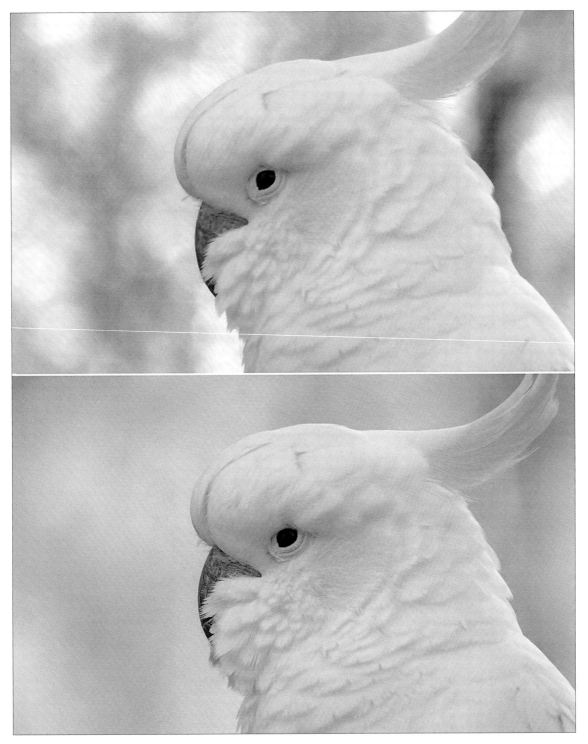

Figure 6.12 Bokeh is less pleasing when the discs are prominent (top) and less obtrusive when they blend into the background (bottom).

If you plan to use selective focus a lot, you should investigate the bokeh characteristics of a particular lens before you buy. Canon user groups and forums will usually be full of comments and questions about bokeh, so the research is fairly easy.

Add-ons and Special Features

After you've purchased your telephoto lens, you'll want to think about some appropriate accessories for it. There are some handy add-ons available that can be valuable. Here are a couple of them to think about.

Lens Hoods

Lens hoods are an important accessory for all lenses, but they're especially valuable with telephotos. As I mentioned earlier, lens hoods do a good job of preserving image contrast by keeping bright light sources outside the field of view from striking the lens and, potentially, bouncing around inside that long tube to generate flare that, when coupled with atmospheric haze, can rob your image of detail and snap. In addition, lens hoods serve as valuable protection for that large, vulnerable, front lens element. It's easy to forget that you've got that long tube sticking out in front of your camera, and accidentally whack the front of your lens into something. It's cheaper to replace a lens hood than it is to have a lens repaired, so you might find that a good hood is valuable protection for your prized optics. Buy one, if you need to.

When choosing a lens hood, it's important to have the right hood for the lens, usually the one offered for that lens by Canon or the third-party manufacturer. You want a hood that blocks precisely the right amount of light: neither too much nor too little. A hood with a front diameter that is too small can show up in your pictures as vignetting. A hood that has a front diameter that's too large isn't stopping all the light it should. Generic lens hoods may not do the job.

When your telephoto is a zoom lens, it's even more important to get the right hood, because you need one that does what it is supposed to at both the wide-angle and telephoto ends of the zoom range. Lens hoods may be cylindrical, rectangular (shaped like the image frame), or petal shaped (that is, cylindrical, but with cutout areas at the corners that correspond to the actual image area). Lens hoods should be mounted in the correct orientation (a bayonet mount for the hood usually takes care of this).

Telephoto Extenders

Telephoto extenders (often called teleconverters outside the Canon world), multiply the actual focal length of your lens, giving you a longer telephoto for much less than the price of a lens with that actual focal length. These extenders fit between the lens and your camera, and they contain optical elements that magnify the image produced by the lens. Available in 1.4X and 2.0X configurations from Canon, an extender transforms, say, a 200mm lens into a 280mm or 400mm optic, respectively. Given the XTi's crop factor, your 200mm lens now has the same field of view as a 448mm or 640mm lens on a full-frame camera. At around $300 each, they're quite a bargain, aren't they?

Actually, there are some downsides. While extenders retain the original closest focusing distance of your original lens, autofocus is maintained only if the lens's original maximum aperture was f/4 or larger (for the 1.4X extender) or f/2.8 or larger (for the 2X extender). The components reduce the effective aperture of any lens they are used with, by one f/stop with the 1.4X extender, and two f/stops with the 2X extender. So, your EF 200mm f/2.8L II USM becomes a 280mm f/4 or 400mm f/5.6 lens. Although Canon extenders are precision optical devices, they do cost you a little sharpness, but improve when you reduce the aperture by a stop or two. Each of the extenders is compatible only with a particular set of lenses of 135mm focal length or greater, so you'll want to check Canon's compatibility chart to see if the component can be used with the lens you want to attach to it.

If your lenses are compatible and you're shooting under bright lighting conditions, the Canon Extender EF 1.4X II and Canon Extender EF 2X II make handy accessories.

Macro Focusing

Some telephotos and telephoto zooms available for the Digital Rebel XTi have particularly close focusing capabilities, making them *macro* lenses. Of course, the object is not necessarily to get close (get too close and you'll find it difficult to light your subject). What you're really looking for in a macro lens is to magnify the apparent size of the subject in the final image. Camera-to-subject distance is most important when you want to back up farther from your subject (say, to avoid spooking skittish insects or small animals). In that case, you'll want a macro lens with a longer focal length to allow that distance while retaining the desired magnification.

Canon makes 50mm, 60mm, 65mm, 100mm, and 180mm lenses with official macro designations. You'll also find macro lenses, macro zooms, and other close-focusing lenses available from Sigma, Tamron, and Tokina. If you want to focus closer with a macro lens, or any other lens, you can add an accessory called an *extension tube*, like the one shown in Figure 6.13. These add-ons move the lens farther from the focal plane, allowing it to focus more closely. You can also use screw-in close-up lenses, like the excellent Canon 500D close-up attachment. (This particular item is so good that it's the most popular close-up attachment among *Nikon* owners, too, if the ecstatic posts I've seen in Nikon user forums are any indication.)

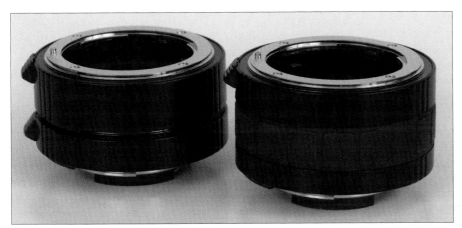

Figure 6.13 Extension tubes enable any lens to focus more closely to the subject.

Image Stabilization

Canon has a burgeoning line of more than a dozen lenses with built-in image sta-bilization (IS) capabilities. This feature uses lens elements that are shifted inter-nally in response to the motion of the lens during handheld photography, countering the shakiness that the camera and photographer produce and which telephoto lenses magnify. However, IS is not limited to long lenses; the feature works like a champ at the 17mm zoom position of Canon's EF-S 17-85mm f/4-5.6 IS USM and EF-S 17-55mm f/2.8 IS USM lenses. Other Canon IS lenses provide stabilization with zooms that are as wide as 24-28mm.

Image stabilization provides you with camera steadiness that's the equivalent of at least two shutter speed increments, which can be invaluable when you're shooting under dim lighting conditions or handholding a long lens for, say, wildlife pho-tography. Perhaps that shot of a fleeing deer calls for a shutter speed of 1/1000th second at f/5.6 with your EF 100-400mm f/4.5-5.6L IS USM lens. Relax. You can shoot at 1/250th second at f/11 and get virtually the same camera-steadying results.

Or, maybe you're shooting a high-school play without a tripod or monopod, and you'd really, really like to use 1/15th second at f/4. Assuming the actors aren't flitting around the stage at high speed, your 17mm-85mm IS lens can grab the shot for you at its wide-angle position. Figure 6.14 was shot from my seat in about the fifteenth row of a concert at ISO 800 with an exposure 1/125th second at f/4 at 200mm with an image-stabilized lens. Without the lens's IS feature, I probably would have needed to use a monopod and a 1/250th second shutter speed (just to be safe) and either opened up to f/2.8 (with less depth-of-field and image sharpness) or boosted the sensitivity to ISO 1600. But with image stabilization, I didn't need the monopod, the larger f/stop, or the higher ISO setting.

However, image stabilization is not a cure-all. Keep these facts in mind:

- **IS doesn't stop action.** Unfortunately, no IS lens is a panacea to replace the action-stopping capabilities of a higher shutter speed. Image stabilization applies only to camera shake. You still need a fast shutter speed to freeze action. IS works great in low light, when you're using long lenses, and for macro photography. It's not always the best choice for action photography unless there's enough light to allow a sufficiently high shutter speed. If so, IS can make your shot even sharper.

- **IS slows you down.** The process of adjusting the lens elements takes time, just as autofocus does, so you might find that IS adds to the lag between when you press the shutter and when the picture is actually taken. That's another reason why image stabilization might not be a good choice for sports.

- **Use when appropriate.** Some IS lenses produce worse results if you use them while you're panning, although newer Canon IS lenses have a mode that works fine when the camera is deliberately moved from side to side during exposure. Older lenses can confuse the motion with camera shake and overcompensate. You might want to switch off IS when panning or when your camera is mounted on a tripod.

- **Do you need IS at all?** Remember that an inexpensive monopod might be able to provide the same additional steadiness as an IS lens, at much lower cost. If you're out in the field shooting wild animals or flowers and you think a tripod isn't practical, try a monopod first.

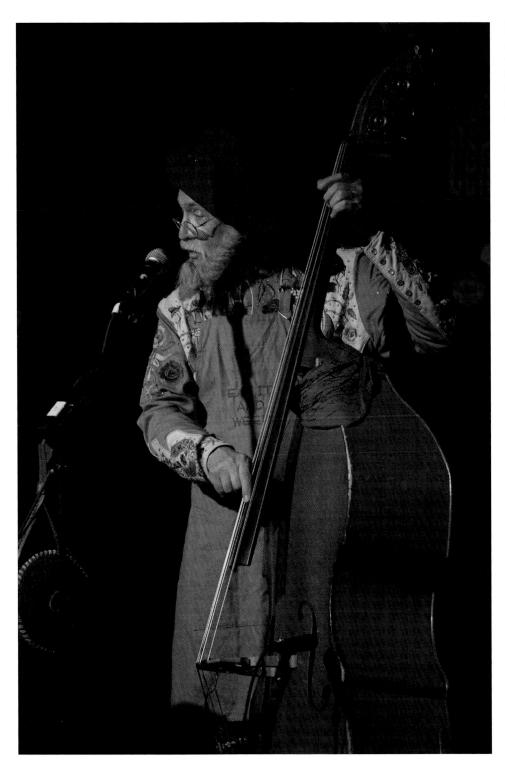

Figure 6.14 Image stabilization let me capture this 200mm shot at 1/125th second and f/4 without the need for a monopod or other steadying aid.

IMAGE STABILIZATION: IN THE CAMERA OR IN THE LENS?

Sony's acquisition of Konica Minolta's dSLR assets and the introduction of an improved in-camera image stabilization system has revived an old debate about whether IS belongs in the camera or in the lens. Other vendors, including Panasonic and Pentax also include image stabilization in the camera, rather than in individual lenses. Perhaps it's my Canon bias showing, but I am quite happy not to have image stabilization available in the body itself. Here are some reasons:

- Should in-camera IS fail, you must send the whole camera in for repair, and camera repairs are generally more expensive than lens repairs. I like being able to simply switch to another lens if I have an IS problem.

- IS in the camera doesn't steady your view in the viewfinder, whereas an IS lens shows you a steadied image as you shoot.

- You're stuck with the IS system built into your camera. If an improved system is incorporated into a lens and the improvements are important to you, just trade in your old lens for the new one.

7

Working with Light

One famous, popular artist describes himself as a "Painter of Light" to add a distinguished touch to the canvases, tote bags, and even screensavers that bear his images. In the real world, however, *all* painters and photographers use light as their medium to create images. The direction and intensity of the light sources create the shapes and textures that we see. The distribution and proportions determine the contrast and tonal values: whether the image is stark or high-key, or muted and low in contrast. The colors of the light (because even "white" light has a color balance that the sensor can detect), and how much of those colors the subject reflects or absorbs, paint the hues visible in the image.

As a Canon Digital Rebel XTi photographer, you, too, must learn to be a "painter of light" if you want to move from *taking* a picture to *making* a photograph. This chapter provides an introduction to using the two main types of illumination: *continuous* lighting (such as daylight, incandescent, or fluorescent sources) and the brief, but brilliant snippets of light we call *electronic flash.*

Continuous Illumination versus Electronic Flash

Continuous lighting is light that is available all the time during a shooting session, such as daylight or the artificial lighting encountered both indoors and outdoors. The latter sources embrace both the lights that are there already (such as lamps or overhead fluorescent lights indoors) and fixtures you supply yourself, including photoflood lamps or reflectors you supply to provide light for photography.

Electronic flash includes the flip-up flash unit built into your Digital Rebel XTi (see Figure 7.1) or any external flash you choose to couple with it, including those that mount on the accessory shoe on top of the camera and units that are used

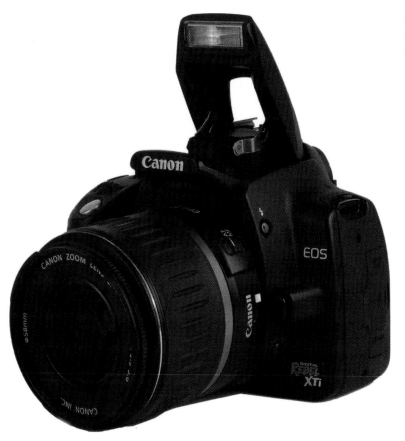

Figure 7.1 One form of light that's always available is the flip-up flash on your Digital Rebel XTi.

off-camera. Studio flash units count, too, and aren't limited to "professional" shooters, as there are economical *monolight* (one-piece flash/power supply) flash available in the $200 price range.

There are advantages and disadvantages to each type of illumination. Here's a quick checklist of pros and cons:

■ **Lighting preview.** With continuous lighting, you always know exactly what kind of lighting effect you're going to get and, if multiple lights are used, how they will interact with each other, as shown in Figure 7.2. With electronic flash, the general effect you're going to see may be a mystery until you've built some experience (unless you're using a flash with a built-in incandescent *modeling light*). You might need to review a shot on the LCD, make some adjustments, and then reshoot to get the look you want. (In this sense, a digital camera's review capabilities replace the Polaroid test shots pro photographers relied on in decades past.)

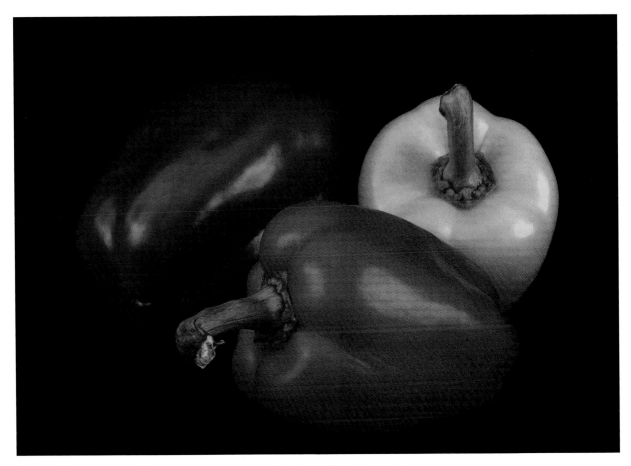

Figure 7.2 Continuous light sources let you see exactly how highlights and shadows interact.

- **Exposure calculation.** Your XTi has no problem calculating exposure for continuous lighting, because it remains constant. The amount of light available just before the exposure will, in almost all cases, be the same amount of light present when the shutter is released. You can even use a handheld light meter to measure the light yourself, say, when you want to compare the illumination falling on the highlight areas of a subject with the light reaching the shadows in order to calculate the exact amount of contrast to expect. Electronic flash illumination, on the other hand, doesn't exist until the flash fires, and so it must be measured using a preflash an instant before the main flash, or measured *during the actual exposure.* In the case of a digital SLR, that is tricky to do in-camera because the mirror has flipped up and is blocking the metering system built into the camera; it's more common, when such a system is used at all, to measure the light by non-through-the-lens means using a light sensor in an external flash unit. If you have a do-it-yourself bent, there are handheld flash meters, too, including models that measure both flash and continuous light.

- **Evenness of illumination.** Of continuous light sources, daylight, in particular, provides illumination that tends to fill an image completely, lighting up the foreground, background, and your subject almost equally. Shadows do come into play, of course, so you might need to use reflectors or fill-in light sources to even out the illumination further, but barring objects that block large sections of your image from daylight, the light is spread fairly evenly. Electronic flash units (as well as continuous light sources such as lamps that don't have the advantage of being 93 million miles from the subject) suffer from the effects of their proximity: the *inverse square law* dictates that as a light source's position increases from the subject, the amount of light reaching the subject falls off proportionately to the square of the distance. In plain English, that means that a flash or lamp that's eight feet away from a subject provides only one-quarter as much illumination as a source that's four feet away (rather than half as much). This translates into relatively shallow "depth-of-light."

- **Action stopping.** When it comes to the ability to freeze moving objects in their tracks, the advantage goes to electronic flash. As I explained in Chapter 4, the brief duration of electronic flash serves as a very high "shutter speed" when the flash is the main or only source of illumination for the photo. Your Digital Rebel XTi's shutter speed may be set for 1/200th second during a flash exposure, but if the flash illumination predominates, the *effective* exposure time will be the 1/1,000th to 1/50,000th second or less duration of the flash, because the flash unit reduces the amount of light released when the metering system senses that the correct exposure has been reached by reducing the duration of the flash. (Some of the power that would go to the flash tube is diverted, producing a burst that is lower in light output, and also briefer.) Action stopping with continuous light sources, on the other hand, is completely dependent on the shutter speed you've dialed in on the camera. And the speeds available are dependent on the amount of light available and your ISO sensitivity setting. For example, if you're shooting sports indoors, there probably won't be enough available light to allow you to use a 1/2000th second shutter speed, but applying that effective speed by using a flash unit is no problem at all.

- **Cost.** Incandescent lamps are generally much less expensive than electronic flash units, which can easily cost several hundred dollars. If you want to use more than one light source, the costs mount more quickly with flash.

- **Flexibility.** Because incandescent lamps are not as bright as electronic flash, the slower shutter speeds required (see Action stopping, on the previous page) mean that you may have to use a tripod more often, especially when shooting portraits. Electronic flash's action-freezing power allows you to work without a tripod, adding flexibility and speed when choosing angles and positions.

Continuous Lighting Basics

While continuous lighting and its effects are generally much easier to visualize and use than electronic flash, there are some factors you need to take into account, particularly the color temperature of the light. (Color temperature concerns aren't exclusive to continuous light sources, of course, but the variations tend to be more extreme and less predictable than those of electronic flash.)

Color temperature, in practical terms, is how "bluish" or how "reddish" the light appears to be to the digital camera's sensor. Indoor illumination is quite warm, comparatively, and appears reddish to the sensor. Daylight, in contrast, seems much bluer to the sensor. Our eyes (our brains, actually) are quite adaptable to these variations, so white objects don't appear to have an orange tinge when viewed indoors, nor do they seem excessively blue outdoors in full daylight. Yet these color temperature variations are real and the sensor is not fooled. To capture the most accurate colors, we need to take the color temperature into account in setting the color balance (or *white balance*) of the XTi—either automatically using the camera's smarts, or manually, using our own knowledge and experience.

The only time you need to think in terms of actual color temperature is when you're making adjustments to RAW files using a converter that allows specifying exact color temperatures. So, those occasions are the only times you're likely to be confused by a seeming contradiction in how color temperatures are named: warmer (more reddish) color temperatures (measured in degrees Kelvin) are the *lower* numbers, while cooler (bluer) color temperatures are *higher* numbers. It might not make sense to say that 3,400K is warmer than 6,000K, but that's the way it is. If it helps, think of a glowing red ember contrasted with a white-hot welder's torch, rather than fire and ice.

The confusion comes from physics. Scientists calculate color temperature from the light emitted by a mythical object called a black body radiator, which absorbs all the radiant energy that strikes it, and reflects none at all. Such a black body not only *absorbs* light perfectly, but it *emits* it perfectly when heated (and since nothing in the universe is perfect, that makes it mythical).

At a particular physical temperature, this imaginary object always emits light of the same wavelength or color. That makes it possible to define color temperature in terms of actual temperature in degrees on the Kelvin scale that scientists use (described in more detail in Chapter 5). Incandescent light, for example, typically has a color temperature of 3,200K to 3,400K. Daylight might range from 5,500K to 6,000K. Each type of illumination we use for photography has its own color temperature range—with some cautions. The next sections will summarize everything you need to know about the qualities of these light sources.

Daylight

Daylight is produced by the sun, and so is moonlight (which is just reflected sunlight). Daylight is present, of course, even when you can't see the sun. When sunlight is direct, it can be bright and harsh. If daylight is diffused by clouds, softened by bouncing off objects such as walls or your photo reflectors, or filtered by shade, it can be much dimmer and less contrasty.

Daylight's color temperature can vary quite widely. It is highest (most blue) at noon when the sun is directly overhead, because the light is traveling through a minimum amount of the filtering layer we call the atmosphere. The color temperature at high noon may be 6,000K. At other times of day the sun is lower in the sky and the particles in the air provide a filtering effect that warm the illumination to about 5,500K for most of the day. Starting an hour before dusk and for an hour after sunrise, the warm appearance of the sunlight is even visible to our eyes when the color temperature may dip to 5,000-4,500K, as shown in Figure 7.3.

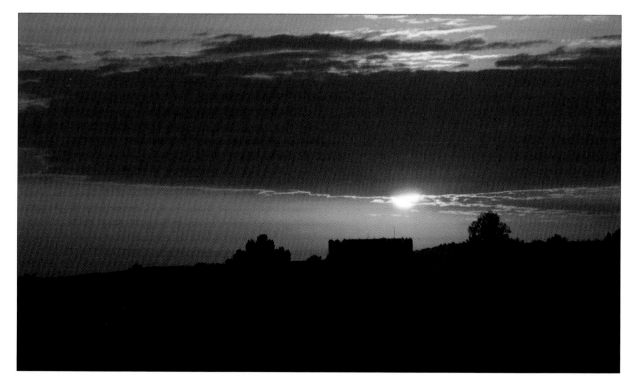

Figure 7.3 At dawn and dusk, the color temperature of daylight may dip as low as 4,500K.

Because you'll be taking so many photos in daylight, you'll want to learn how to use or compensate for the brightness and contrast of sunlight, as well as how to deal with its color temperature. I'll provide some hints later in this chapter.

Incandescent/Tungsten Light

The term incandescent or tungsten illumination is usually applied to the direct descendents of Thomas Edison's original electric lamp. Such lights consist of a glass bulb that contains a vacuum, or is filled with a halogen gas, and contains a tungsten filament that is heated by an electrical current, producing photons and heat. Tungsten-halogen lamps are a variation on the basic lightbulb, using a more rugged (and longer-lasting) filament that can be heated to a higher temperature, housed in a thicker glass or quartz envelope, and filled with iodine or bromine ("halogen") gases. The higher temperature allows tungsten-halogen (or quartz-halogen/quartz-iodine, depending on their construction) lamps to burn "hotter" and whiter. Although popular for automobile headlamps today, they've also been popular for photographic illumination.

Although incandescent illumination isn't a perfect black body radiator, it's close enough that the color temperature of such lamps can be precisely calculated and used for photography without concerns about color variation (at least, until the very end of the lamp's life).

The other qualities of this type of lighting, such as contrast, are dependent on the distance of the lamp from the subject, type of reflectors used, and other factors that I'll explain later in this chapter.

Fluorescent Light/Other Light Sources

Fluorescent light has some advantages in terms of illumination, but some disadvantages from a photographic standpoint. This type of lamp generates light through an electro-chemical reaction that emits most of its energy as visible light, rather than heat, which is why the bulbs don't become as hot. The type of light produced varies depending on the phosphor coatings and type of gas in the tube. So, the illumination that fluorescent bulbs produce can vary widely in its characteristics.

That's not great news for photographers. Different types of lamps have different "color temperatures" that can't be precisely measured in degrees Kelvin, because the light isn't produced by heating. Worse, fluorescent lamps have a discontinuous spectrum of light that can have some colors missing entirely. A particular type of tube can lack certain shades of red or other colors (see Figure 7.4), which is why fluorescent lamps (which are seeing increased use as a power-saving measure) and other alternative technologies such as sodium-vapor illumination can produce ghastly looking human skin tones. Their spectra can lack the reddish tones we associate with healthy skin and emphasize the blues and greens popular in horror movies.

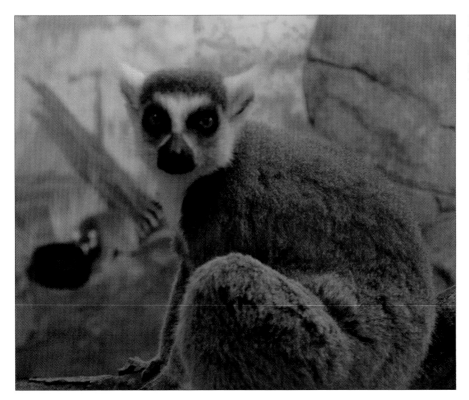

Figure 7.4 The fluorescent supplementary lighting may not bother this lemur, but the greenish cast adds an eerie note to this photo.

Adjusting White Balance

I showed you how to adjust white balance in Chapter 3, using the XTi's built-in presets, white balance shift capabilities, and white balance bracketing (there's more on bracketing in Chapter 4, too).

In most cases, however, the Digital Rebel XTi will do a good job of calculating white balance for you, so Auto can be used as your choice most of the time. Use the preset values or set a custom white balance that matches the current shooting conditions when you need to. The only really problematic light sources are likely to be fluorescents. Vendors, such as GE and Sylvania, may actually provide a figure known as the *color rendering index* (or CRI), which is a measure of how accurately a particular light source represents standard colors, using a scale of 0 (some sodium-vapor lamps) to 100 (daylight and most incandescent lamps). Daylight fluorescents and deluxe cool white fluorescents might have a CRI of about 79 to 95, which is perfectly acceptable for most photographic applications. Warm white fluorescents might have a CRI of 55. White deluxe mercury vapor lights are less suitable with a CRI of 45, while low pressure sodium lamps can vary from CRI 0-18.

Remember that if you shoot RAW, you can specify the white balance of your image when you import it into Photoshop, Photoshop Elements, or another image editor. While color-balancing filters that fit on the front of the lens exist, they are primarily useful for film cameras, because film's color balance can't be tweaked as extensively as that of a sensor.

Electronic Flash Basics

Until you delve into the situation deeply enough, it might appear that serious photographers have a love/hate relationship with electronic flash. You'll often hear that flash photography is less natural looking, and that the built-in flash in most cameras should never be used as the primary source of illumination because it provides a harsh, garish look. Indeed, most "pro" cameras like the Canon EOS 1D Mark II N and 1Ds Mark II don't have a built-in flash at all. Available ("continuous") lighting is praised, and flash photography seems to be roundly denounced.

In truth, however, the bias is against *bad* flash photography. Indeed, flash has become the studio light source of choice for pro photographers, because it's more intense (and its intensity can be varied to order by the photographer), freezes action, frees you from using a tripod (unless you want to use one to lock down a composition), and has a snappy, consistent light quality that matches daylight. (While color balance changes as the flash duration shortens, some Canon flash units can communicate to the camera the exact white balance provided for that shot.) And even pros will cede that the built-in flash of the Canon Digital Rebel XTi has some important uses as an adjunct to existing light, particularly to fill in dark shadows.

But electronic flash isn't as inherently easy to use as continuous lighting. As I noted earlier, electronic flash units are more expensive, don't show you exactly what the lighting effect will be (unless you use a second source called a *modeling light* for a preview), and the exposure of electronic flash units is more difficult to calculate accurately.

How Electronic Flash Works

The bursts of light we call electronic flash are produced by a flash of photons generated by an electrical charge that is accumulated in a component called a *capacitor* and then directed through a glass tube containing xenon gas, which absorbs the energy and emits the brief flash. For the pop-up flash built into the Digital

Rebel XTi, the full burst of light lasts about 1/1000th second and provides enough illumination to shoot a subject 10 feet away at f/4 using the ISO 100 setting. In a more typical situation, you'd use ISO 200, f/5.6 to f/8 and photograph something 8 to 10 feet away. As you can see, the built-in flash is somewhat limited in range; you'll see why external flash units are often a good idea later in this chapter. In all cases, though, flash illumination is usually fast enough to stop the quickest action, such as the water drop frozen in mid-splash in Figure 7.5.

An electronic flash (whether built in or connected to the Digital Rebel XTi through a cable or the hot shoe) is triggered at the instant of exposure, during a period when the sensor is fully exposed by the shutter. As I mentioned earlier in this book, the XTi has a vertically traveling shutter that consists of two curtains. The first curtain opens and moves to the opposite side of the frame, at which point the shutter is completely open. The flash can be triggered at this point (so-called *first-curtain sync*), making the flash exposure. Then, after a delay that can vary from 30 seconds to 1/200th second (with the Digital Rebel XTi; other cameras may sync at a faster or slower speed), a second curtain begins moving across the sensor plane, covering up the sensor again. If the flash is triggered just before the second curtain starts to close, then *second-curtain sync* is used. In both cases, though, a shutter speed of 1/200th second is the maximum that can be used to take a photo.

If you happen to set the XTi's shutter to a faster speed in Tv or M mode, the camera will automatically adjust the shutter speed down to 1/200th second. In Av, P, or any of the Basic Zone modes, the XTi will never select a shutter speed higher than 1/200th second when using flash. Actually, in P mode, shutter speed is automatically set between 1/60th and 1/200th second when using flash.

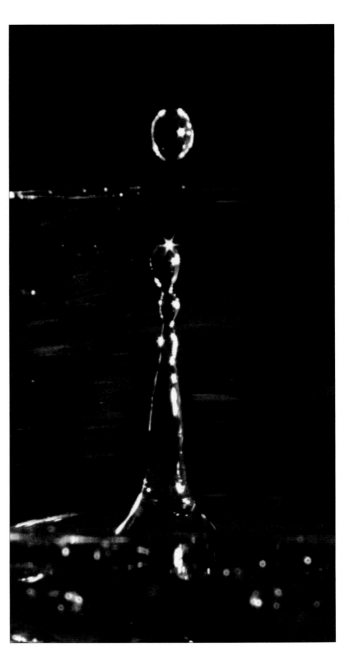

Figure 7.5 Electronic flash can freeze almost any action.

Ghost Images

The difference might not seem like much, but whether you use first-curtain sync (the default setting) or second-curtain sync (an optional setting) can make a significant difference to your photograph *if the ambient light in your scene also contributes to the image.* At faster shutter speeds, particularly 1/200th second, there isn't much time for the ambient light to register, unless it is very bright. It's likely that the electronic flash will provide almost all the illumination, so first-curtain sync or second-curtain sync isn't very important.

However, at slower shutter speeds, or with very bright ambient light levels, there is a significant difference, particularly if your subject is moving or the camera isn't steady. In any of those situations, the ambient light will register as a second image accompanying the flash exposure, and if there is movement (camera or subject), that additional image will not be in the same place as the flash exposure. It will show as a ghost image and, if the movement is significant enough, as a blurred ghost image trailing in front of or behind your subject in the direction of the movement.

When you're using first-curtain sync, the flash goes off the instant the shutter opens, producing an image of the subject on the sensor. Then, the shutter remains open for an additional period (30 seconds to 1/200th second, as I noted). If your subject is moving, say, toward the right side of the frame, the ghost image produced by the ambient light will produce a blur on the right side of the original subject image, making it look as if your sharp (flash-produced) image is chasing the ghost. For those of us who grew up with lightning-fast superheroes who always left a ghost trail *behind them*, that looks un-natural (see Figure 7.6).

So, Canon provides second-curtain sync to remedy the situation. In that mode, the shutter opens, as before, but the electronic flash doesn't fire immediately. Instead, the shutter remains open for its designated duration, and the ghost image forms. If your subject moves from the left side of the frame to the right side, the ghost will move from left to right, too. *Then*, about 1.5 milliseconds before the second shutter curtain closes, the flash is triggered, producing a nice, sharp flash image *ahead* of the ghost image. Voilà! We have monsieur *le Flash* outrunning his own trailing image.

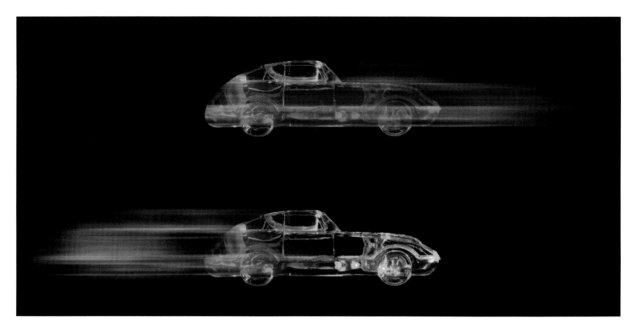

Figure 7.6 First-curtain sync produces an image that trails in front of the flash exposure (top), while second-curtain sync creates a more "natural looking" trail behind the flash image.

Exception to the Sync Rule

Triggering the electronic flash only when the shutter is completely open makes a lot of sense if you think about what's going on. To obtain shutter speeds faster than 1/200th second, the XTi exposes only part of the sensor at one time, by starting the second curtain on its journey before the first curtain has completely opened. That effectively provides a briefer exposure as the open portion between the two curtains passes over the surface of the sensor. If the flash were to fire during the time when the first and second curtains partially obscured the sensor, only the slit that was actually open would be exposed.

However, the XTi and certain Canon flashes provide a partial solution, called *high-speed sync* or *FP sync* (focal plane sync). Those flash units can fire a series of flashes consecutively in rapid succession, producing the illusion of a longer continuous flash, although at reduced intensity. These multiple flashes have a duration long enough to allow exposing the area of the sensor revealed by the traveling slit as it makes its full pass. However, the reduced intensity means that your flash's range is greatly reduced.

Determining Exposure

Calculating the proper exposure for an electronic flash photograph is a bit more complicated than determining the settings for an exposure by continuous light. The right exposure isn't simply a function of how far your subject is (which the XTi can figure out based on the autofocus distance that's locked in just prior to taking the picture). Various objects reflect more or less light at the same distance so, obviously, the camera needs to measure the amount of light reflected back and through the lens. Yet, because the flash itself isn't available for measuring until it's triggered, the XTi has nothing to measure.

The solution is to fire the flash twice. The initial shot is a preflash that can be analyzed, followed by a main flash that's given exactly the calculated intensity needed to provide a correct exposure. As a result, the primary flash may be longer for distant objects and shorter for closer subjects, depending on the required intensity for exposure. This through-the-lens evaluative flash exposure system is called E-TTL II, and it operates whenever the pop-up internal flash is used, or you have attached a Canon dedicated flash unit to the XTi.

Guide Numbers

Guide numbers, usually abbreviated GN, are a way to specify the power of an electronic flash in a way that can be used to determine the correct f/stop to use at a particular shooting distance and ISO setting. In fact, before automatic flash units became prevalent, the GN was actually used to do just that. A GN is usually given as a pair of numbers for both feet and meters that represent the range at ISO 100. For example, the Digital Rebel XTi's built-in flash has a GN of 12/39 (meters/feet) at ISO 100. To calculate the right exposure at that ISO setting, you'd divide the guide number by the distance to arrive at the appropriate f/stop.

Using the XTi's built-in flash as an example, at ISO 100 with its GN of 43, if you wanted to shoot a subject at a distance of 10 feet, you'd use f/4.3 (43 divided by 10; round to f/4 for simplicity's sake). At 8 feet, an f/stop of f/5.4 (round up to f/5.6) would be used. Some quick mental calculations with the GN will give you any particular electronic flash's range. You can easily see that the built-in flash would begin to peter out at about 15 feet, where you'd need an aperture of f/2.8 at ISO 100. Of course, in the real world you'd probably bump the sensitivity up to a setting of ISO 400 so you could use a more practical f/5.6 at that distance.

Today, guide numbers are most useful for comparing the power of various flash units. You don't need to be a math genius to see that an electronic flash with a GN of, say, 165 would be *a lot* more powerful than your built-in flash (at ISO 100, you could use f/11 instead of f/2.8 at 15 feet).

Using the Built-In Flash

The Canon Digital Rebel XTi's built-in flash is a handy accessory because it is available as required, without the need to carry an external flash around with you constantly. This section explains how to use the flip-up flash in the various Basic Zone and Creative Zone modes.

Basic Zone Flash

When the XTi is set to one of the Basic Zone modes (except for Landscape, Sports, or Flash Off modes), the built-in flash will pop up when needed to provide extra illumination in low-light situations, or when your subject matter is backlit and could benefit from some fill flash. The flash doesn't pop up in Landscape mode because the flash doesn't have enough reach to have much effect for pictures of distant vistas in any case; nor does the flash pop up automatically in Sports mode, because you'll often want to use shutter speeds faster than 1/200th second and/or be shooting subjects that are out of flash range. Pop-up flash is disabled in Flash Off mode for obvious reasons.

If you happen to be shooting a landscape photo and do want to use flash (say, to add some illumination to a subject that's closer to the camera), or you want flash with your sports photos, or you *don't* want the flash popping up all the time when using one of the other Basic Zone modes, switch to an appropriate Creative Zone mode and use that instead.

Creative Zone Flash

When you're using a Creative Zone mode, you'll have to judge for yourself when flash might be useful, and flip it up yourself by pressing the Flash button on the side of the pentaprism. The behavior of the internal flash varies, depending on which Creative Zone mode you're using.

- **P/A-DEP.** In these modes, the XTi fully automates the exposure process, giving you subtle fill flash effects in daylight and fully illuminating your subject under dimmer lighting conditions. The camera selects a shutter speed from 1/60th to 1/200th second, and it sets an appropriate aperture.

- **Av.** In aperture priority mode, you set the aperture as always, and the XTi chooses a shutter speed from 30 seconds to 1/200th second. Use this mode with care, because if the camera detects a dark background, it will use the flash to expose the main subject in the foreground, and then leave the shutter open long enough to allow the background to be exposed correctly, too. If you're not using an image-stabilized lens, you can end up with blurry ghost images even of non-moving subjects at exposures longer than 1/30th second, and if your camera is not mounted on a tripod, you'll see these blurs at exposures longer than about 1/8th second even if you are using IS. You can prevent Av mode from using shutter speeds slower than 1/200th second by using Custom Function 03, as described in Chapter 3.

- **Tv.** When using flash in Tv mode, you set the shutter speed from 30 seconds to 1/200th second, and the XTi will choose the correct aperture for the correct flash exposure. If you accidentally set the shutter speed higher than 1/200th second, the camera will reduce it to 1/200th second when you're using the flash.

- **M.** In Manual mode, you select both shutter speed (30 seconds to 1/200th second) and aperture. The camera will adjust the shutter speed to 1/200th second if you try to use a faster speed with flash. The E-TTL II system will provide the correct amount of exposure for your main subject at the aperture you've chosen (if the subject is within the flash's range, of course).

When using Creative Zone modes (or any Basic Zone mode in which flash is used), if Red-Eye Reduction is turned on in the Shooting menu (as described in Chapter 3), the red-eye reduction lamp will illuminate for about 1.5 seconds when you press down the shutter release halfway, theoretically causing your subjects' irises to contract (if they are looking toward the camera), and thereby reducing the red-eye effect in your photograph.

Using FE Lock and Flash Exposure Compensation

If you want to lock flash exposure for a subject that is not centered in the frame, you can use the FE Lock button (*) to lock in a specific flash exposure. Just depress and hold the shutter button halfway to lock in focus, then center the viewfinder on the subject you want to correctly expose and press the * button. The preflash fires and calculates exposure, displaying the FEL (flash exposure lock) message in the viewfinder. Then, recompose your photo and press the shutter down the rest of the way to take the photo.

You can also manually add or subtract exposure to the flash exposure calculated by the XTi. Just use the Flash exp comp setting in the Shooting 2 menu, with the left/right cross keys used to add or subtract flash exposure. The exposure index scale on the status LCD and in the viewfinder will indicate the change you've made. As with non-flash exposure compensation, the adjustment you make remains in effect for the pictures that follow, and even when you've turned the camera off, remember to cancel the flash exposure compensation adjustment by reversing the steps used to set it when you're done using it.

Using External Electronic Flash

Canon offers a broad range of accessory electronic flash units for the Digital Rebel XTi. They can be mounted to the flash accessory shoe, or used off-camera with a dedicated cord that plugs into the flash shoe to maintain full communications with the camera for all special features. They range from the Speedlite 580EX (see Figure 7.7), which can correctly expose subjects up to 24 feet away at f/11 and ISO 200, to the 220EX, which is good out to 9 feet at f/11 and ISO 200. (You'll get greater ranges at even higher ISO settings, of course.)

Speedlite 580EX

This flagship of the Canon accessory flash line is the most powerful unit the company offers, with a GN of 190, and a manual/automatic zoom flash head that covers the full frame of lenses from 24mm wide angle to 105mm tele-photo. (There's a flip-down wide-angle diffuser that spreads the flash to cover a 14mm lens's field of view, too.) All angle specifications given by Canon refer to full-frame sensors, but this flash unit automatically converts its field of view coverage to accommodate the crop factor of the Digital Rebel XTi and the other 1.6X crop Canon dSLRs.

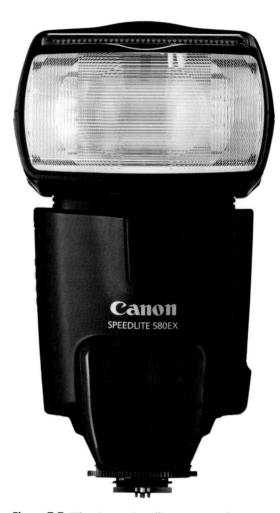

The unit offers full swivel, 180 degrees in either direction, and has its own built-in AF assist beam and an exposure system that's compatible with the nine focus points of the XTi. The 580EX automatically communicates white balance information to your camera, allowing it to automatically adjust WB to match the flash output. You can even simulate a modeling light effect: when you press the depth-of-field preview button on the XTi, the 580EX emits a one-second burst of light that allows you to judge the flash effect. If you're using multiple flash units with Canon's wireless E-TTL system, this model can serve as a master flash that controls the slave units you've set up (more about this later), or function as a slave itself.

It's easy to access all the features of this unit, because it has a large backlit LCD panel on the back that provides information about all flash settings. Powered by economical AA-size batteries, the unit recycles in 0.1 to 6 seconds, and can squeeze 100 to 700 flashes from a set of alkaline or rechargeable AA cells.

Figure 7.7 The Canon Speedlite 580EX is the most powerful shoe-mount flash Canon offers.

Speedlite 430EX

This less pricey electronic flash has a GN of 141, with automatic and manual zoom coverage from 24mm to 105mm, and the same wide-angle pullout panel found on the 580EX that covers the area of a 14mm lens on a full-frame camera, and automatic conversion to the cropped frame area of the XTi and other 1.6X crop Canon dSLRs. The 430EX also communicates white balance information with the camera, and has its own AF assist beam. Compatible with Canon's wireless E-TTL system, it makes a good slave unit, but it cannot serve as a master flash. It, too, uses AA batteries, and offers recycle times of 0.1 to 3.7 seconds for 200 to 1,400 flashes, depending on subject distance.

Speedlite 220EX

Unlike the other two units, this one offers automatic operation only, and none of the fancy features of its more expensive siblings. Its 72 guide number is a little beefier than the XTi's built-in flash, making it a good choice as a low-power auxiliary flash unit. It lacks a zoomable flash head, and offers fixed coverage equivalent to the field of view of a 28mm full-frame lens. Expect 250 to 1,700 flashes from a set of four AA batteries, and recycle times of 0.1 to 4.5 seconds. The built-in AF assist beam is linked to the center focusing point of the XTi only.

More Advanced Lighting Techniques

As you advance in your Canon Digital Rebel XTi photography, you'll want to learn more sophisticated lighting techniques, using more than just straight-on flash, or a single flash unit. Entire books have been written on lighting techniques, and I've written multiple chapters on them in books of my own. I'm going to provide a quick introduction to some of the techniques you should be considering.

Fill Flash

Who says that electronic flash can't be used in full daylight? Even when there is plenty of illumination to make an exposure, you still can benefit from adding a little more with electronic flash. A perfect example can be found in contrasty daylight situations in which bright sunlight forms deep shadows that could use a bit of brightening. Indoors, you might have enough light to take a photo, but still be plagued by dark shadows that ruin your shot. In either case, your Rebel XTi's built-in flash (or an external flash you connect to the camera) can provide that extra bit of light that brightens those shadows.

Figure 7.8 shows a parrot photographed under direct sunlight. At left, a shadow darkens the bird's left eye, possibly a bit too much for most tastes. At right, a tiny

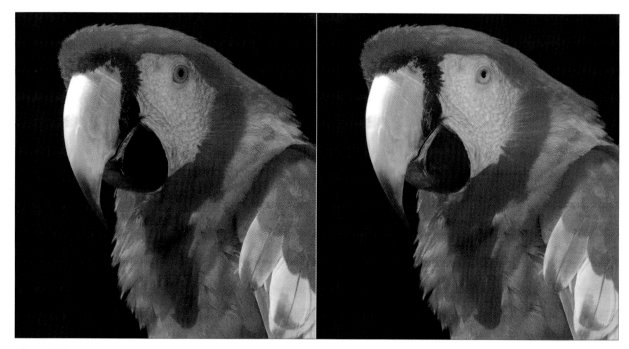

Figure 7.8 Dark shadows obscuring the parrot's eye can be brightened using fill flash.

burst of light from the camera's flash brightens the shadows and, as a bonus, contributes a catch light to the parrot's eye (at roughly the 11 o'clock position) that adds some sparkle.

If you've set the Rebel XTi to use evaluative exposure for electronic flash (set Custom Function 8 to 0), fill flash is virtually automatic in Programmed, Aperture Priority, Shutter Priority, and Manual modes. Just remember to flip up the flash and take your picture. The camera will evaluate the scene and adjust the amount of flash to just enough to fill in the dark shadows.

Diffusing and Softening the Light

Direct light can be harsh and glaring, especially if you're using the flash built into your camera, or an auxiliary flash mounted in the hot shoe and pointed directly at your subject. The first thing you should do is stop using direct light (unless you're looking for a stark, contrasty appearance as a creative effect). There are a number of simple things you can do with both continuous and flash illumination.

- **Use window light.** Light coming in a window can be soft and flattering, and a good choice for human subjects. Move your subject close enough to the window that its light provides the primary source of illumination. You might want to turn off other lights in the room, particularly to avoid mixing daylight and incandescent light.

- **Bounce the light.** External electronic flash units mounted on the XTi usually have a swivel that allows them to be pointed up at a ceiling for a bounce light effect. You can also bounce the light off a wall. You'll want the ceiling or wall to be white or have a neutral gray color to avoid a color cast.

- **Use reflectors.** Another way to bounce the light is to use reflectors or umbrellas that you can position yourself to provide a greater degree of control over the quantity and direction of the bounced light. Good reflectors can be pieces of foamboard, Mylar, or a reflective disk held in place by a clamp and stand. Although some expensive umbrellas and reflectors are available, spending a lot isn't necessary. A simple piece of white foamboard does the job beautifully. Umbrellas have the advantage of being compact and foldable, while providing a soft, even kind of light. They're relatively cheap, too, with a good 40-inch umbrella available for as little as $20.

- **Use diffusers.** Sto-Fen and some other vendors offer clip-on diffusers like the one shown in Figure 7.9, that fit over your electronic flash head and provide a soft, flattering light. These add-ons are more portable than umbrellas and other reflectors, yet provide a nice diffuse lighting effect. Slide-on diffusers are available in colors, too, for warming, cooling, or special effects.

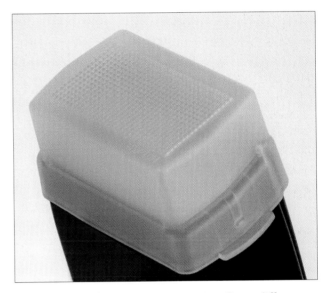

Figure 7.9 The Sto-Fen OmniBounce is a clip-on diffuser that softens the light of an external flash unit.

Using Multiple Light Sources

Once you gain control over the qualities and effects you get with a single light source, you'll want to graduate to using multiple light sources. Using several lights allows you to shape and mold the illumination of your subjects to provide a variety of effects, from backlighting to side lighting to more formal portrait lighting. You can start simply with several incandescent light sources, bounced off umbrellas or reflectors that you construct. Or you can use more flexible multiple electronic flash setups.

Effective lighting is the one element that differentiates great photography from candid or snapshot shooting. Lighting can make a mundane subject look a little more glamorous. Make subjects appear to be soft when you want a soft look, or bright and sparkly when you want a vivid look, or strong and dramatic if that's what you desire. As you might guess, having control over your lighting means that you probably can't use the lights that are already in the room. You'll need separate, discrete lighting fixtures that can be moved, aimed, brightened, and dimmed on command.

Selecting your lighting gear will depend on the type of photography you do, and the budget you have to support it. It's entirely possible for a beginning XTi photographer to create a basic, inexpensive lighting system capable of delivering high-quality results, just as you can spend megabucks for a sophisticated lighting system.

Basic Flash Setups

If you want to use multiple electronic flash units, the Canon Speedlites described earlier will serve admirably. The two higher-end models can be used with Canon's wireless E-TTL feature, which allows you to set up to three separate groups of flash units (several flashes can be included in each group) and trigger them using a master flash (such as the 580EX) and the camera. Just set up one master unit (there's a switch on the unit's foot that sets it for master mode) and arrange the compatible slave units around your subject. You can set the relative power of each unit separately, thereby controlling how much of the scene's illumination comes from the main flash, and how much from the auxiliary flash units, which can be used as fill flash, background lights, or, if you're careful, to illuminate the hair of portrait subjects.

Studio Flash

If you're serious about using multiple flash units, a studio flash setup might be more practical. The traditional studio flash is a multi-part unit, consisting of a flash head that mounts on your light stand and is tethered to an AC (or sometimes battery) power supply. A single power supply can feed two or more flash heads at a time, with separate control over the output of each head.

When they are operating off AC power, studio flash units don't have to be frugal with the juice, and are often powerful enough to illuminate very large subjects, or to supply lots and lots of light to smaller subjects. The output of such units is measured in watt seconds (ws), so you could purchase a 200ws, 400ws, or 800ws unit, and a power pack to match.

Their advantages include greater power output, much faster recycling, built-in modeling lamps, multiple power levels, and ruggedness that can stand up to transport, because many photographers pack up these kits and tote them around as location lighting rigs. Studio lighting kits can range in price from a few hundred dollars for a set of lights, stands, and reflectors, to thousands for a high-end lighting system complete with all the necessary accessories.

A more practical choice these days is *monolights* (see Figure 7.10), which are "all-in-one" studio lights that sell for about $200. They have the flash tube, modeling light, and power supply built into a single unit that can be mounted on a light stand. Monolights are available in AC-only and battery-pack versions, although an external battery eliminates some of the advantages of having a flash with everything in one unit. They are very portable, because all you need is a case for the monolight itself, plus the stands and other accessories you want to carry along. Because these units are so popular with photographers who are not full-time professionals, the lower-cost monolights are often designed more for lighter duty than professional studio flash. That doesn't mean they aren't rugged; you'll just need to handle them with a little more care, and, perhaps, not expect them to be used eight hours a day for weeks on end. In most other respects, however, monolights are the equal of traditional studio flash units in terms of fast recycling, built-in modeling lamps, adjustable power, and so forth.

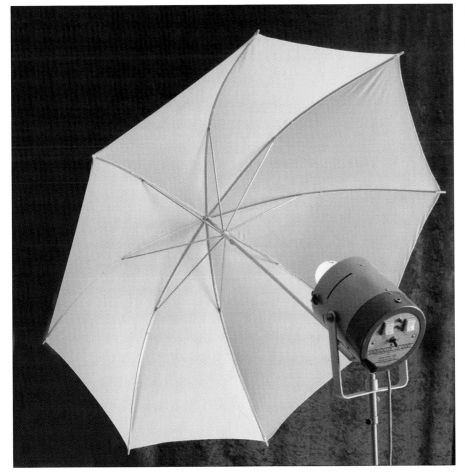

Figure 7.10 All-in-one "monolights" contain flash, power supply, and a modeling light in one compact package (umbrella not included).

Connecting Multiple Units to Your Canon Digital Rebel XTi

Non-dedicated electronic flash units can't use the automated E-TTL II features of your Digital Rebel XTi; you'll need to calculate exposure manually, through test shots evaluated on your camera's LCD or by using an electronic flash meter. Moreover, you don't have to connect them to the accessory shoe on top of the camera, because they use a PC/X connector, which the XTi lacks. You'll need a hot shoe/PC adapter to provide a connection for studio and other flash that require a PC/X connector.

You should be aware that older electronic flash units sometimes use a triggering voltage that is too much for your XTi to handle. You can actually damage the camera's electronics if the voltage is too high. You won't need to worry about this if you purchase brand new units from Alien Bees, Adorama, or other vendors. But if you must connect an external flash with an unknown triggering voltage, I recommend using a Wein Safe Sync (see Figure 7.11), which isolates the flash's voltage from the camera triggering circuit. It makes an excellent hot shoe/PC adapter, so this one gadget can serve all your flash connection needs.

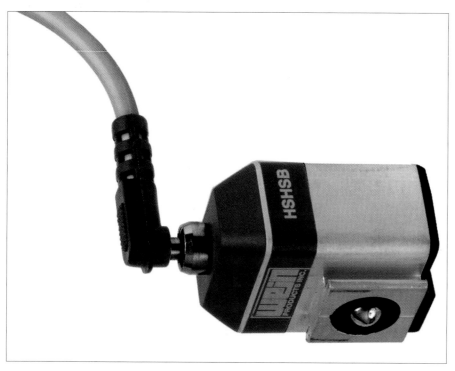

Figure 7.11 A voltage isolator can prevent frying your XTi's flash circuits if you use an older electronic flash.

Another safe way to connect external cameras is through a radio-control device, such as the transmitter/receiver set shown in Figure 7.12. One piece clips on the hot shoe and plugs into the hot shoe/PC adapter and transmits a signal to a matching receiver that's connected to your flash unit. The receiver has both a PC connector of its own as well as a "monoplug" connector (it looks like a headphone plug) that links to a matching port on compatible flash units.

Finally, some flash units have an optical slave trigger built in, or can be fitted with one, so that they fire automatically when another flash, including your camera's built-in unit, fires. The Canon Speedlite Transmitter ST-E2, at about $200, is another option. It's a dedicated E-TTL II wireless autoflash transmitter that can control an unlimited number of 420EX, 550EX, or 580EX flash units, allocated to three separate groups so you can set the output levels of flash units in each group separately, if you like, to produce various lighting ratios. The unit also can be used with MR-14EX and MT-24EX flashes, which are ringlights mounted *around* the lens to provide soft lighting for photography at close-up and portrait distances.

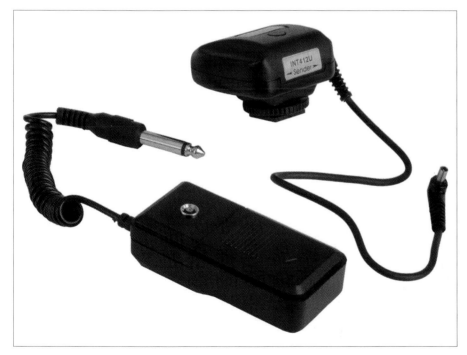

Figure 7.12 A radio-control device frees you from a sync cord tether between your flash and camera.

Other Lighting Accessories

Once you start working with light, you'll find there are plenty of useful accessories that can help you. Here are some of the most popular that you might want to consider.

Soft Boxes

Soft boxes are large square or rectangular devices that may resemble a square umbrella with a front cover, and produce a similar lighting effect. They can extend from a few feet square to massive boxes that stand five or six feet tall—virtually a wall of light. With a flash unit or two inside a soft box, you have a very large, semi-directional light source that's very diffuse and very flattering for portraiture and other people photography. (See Figure 7.13, taken with a soft box and a background light.)

Soft boxes are also handy for photographing shiny objects. They not only provide a soft light, but if the box itself happens to reflect in the subject (say you're photographing a chromium toaster), the box will provide an interesting highlight that's indistinct and not distracting.

You can buy soft boxes or make your own. Some lengths of friction-fit plastic pipe and a lot of muslin cut and sewed just so may be all that you need.

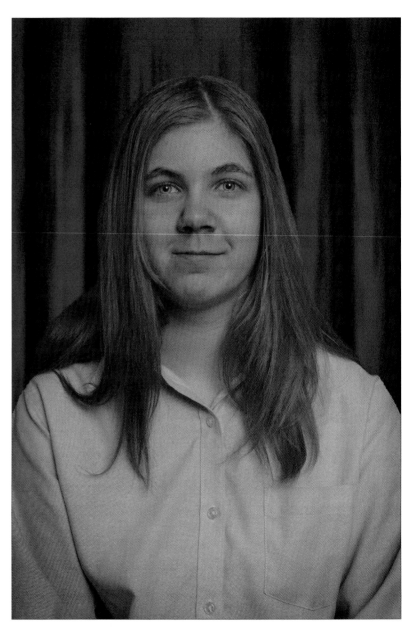

Figure 7.13 A soft box can produce diffuse, flattering lighting like this for portraits.

Light Stands

Both electronic flash and incandescent lamps can benefit from light stands. These are lightweight, tripod-like devices (but without a swiveling or tilting head) that can be set on the floor, tabletops, or other elevated surfaces and positioned as needed. Light stands should be strong enough to support an external lighting unit, up to and including a relatively heavy flash with soft box or umbrella reflectors. You want the supports to be capable of raising the lights high enough to be effective. Look for light stands capable of extending six to seven feet high. The nine-foot units usually have larger, steadier bases, and extend high enough that you can use them as background supports. You'll be using these stands for a lifetime, so invest in good ones. I bought the light stand shown in Figure 7.14 when I was in college, and I have been using it for decades.

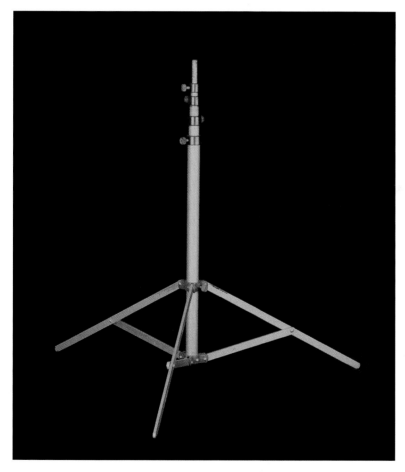

Figure 7.14 Light stands can hold lights, umbrellas, backdrops, and other equipment.

Backgrounds

Backgrounds can be backdrops of cloth, sheets of muslin you've painted yourself using a sponge dipped in paint, rolls of seamless paper, or any other suitable surface your mind can dream up. Backgrounds provide a complementary and non-distracting area behind subjects (especially portraits) and can be lit separately to provide contrast and separation that outlines the subject, or which helps set a mood.

I like to use plain-colored backgrounds for portraits, and white seamless backgrounds for product photography. You can usually construct these yourself from cheap materials and tape them up on the wall behind your subject, or mount them on a pole stretched between a pair of light stands.

Snoots and Barn Doors

These fit over the flash unit and direct the light at your subject. Snoots are excellent for converting a flash unit into a hair light, whereas barn doors give you enough control over the illumination by opening and closing their flaps so that you can use another flash as a background light, with the capability of feathering the light exactly where you want it on the background. Both are shown in Figure 7.15.

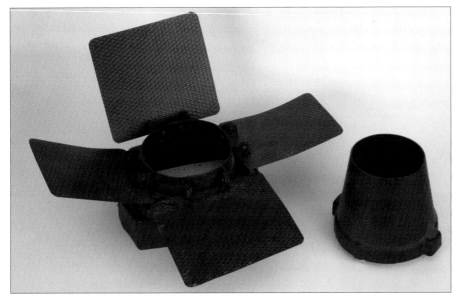

Figure 7.15 Snoots and barn doors allow you to modulate the light from a flash or lamp, and they are especially useful for hair lights and background lights.

8

Downloading and Editing Your Images

Taking the picture is only half the work and, in some cases, only half the fun. After you've captured some great images and have them safely stored on your Canon Digital Rebel XTi's memory card, you'll need to transfer them from your camera and Compact Flash card to your computer, where they can be organized, fine-tuned in an image editor, and prepared for web display, printing, or some other final destination.

Fortunately, there are lots of software utilities and applications to help you do all these things. This chapter will introduce you to a few of them.

What's in the Box?

Your Canon Digital Rebel XTi came with a set of EOS Digital Solutions CDs with software programs for both Windows PCs and Macs. Pop the CD into your computer and it will self-install a selection of these useful applications and utilities. Manuals for all these programs are included on a CD, too, but here's a summary of what you get:

EOS Utility

Both Windows and Mac versions are provided for this useful program, which has several functions. It serves as an image downloading module that can automatically copy photos from your XTi and transfer them to either Digital Photo

Professional or ZoomBrowser EX. It also includes a camera settings/remote shooting module that allows you to link your computer with the XTi and use a dialog box to change camera settings and to control the camera for remote shooting. The settings feature is especially useful for changing Picture Styles quickly, while you'll find the remote shooting capabilities useful when you want to program a delay before the camera takes a picture, or do some interval (time-lapse) shooting.

ZoomBrowser/ImageBrowser

ZoomBrowser is an image viewing and editing application for Windows PCs (the equivalent program for Macs is called ImageBrowser). You can organize, sort, classify, and rename files, and convert JPEG files in batches. This utility is especially useful for printing index sheets of groups of images (see Figure 8.1). It can also prepare images for e-mailing. It works with RAW Image Task for converting CR2 files to some other format, and it can be used to select images for merging using PhotoStitch.

The simple image-editing facilities of ZoomBrowser allow red-eye correction, brightness/contrast and color correction, manipulating sharpness, trimming photos, and a few other functions. For more complex editing, you can transfer images directly from this application to Photoshop or another image editor.

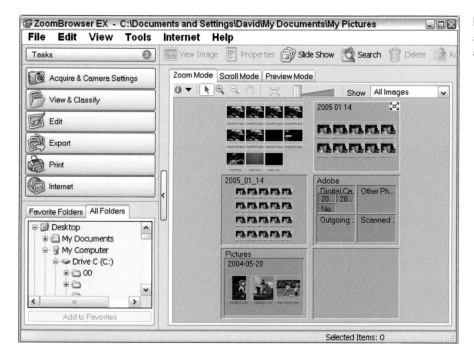

Figure 8.1 ZoomBrowser allows organizing your images and performing simple fixes.

RAW Image Task

This is a simple RAW converter that can be used to create TIFF or JPEG images from RAW files, using the settings you specified in the camera, or tweaked settings that you choose. It can also transfer the converted files to another image editor, such as Photoshop or Photoshop Elements. These functions are available for both Windows PCs and Macs.

PhotoStitch

This Windows/Mac utility allows you to take several JPEG images and combine them to create a panorama in a single new file. You can choose the images to be merged in ZoomBrowser and then transfer them to PhotoStitch, or operate the utility as a stand-alone module and select the images using the standard File Open commands. (See Figure 8.2.)

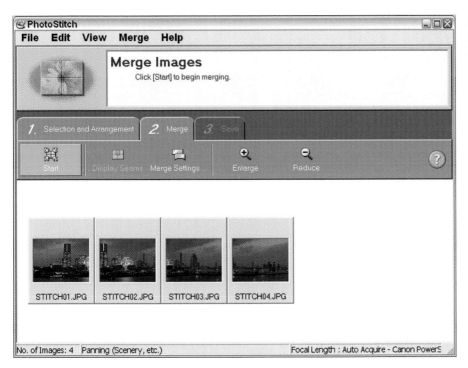

Figure 8.2 Panoramas are easy to create with PhotoStitch.

Digital Photo Professional

While far from a Photoshop replacement, Digital Photo Professional is a useful image-editing program that helps you organize, trim, correct, and print images. You can make RAW adjustments, correct tonal curves, color tone, color saturation, sharpness, as well as brightness and contrast. Especially handy are the "recipes" that can be developed and saved so that a given set of corrections can be kept separate from the file itself, and, if desired, applied to other images. (See Figure 8.3.)

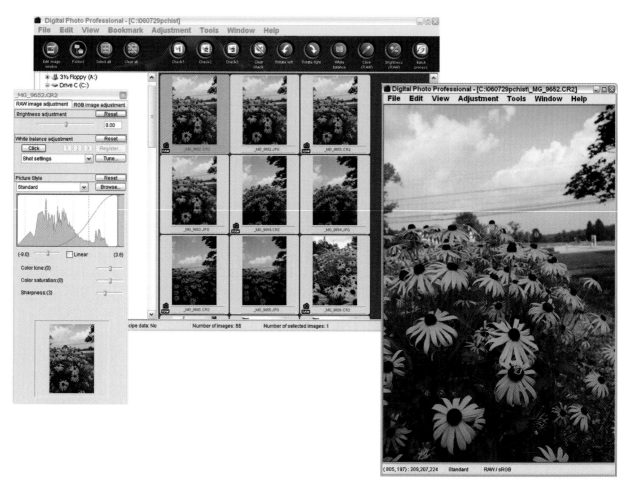

Figure 8.3 Digital Photo Professional will never replace Photoshop, but it has some basic image-editing features.

Transferring Your Photos

While it's rewarding to capture some great images and have them ensconced in your camera, eventually you'll be transferring them to your laptop or PC, whether you're using a Windows or Macintosh machine. You have three options for image transfer: direct transfer over a USB cable, automated transfer using a card reader and transfer software such as the EOS Utility or Adobe Photoshop Elements Photo Downloader, or manual transfer using drag and drop from a memory card inserted in a card reader.

Direct Transfer

There are some advantages to transferring photos directly from your Digital Rebel XTi to a computer. The destination computer doesn't need to have a card reader; all it requires is a USB port. So, if you have the USB cable that came with your camera, you can transfer photos to any computer that has the Canon utility software (discussed later) installed. However, direct transfer uses your XTi's internal battery power (whereas removing the card and transferring the photos with a card reader installed on the destination computer does not).

You can select which images are transferred to the computer, or transfer all the images, both RAW and JPEG, that are on the Compact Flash card. This method requires that you install the software furnished with the Digital Rebel XTi, including the EOS Utility and Digital Photo Professional. The CD bundled with your camera has versions of each for both Macintosh and Windows.

Just follow these steps:

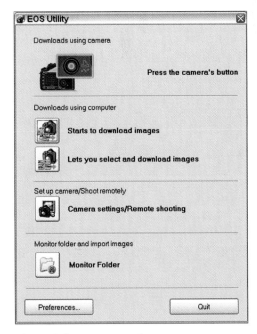

Figure 8.4 The EOS Utility can automate transfer of pictures to your computer.

1. Press the Menu button and in Set-up 2 menu, make sure Communication is set to PC Connection, and then turn the camera off.

2. Connect the USB cable to the DIGITAL terminal on the left side of the Digital Rebel XTi (under the rubber cover), and plug the other end into a USB port on the destination computer.

3. Turn on the Digital Rebel XTi. The EOS Utility, shown in Figure 8.4, will appear on your computer screen, ready to download your photos. (If you have another program installed that also has a transfer utility, such as Adobe Photoshop Elements 5.0's Photo Downloader, it may pop up as well. Close that window if you want to use the EOS Utility.)

4. Use the controls within the EOS Utility to activate the transfer process.

Using a Card Reader and Software

You can also use a Compact Flash memory card reader and software to transfer photos, and automate the process using the EOS Utility, Photoshop Elements 5.0's Photo Downloader, or the downloading program supplied with some other third-party applications. This method is more frugal in its use of your XTi's battery, and it can be faster if you have a speedy USB 2.0 or FireWire card reader attached to an appropriate port.

The installed software automatically remains in memory as you work and recognizes when a Compact Flash card is inserted in your card reader; you don't need to launch it yourself. With the EOS Utility, you'll see a dialog box like the one shown in Figure 8.4. You can click the Starts to Download Images button to begin the transfer of all images immediately, or click the Lets You Select and Download Images button to produce a dialog box like the one shown in Figure 8.5 that allows you to choose which images to download from the memory card.

When you start the download, the status box shown in Figure 8.6 appears to let you know how the transfer is progressing.

If you're using a third-party utility, such as Elements 5.0 Photo Downloader, thumbnails of the images on the card will appear in a dialog box like the one shown in Figure 8.7. You can select the photos you want to transfer, plus options such as Automatically Fix Red Eyes. Start the download, and a confirmation dialog box like the one shown in Figure 8.8 shows the progress.

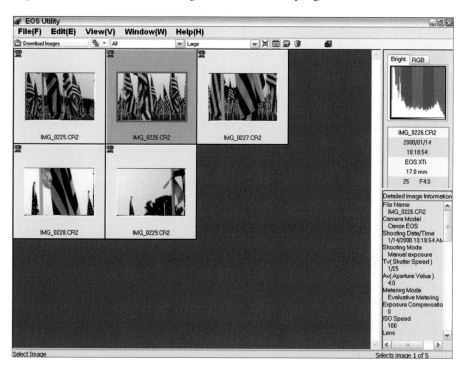

Figure 8.5 If you don't want to transfer all images, you can select the ones you want to copy.

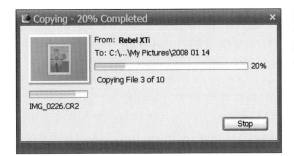

Figure 8.6 During the transfer, the EOS Utility provides an updated status showing the progress.

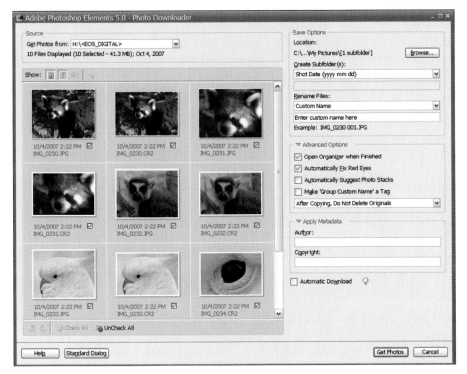

Figure 8.7 Photoshop Elements 5.0's Photo Downloader allows you to select the photos you want to copy to your computer, and apply some options such as new file names or red-eye fixes automatically.

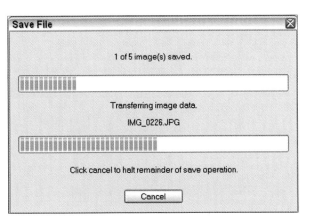

Figure 8.8 Photo Downloader also shows you the progress as images are downloaded to your computer.

Dragging and Dropping

The final way to move photos from your memory card to your computer is the old-fashioned way: manually dragging and dropping the files from one window on your computer to another. The procedure works pretty much the same whether you're using a Mac or a PC.

1. Remove the Compact Flash card from the Digital Rebel XTi and insert it in your memory card reader.

2. Using Windows Explorer, My Computer, or your Mac desktop, open the icon representing the memory card, which appears on your desktop as just another disk drive.

3. Open a second window representing the folder on your computer that you want to use as the destination for the files you are copying or moving.

4. Drag and drop the files from the Compact Flash card window to the folder on your computer (see Figure 8.9). You can select individual files, press Ctrl/Command+A to select all the files or Ctrl/Command+click to select multiple files.

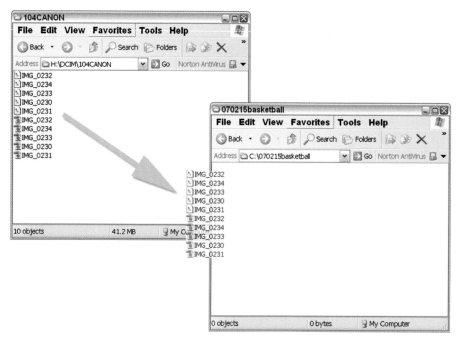

Figure 8.9 Dragging and dropping files is an easy way to transfer photos from a Compact Flash card to your computer.

Editing Your Photos

Image manipulation tasks fall into several categories. You might want to fine-tune your images, retouch them, change color balance, composite several images together, and perform other tasks we know as image editing with a program like Adobe Photoshop, or Photoshop Elements, or Corel Photo-Paint.

You might want to play with the settings in RAW files, too, as you import them from their .CR2 state into an image editor. There are specialized tools expressly for tweaking RAW files, ranging from Canon's own Digital Photo Professional to Adobe Camera RAW, and PhaseOne's Capture One Pro (C1 Pro). A third type of manipulation is the specialized task of noise reduction, which can be performed within Photoshop, Adobe Camera RAW, or tools like Bibble Professional. There are also specialized tools just for noise reduction, such as Noise Ninja (now furnished with Bibble) and Neat Image.

Each of these utilities and applications deserves a chapter of its own, so I'm simply going to enumerate some of the most popular image-editing and RAW conversion programs here and tell you a little about what they do.

Image Editors

Image editors are general-purpose photo editing applications that can do color correction, tonal modifications, retouching, combining of several images into one, and usually include tools for working with RAW files and reducing noise. So, you'll find programs like those listed here good for all-around image manipulation. The leading programs are:

Adobe Photoshop CS3/Photoshop Elements 5.0. Photoshop CS3 Standard and Extended versions are the serious photographer's number one choice for image editing, and Elements is an excellent option for those who need most of Photoshop's power, but not all of its professional-level features. Both use the latest version of Adobe's Camera Raw plug-in, which makes it easy to adjust things like color space profiles, color depth (either 8 bits or 16 bits per color channel), image resolution, white balance, exposure, shadows, brightness, sharpness, luminance, and noise reduction. One plus with the Adobe products is that they are (eventually) available in identical versions for both Windows and Macs. In recent years the Mac version of each Elements release has lagged a bit behind the introduction of the Windows version, and it has often included a slightly different mix of features.

Adobe Fireworks. This is the Windows/Mac image-editing program formerly from Macromedia, and now owned by Adobe, and is most useful when used with web development and animation software like Dreamweaver and Flash. If you're using your Digital Rebel XTi images on web pages, you'll like this program's capabilities in the web graphics arena, such as banners, image maps, and rollover buttons. Some of Adobe's Creative Suite packages (which include multiple programs like Adobe Illustrator CS and Fireworks) substitute this image editor for Photoshop. So, it appears that Fireworks, which many users love, will continue as a viable product.

Corel Photo-Paint. This is the image-editing program that is included in the popular CorelDRAW Graphics suite. Although a Mac version was available in the past, this is primarily a Windows application today. It's a full-featured photo retouching and image-editing program with selection, retouching, and painting tools for manual image manipulations, and it also includes convenient automated commands for a few common tasks, such as red-eye removal. Photo-Paint accepts Photoshop plug-ins to expand its assortment of filters and special effects.

Corel Paint Shop Pro. This is a general-purpose Windows image editor that has gained a reputation as the "poor man's Photoshop" for providing a substantial portion of Photoshop's capabilities at a fraction of the cost. It includes a nifty set of wizard-like commands that automate common tasks, such as removing red-eye and scratches, as well as filters and effects that can be expanded with other Photoshop plug-ins.

Corel Painter. Here's another image-editing program for Windows PCs from Corel. This one's strength is in mimicking natural media, such as charcoal, pastels, and various kinds of paint. Painter includes a basic assortment of tools that you can use to edit existing images, but the program is really designed for artists to use in creating original illustrations. As a photographer, you might prefer another image editor, but if you like to paint on top of your photographic images, nothing else really does the job of Painter.

Ulead PhotoImpact. Although still bearing the Ulead name, this application has been assimilated into the Corel fold as a low-end product. (Resistance is futile!) But PhotoImpact is far from low-end in its capabilities. This is a Windows general-purpose photo editing program with a huge assortment of brushes for painting, retouching, and cloning, in addition to the usual selection, cropping, and fill tools. If you frequently find yourself performing the same image manipulations on a number of files, you'll appreciate PhotoImpact's batch operations. Using this feature, you can select multiple image files and then apply any one of a long list of filters, enhancements, or auto-process commands to all the selected files.

RAW Utilities

Because in the past digital camera vendors offered RAW converters that weren't very good (Canon's File View Utility comes to mind), there is a lively market for third-party RAW utilities available at extra cost. However, the EOS Utility and Digital Photo Professional do a good job and may be all that you need.

The third-party solutions are usually available as standalone applications (often for both Windows and Macintosh platforms), as Photoshop-compatible plug-ins, or both. Because the RAW plug-ins often displace Photoshop's own RAW converter, I tend to prefer to use most RAW utilities in standalone mode. That way, if I choose to open a file directly in Photoshop it automatically opens using Photoshop's fast and easy-to-use Adobe Camera Raw (ACR) plug-in. If I have more time or need the capabilities of another converter, I can load that, open the file, and make my corrections there. Most are able to transfer the processed file directly to Photoshop even if you aren't using plug-in mode.

This section provides a quick overview of the range of RAW file handlers, so you can get a better idea of the kinds of information available with particular applications. I'm going to include both high-end and low-end RAW browsers so you can see just what is available.

EOS Utility/Digital Photo Professional

Canon provides these software utilities for viewing/converting images taken with Canon cameras, and for controlling the camera remotely through a linked computer. Digital Photo Professional, introduced earlier in this chapter, is preferred by many for Canon dSLR cameras like the Digital Rebel XTi.

DPP offers much higher-speed processing of RAW images than was available with the late, not lamented, sluggardly File Viewer Utility (as much as six times faster). Canon says this utility rivals third-party standalone and plug-in RAW converters in speed and features. It supports both Canon's original CRW format and the newer CR2 RAW format used by the XTi, along with TIFF, Exif TIFF, and JPEG.

You can save settings that include multiple adjustments and apply them to other images, and use the clever comparison mode to compare your original and edited versions of an image either side by side or within a single split image. The utility allows easy adjustment of color channels, tone curves, exposure compensation, white balance, dynamic range, brightness, contrast, color saturation, ICC Profile embedding, and assignment of monitor profiles. A new feature is the ability to continue editing images while batches of previously adjusted RAW files are rendered and saved in the background.

IrfanView

At the low (free) end of the price scale is IrfanView, a Windows freeware program you can download at www.irfanview.com. It can read many common RAW photo formats. It's a quick way to view RAW files (just drag and drop to the IrfanView window) and make fast changes to the unprocessed file. You can crop, rotate, or correct your image, and do some cool things like swapping the colors around (red for blue, blue for green, and so forth) to create false color pictures.

The price is right, and IrfanView has some valuable capabilities (see Figure 8.10).

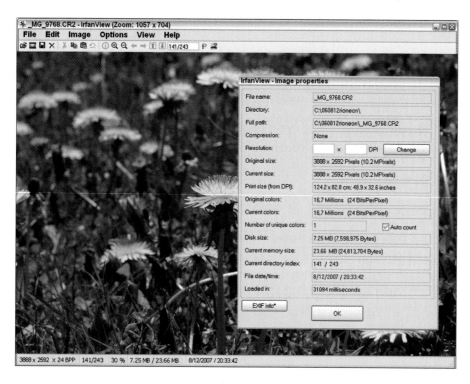

Figure 8.10 IrfanView is a freeware program that can read many RAW file formats, including the XTi's CR2 format.

Phase One Capture One Pro (C1 Pro)

If there is a Cadillac of RAW converters for Canon digital SLR cameras, C1 Pro has to be it. This premium-priced program does everything, does it well, and does it quickly. If you can't justify the price tag of this professional-level software, there are "lite" versions for serious amateur and cash-challenged professionals called Capture One dSLR and Capture One dSLR SE.

Aimed at photographers with high-volume needs (that would include school and portrait photographers, as well as busy, commercial photographers), C1 Pro (shown in Figure 8.11) is available for both Windows and Mac OS X, and it supports a broad range of Canon digital cameras. Phase One is a leading supplier of

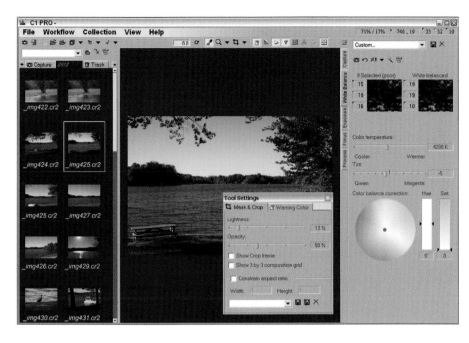

Figure 8.11 Phase One's C1 Pro is fast and sophisticated.

megabucks digital camera backs for medium and larger format cameras, so they really understand the needs of photographers.

The latest features include individual noise reduction controls for each image, automatic levels adjustment, a "quick develop" option that allows speedy conversion from RAW to TIFF or JPEG formats, dual-image side-by-side views for comparison purposes, and helpful grids and guides that can be superimposed over an image. Photographers concerned about copyright protection will appreciate the ability to add watermarks to the output images.

Bibble Pro

One of my personal favorites among third-party RAW converters is Bibble Pro (shown in Figure 8.12), which just came out with a new version as I was writing this book. It supports one of the broadest ranges of RAW file formats available (which can be handy if you find yourself with the need to convert a file from a friend or colleague's non-Canon camera, including NEF files from Nikon D1, D1x/h, D2H, and D100; CRW files from the Canon C30, D60, 10D, and 300D; CR2 files from the Canon Digital Rebel XTi/XTi and other newer models; ORF files from the Olympus E10, E20, E1, C5050, and C5060; DCR files from the Kodak 720x, 760, and 14n; RAF files from the Fuji S2Pro; PEF files from Pentax ISTD; MRW files from the Minolta Maxxum; and TIF files from Canon 1D/1DS).

The utility supports lots of different platforms, too. It's available for Windows, Mac OS X, and, believe it or not, Linux.

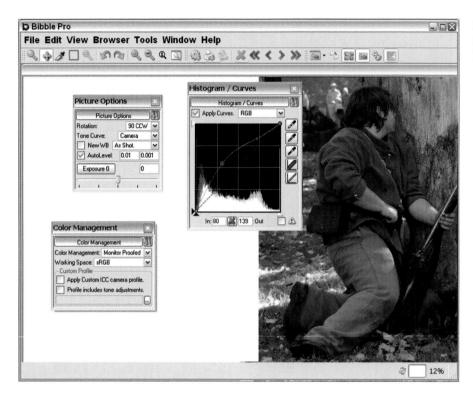

Figure 8.12 Bibble Pro supports a broad range of RAW file formats.

Bibble works fast because it offers instantaneous previews and real-time feedback as changes are made. That's important when you need to convert many images in a short time (event photographers will know what I am talking about!). Bibble's batch-processing capabilities also let you convert large numbers of files using settings you specify without further intervention.

Its customizable interface lets you organize and edit images quickly, and then output them in a variety of formats, including 16-bit TIFF and PNG. You can even create a Web gallery from within Bibble. I often find myself disliking the generic filenames applied to digital images by cameras, so I really like Bibble's ability to rename batches of files using new names that you specify.

Bibble is fully color managed, which means it can support all the popular color spaces (Adobe sRGB, and so forth) and use custom profiles generated by third-party color-management software. There are two editions of Bibble, a Pro version and a Lite version. Because the Pro version is reasonably priced at $129, I don't really see the need to save $60 with the Lite edition, which lacks the top-line's options for tethered shooting, embedding IPTC-compatible captions in images, and can also be used as a Photoshop plug-in (if you prefer not to work with the application in its standalone mode). Bibble Pro now incorporates Noise Ninja technology, so you can get double-duty from this valuable application.

BreezeBrowser

BreezeBrowser, shown in Figure 8.13, was long the RAW converter of choice for Canon dSLR owners who run Windows and who were dissatisfied with Canon's lame antique File Viewer Utility. It works quickly, and it has lots of options for converting CRW and CR2 files to other formats. You can choose to show highlights that will be blown out in your finished photo as flashing areas (so they can be more easily identified and corrected), use histograms to correct tones, add color profiles, auto-rotate images, and adjust all those raw image parameters, such as white balance, color space, saturation, contrast, sharpening, color tone, EV compensation, and other settings.

You can also control noise reduction (choosing from low, normal, or high reduction), evaluate your changes in the live preview, and then save the file as a compressed JPEG or as either an 8-bit or 16-bit TIFF file. BreezeBrowser also can create HTML Web galleries directly from your selection of images.

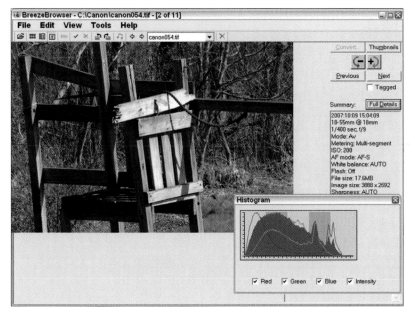

Figure 8.13 BreezeBrowser makes converting Canon RAW files a breeze.

Photoshop CS3

The latest version of Photoshop includes a built-in RAW plug-in that is compatible with the proprietary formats of a growing number of digital cameras, both new and old. This plug-in also works with Photoshop Elements 5.0.

To open a RAW image in Photoshop CS3, just follow these steps (Elements 5.0 users can use much the same workflow, although fewer settings are available):

1. Transfer the RAW images from your camera to your computer's hard drive.

2. In Photoshop, choose Open from the File menu, or use Bridge.

3. Select a RAW image file. The Adobe Camera Raw plug-in will pop up, showing a preview of the image, like the one shown in Figure 8.14.

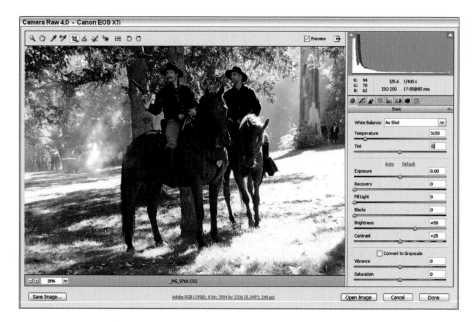

Figure 8.14 The basic ACR dialog box looks like this when processing a single image.

4. If you like, use one of the tools found in the toolbar at the top left of the dialog box. From left to right, they are:

■ **Zoom.** Operates just like the Zoom tool in Photoshop.

■ **Hand.** Use like the Hand tool in Photoshop.

■ **White Balance.** Click an area in the image that should be neutral gray or white to set the white balance quickly.

■ **Color Sampler.** Use to determine the RGB values of areas you click with this eyedropper.

■ **Crop.** Pre-crops the image so that only the portion you specify is imported into Photoshop. This option saves time when you want to work on a section of a large image, and you don't need the entire file.

■ **Straighten.** Drag in the preview image to define what should be a horizontal or vertical line, and ACR will realign the image to straighten it.

■ **Retouch.** Used to heal or clone areas you define.

■ **Red-Eye Removal.** Quickly zap red pupils in your human subjects.

- **ACR Preferences.** Produces a dialog box of Adobe Camera Raw preferences.

- **Rotate Counter-clockwise.** Rotates counter-clockwise in 90-degree increments with a click.

- **Rotate Clockwise.** Rotates clockwise in 90-degree increments with a click.

5. Using the Basic tab, you can have ACR show you red and blue highlights in the preview that indicate shadow areas that are clipped (too dark to show detail) and light areas that are blown out (too bright). Click the triangles in the upper-left corner of the histogram display (shadow clipping) and upper-right corner (highlight clipping) to toggle these indicators on or off.

6. Also in the Basic tab you can choose white balance, either from the drop-down list or by setting a color temperature and green/magenta color bias (tint) using the sliders.

7. Other sliders are available to control exposure, recovery, fill light, blacks, brightness, contrast, vibrance, and saturation. A checkbox can be marked to convert the image to grayscale.

8. Make other adjustments (described in more detail below).

9. If you want ACR to make adjustments for you automatically, click the Auto link (located just above the Exposure slider).

10. If you've marked more than one image to be opened, the additional images appear in a "filmstrip" at the left side of the screen. You can click on each thumbnail in the filmstrip in turn and apply different settings to each.

11. Click Open Image/Open Images image(s) into Photoshop using the settings you've made.

The Basic tab is displayed by default when the ACR dialog box opens, and it includes most of the sliders and controls you'll need to fine-tune your image as you import it into Photoshop. These include:

- **White Balance.** Leave it As Shot or change to a value such as Daylight, Cloudy, Shade, Tungsten, Fluorescent, or Flash. If you like, you can set a custom white balance using the Temperature and Tint sliders.

- **Exposure.** This slider adjusts the overall brightness and darkness of the image.

- **Recovery.** Restores detail in the red, green, and blue color channels.

- **Fill Light.** Reconstructs detail in shadows.

- **Blacks.** Increases the number of tones represented as black in the final image, emphasizing tones in the shadow areas of the image.

■ **Brightness.** This slider adjusts the brightness and darkness of an image.

■ **Contrast.** Manipulates the contrast of the midtones of your image.

■ **Convert to Grayscale.** Mark this box to convert the image to black and white.

■ **Vibrance.** Prevents over-saturation when enriching the colors of an image.

■ **Saturation.** Manipulates the richness of all colors equally, from zero saturation (gray/black, no color) at the -100 setting to double the usual saturation at the +100 setting.

Additional controls are available on the Tone Curve, Detail, HSL/Grayscale, Split Toning, Lens Corrections, Camera Calibration, and Presets tabs, shown in Figure 8.15. The Tone Curve tab can change the tonal values of your image. The Detail tab lets you adjust sharpness, luminance smoothing, and apply color noise reduction. The HSL/Grayscale tab offers controls for adjusting hue, saturation, and lightness and converting an image to black-and-white. The Split Toning tab helps you colorize an image with sepia or cyanotype (blue) shades. The Lens Corrections tab has sliders to adjust for chromatic aberrations and vignetting. The Camera Calibration tab provides a way for calibrating the color corrections made in the Camera Raw plug-in. The Presets tab is used to load settings you've stored for reuse.

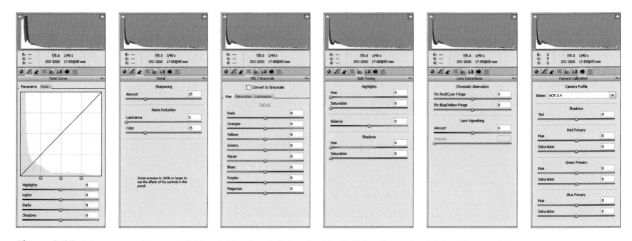

Figure 8.15 More controls are available within the additional tabbed dialog boxes in Adobe Camera Raw.

9

Canon Digital Rebel XTi: Troubleshooting and Prevention

One of the nice things about modern electronic cameras like the Canon Digital Rebel XTi is that they have fewer mechanical moving parts to fail, so they are less likely to "wear out." No film transport mechanism, no wind lever or motor drive, no complicated mechanical linkages from camera to lens to physically stop down the lens aperture. Instead, tiny, reliable motors are built into each lens (and you lose the use of only that lens should something fail), and one of the few major moving parts in the camera itself is a lightweight mirror (its small size is one of the advantages of the XTi's 1.6X crop factor) that flips up and down with each shot.

Of course, the camera also has a moving shutter that can fail, but the shutter is built rugged enough that Canon confidently predicts its useful life at tens of thousands of shutter cycles. Unless you're shooting sports in continuous mode day in and day out, the shutter on your XTi is likely to last as long as you expect to use the camera.

The only other things on the camera that move are switches, dials, buttons, the flip-up electronic flash, and the door that slides open to allow you to remove and re-insert the Compact Flash card. Unless you're extraordinarily clumsy or unlucky and manage to bend the internal pins in the CF card slot, or give your built-in flash a good whack while it is in use, there's not a lot that can go wrong mechanically with your Digital Rebel XTi.

Of course, there is a flip-side. One of the chief drawbacks of modern electronic cameras is that they are modern *electronic* cameras. Your XTi is fully dependent on its battery. Without it, the camera can't be used. There are many other electrical and electronic connections in the camera (many connected to those mechanical switches and dials) and components like the color LCD that can potentially fail or suffer damage. The camera also relies on its "operating system," or *firmware*, that can be plagued by bugs that cause unexpected behavior. Luckily, electronic components are generally more reliable and trouble-free, especially when compared to any mechanical counterparts from back in the pre-electronic film camera days. (Film cameras of the last 10 to 20 years have had almost as many electronic features as digital cameras, but, believe it or not, there were whole generations of film cameras that had *no* electronics or batteries.)

Digital cameras have problems unique to their breed, too; the most troublesome being the need to clean the sensor of dust and grime periodically. This chapter will show you how to diagnose problems, fix some common ills, and, more importantly, learn how to avoid them in the future.

Update Your Firmware

As I said, the firmware in your Digital Rebel XTi is the camera's operating system, which handles everything from menu display (including fonts, colors, and the actual entries themselves), what languages are available, and even support for specific devices and features. Upgrading the firmware to a new version makes it possible to add new features while fixing some of the bugs that sneak in. For example, updates to the XTi's firmware eliminated a condition that prevented the camera from using the remote controller RC-1, fixed a bug in the auto play function that prevented it from stopping during playback, and improved communication reliability when using certain CF cards.

Even more interesting are some of the "bootleg" firmware upgrades that become available from time to time. The most notorious examples apply to the original Digital Rebel, which was basically equipped with the same firmware (and much of the electronics) found in the contemporary Canon EOS 10D. Clever souls produced hacked firmware (which was unsupported by Canon) that restored to the Digital Rebel/300D features that had been disabled, such as ISO 3200 capabilities, flash exposure control, mirror lockup, and single-shot autofocus. (Quite an impressive list!) Hacked firmware can be dangerous—potentially killing your camera if the unauthorized "operating system" has bugs in it that might prevent reloading the factory firmware in case of failure.

Official Firmware

Official firmware for your XTi is given a version number that you can view by turning on the power, pressing the Menu button, and scrolling to Firmware Ver. x.x.x in the Set-up 2 menu with the camera set to one of the Creative Zone modes. As I write this, the current version is 1.0.5, as shown in Figure 9.1. The first number in the string represents the major release number, while the second and third represent less significant upgrades and minor tweaks, respectively. Theoretically, a camera should have a Firmware Version number of 1.0.0 when it is introduced, but vendors have been known to do some minor fixes during testing and unveil a camera with a 1.0.1 firmware designation (in the case of the XTi). If a given model is available long enough, as the EOS 20D was, it can evolve into significant upgrades, such as 2.0.3.

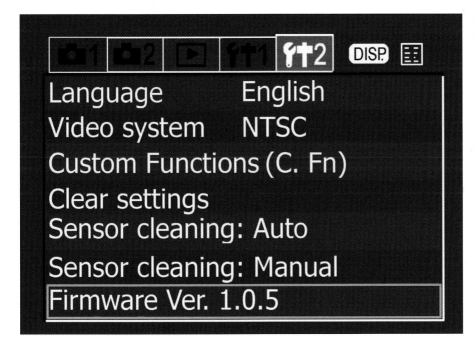

Figure 9.1 You can view the current firmware version in the Set-up 2 menu.

Firmware upgrades are used most frequently to fix bugs in the software, and much less frequently to add or enhance features. For example, previous firmware upgrades for Canon cameras have mended things like incorrect color temperature reporting when using specific Canon Speedlites, or problems communicating with Compact Flash cards under certain conditions. The exact changes made to the firmware are generally spelled out in the firmware release announcement. You can examine the remedies provided and decide whether a given firmware patch is important to you. If not, you can usually safely wait awhile before going through the bother of upgrading your firmware—at least long enough for the early adopters to report whether the bug fixes have introduced new bugs of their own. Each new firmware release incorporates the changes from previous releases, so if you skip a minor upgrade you should have no problems.

Upgrading Your Firmware

If you're computer savvy, you might wonder how your Digital Rebel XTi is able to overwrite its own operating system—that is, how can the existing firmware be used to load the new version on top of itself? It's a little like lifting yourself by reaching down and pulling up on your bootstraps. Not ironically, that's almost exactly what happens: at your command (when you start the upgrade process), the XTi shifts into a special mode in which it is no longer operating from its firmware but, rather, from a small piece of software called a *bootstrap loader*—a separate, protected software program that functions only at startup or when upgrading firmware. The loader's function is to look for firmware to launch or, when directed, to copy new firmware from a Compact Flash card to the internal memory space where the old firmware is located. After the new firmware has replaced the old, you can turn off your camera, and then turn it on again, and the updated operating system will be loaded.

Because the loader software is small in size and limited in function, there are some restrictions on what it can do. For one thing, it recognizes only Compact Flash cards that have been formatted using an organizational system called FAT16 (which again, you might be familiar with if you're comfortable with hard disk technology). To ensure that the Compact Flash card is formatted using FAT16, you must upgrade using a CF card at least 8MB in size and no larger than 2GB, and then format the card in your camera. Memory cards that are smaller or larger might be formatted using a different FAT system (FAT12 or FAT32, respectively).

In addition, the loader software isn't set up to go hunting through your Compact Flash card for the firmware file. It looks only in the top or root directory of your card, so that's where you must copy the firmware you download. Once you've determined that a new firmware update is available for your camera (you'll have to check the Canon website from time to time; they won't be sending you a telegram) and that you want to install it, just follow these steps. (If you chicken out, any Canon Service Center can install the firmware upgrade for you.)

WARNING

Use a fully charged battery or Canon's optional ACK-DC20 AC adapter kit to ensure that you'll have enough power to operate the camera for the entire upgrade. Moreover, you should not turn off the camera while your old firmware is being overwritten. Don't open the Compact Flash card door or do anything else that might disrupt operation of the XTi while the firmware is being installed.

1. Download the firmware from Canon and place it on your computer's hard drive. The firmware is contained in a self-extracting file for either Windows or Mac OS. It will have a name such as e4kr3105.fir.

2. In your camera, format a Compact Flash card that's larger than 8MB and smaller than 2GB to ensure that the proper file system has been formatted onto the card. Choose Format from the Set-up 1 menu, and initialize the card (make sure you don't have images you want to keep before you do this!).

3. You can copy the upgrade software to the card either using a CF card reader or by connecting the camera to your computer with a USB cable.

4. Insert the CF card in the camera and then turn on the camera (if you used a card reader).

5. Select one of the Creative Zone modes.

6. Press Menu and use the cross keys to move to Firmware Ver. x.x.x at the bottom of the Set-up 2 menu and press the Set button. The firmware update screen shown in Figure 9.2 appears. Choose OK, and press the Set button to begin loading the update program (see Figure 9.3).

7. A final confirmation screen will appear. Choose OK, and press Set to confirm. The firmware will be updated (see Figure 9.4).

8. When you see the completion screen, shown in Figure 9.5, press the Set button to complete the process.

9. Turn off the Digital Rebel XTi, remove the AC adapter, if used, and replace the battery. Then turn on the camera to boot up your camera with the new firmware update.

10. Be sure to reformat the card before returning it to regular use to remove the firmware software.

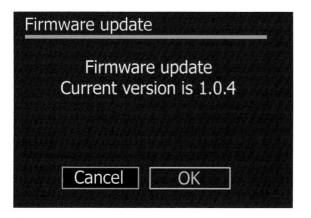

Figure 9.2 The firmware update screen.

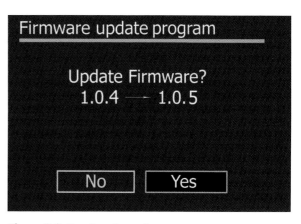

Figure 9.3 Loading the update program.

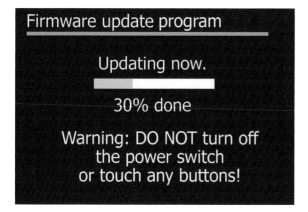

Figure 9.4 While the update is underway, a progress screen appears.

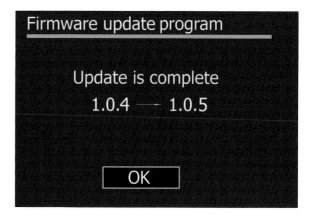

Figure 9.5 When the update is complete, the confirmation screen appears.

Protect Your LCD

The combined color/monochrome status LCD on the back of your Digital Rebel XTi almost seems like a target for banging, scratching, and other abuse. Fortunately, it's quite rugged, and a few errant knocks are unlikely to shatter the protective cover over the LCD, and scratches won't easily mar its surface. However, if you want to be on the safe side, you can purchase a number of protective products to keep your LCD safe—and, in some cases, make it a little easier to view. Here's a quick overview of your options.

- **Plastic overlays.** The simplest solution (although not always the cheapest) is to apply a plastic overlay sheet or "skin" cut to fit your LCD. These adhere either by static electricity or through a light adhesive coating that's even less clingy than stick-it notes. You can cut down overlays made for PDAs (although these can be pricey at up to $19.95 for a set of several sheets) or purchase overlays sold specifically for digital cameras. Vendors such as Hoodman (www.hoodmanusa.com) and Belkin (www.belkin.com) offer overlays of this type. These products will do a good job of shielding your XTi's LCD screen from scratches and minor impacts, but they will not offer much protection from a good whack.

■ **Acrylic shields.** These scratch-resistant acrylic panels, laser-cut to fit your camera perfectly, are my choice as the best protection solution, and they are what I use on my own XTi. At about $6 each, they also happen to be the least expensive option. I get mine, shown in Figure 9.6, from a company called 'da Products (www.daproducts.com). They attach using strips of sticky adhesive that hold the panel flush and tight but allow the acrylic to be pried off and the adhesive removed easily if you want to remove or replace the shield. They don't attenuate your view of the LCD and are non-reflective enough for use under a variety of lighting conditions.

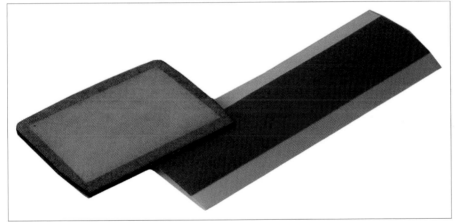

Figure 9.6 A tough acrylic shield, shown here with a set of sticky strips to help it adhere to the camera, can protect your LCD from scratches.

■ **Flip-up hoods.** These protectors slip on using the flanges around your XTi's eyepiece, and they provide a complete cover that completely shields the LCD, but unfolds to provide a three-sided hood that allows viewing the LCD while minimizing the extraneous light falling on it and reducing contrast. They're sold for about $40 by Delkin and Hoodman (Model HX-RTI is specifically for Canon Digital Rebel XTi cameras). If you want to completely protect your LCD from hard knocks and need to view the screen outdoors in bright sunlight, there is nothing better. However, I have a couple problems with these devices. First, with the cover closed, and you can't review your camera settings on the LCD before taking a picture, and can't peek down after taking a shot to see what your image looks like during picture review. You must open the each time you want to look at the LCD. Moreover, with the hood unfolded, it's difficult to look through the viewfinder: don't count on being able to use the viewfinder *and* the LCD at the same time with one of these hoods in place.

■ **Magnifiers.** If you look hard enough, you should be able to find an LCD magnifier that fits over the monitor panel and provides a 2X magnification. These often strap on clumsily, and they serve better as a way to get an enlarged view of the LCD than as protection. Hoodman, Photodon (www.photodon.com), and other suppliers offer these specialized devices.

Troubleshooting Memory Cards

Sometimes good memory cards go bad. Sometimes good photographers can treat their memory cards badly. It's possible that a memory card that works fine in one camera won't be recognized when inserted into another. In the worst case, you can have a card full of important photos and find that the card seems to be corrupted and you can't access any of them. Don't panic! If these scenarios sound horrific to you, there are lots of things you can do to prevent them from happening, and a variety of remedies available if they do occur. You'll want to take some time—before disaster strikes—to consider your options.

All Your Eggs in One Basket?

The debate about whether it's better to use one large memory card or several smaller ones has been going on since even before there were memory cards. I can remember when computer users wondered whether it was smarter to install a pair of 200MB (not *gigabyte*) hard drives in their computer, or if they should go for one of those new-fangled 500MB models. By the same token, a few years ago the user groups were full of proponents who insisted that you ought to use 128MB Compact Flash cards rather than the huge 512MB versions. Today, most of the arguments involve 4GB cards versus 2GB cards or whether 8GB cards are preferable to 4GB media. I expect that as prices for 16GB CF cards continue to drop they'll find their way into the debate, as well.

Why all the fuss? Are 4GB memory cards more likely to fail than 2GB cards? Are you risking all your photos if you trust your images to a larger card? Isn't it better to use several smaller cards, so that if one fails you lose only half as many photos? Or, isn't it wiser to put all your photos onto one larger card, because the more cards you use, the better your odds of misplacing or damaging one and losing at least some pictures?

In the end, the "eggs in one basket" argument boils down to statistics, and how you happen to use your XTi. The rationales can go both ways. If you have multiple smaller cards, you do increase your chances of something happening to one of them, so, arguably, you might be boosting the odds of losing some pictures. If all your images are important, the fact that you've lost 100 rather than 200 pictures isn't very comforting.

Also consider that the eggs/basket scenario assumes that the cards that are lost or damaged are always full. It's actually likely that your 4GB card might suffer a mishap when it's less than half full (indeed, it's more likely that a large card won't be completely filled before it's offloaded to a computer), so you really might not lose any more shots with a single 4GB card than with multiple 2GB cards.

If you shoot photojournalist-type pictures, you probably change memory cards when they're less than completely full in order to avoid the need to do so at a crucial moment. (When I shoot sports, my cards rarely reach 80 to 90 percent of capacity before I change them.) Using multiple smaller cards means you have to change them that much more often, which can be a real pain when you're taking a lot of photos. As an example, if you use 1GB memory cards with a Digital Rebel XTi and shoot RAW+JPEG, you may get only 53 pictures on the card. That's only 1.5X the capacity of a 36-exposure roll of film (remember those?). In my book, I prefer keeping all my eggs in one basket, and then making very sure that nothing happens to that basket.

There are only two really good reasons to justify limiting yourself to smaller memory cards when larger ones can be purchased at the same cost per-gigabyte. One of them is when every single picture is precious to you and the loss of any of them would be a disaster. If you're a wedding photographer, for example, and unlikely to be able to restage the nuptials if a memory card goes bad, you'll probably want to shoot no more pictures than you can afford to lose on a single card, and have an assistant ready to copy each card removed from the camera onto a backup hard drive or DVD on a laptop onsite.

To be even safer, you'd want to alternate cameras or have a second photographer at least partially duplicating your coverage so your shots are distributed over several memory cards simultaneously. (Strictly speaking, the safest route of all is to spend $1,000 on Canon's WFT-E1A Wireless LAN transmitter and beam the images over to a computer as you shoot them. A mandatory accessory for this gadget is a Canon EOS 1-Ds Mark II camera for about $7,000 more, as it won't work with an XTi. Sorry!)

If none of these options is available to you, consider *interleaving* your shots. Say you don't shoot weddings, but you do go on vacation from time to time. Take 50 or so pictures on one card, or whatever number of images might fill about 25 percent of its capacity. Then, replace it with a different card and shoot about 25 percent of that card's available space. Repeat these steps with diligence (you'd have to be determined to go through this inconvenience), and, if you use four or more memory cards you'll find your pictures from each location scattered among the different Compact Flash cards. If you lose or damage one, you'll still have *some* pictures from all the various stops on your trip on the other cards. That's more work than I like to do (I usually tote around a portable hard disk and copy the files to the drive as I go), but it's an option.

The second good reason to use smaller memory cards is if you own a camera that is incompatible with Compact Flash cards larger than 2GB. The Canon Digital Rebel XTi isn't one of these, so you're stuck with reason #1.

What Can Go Wrong?

Lots of things can go wrong with your memory card, but the ones that aren't caused by human stupidity are statistically very rare. Yes, a Compact Flash card's internal bit bin or controller can suddenly fail due to a manufacturing error or some inexplicable event caused by old age. However, if your CF card works for the first week or two that you own it, it should work forever. There's really not a lot that can wear out.

The typical Compact Flash card is rated for a Mean Time Between Failures of 1,000,000 hours of use. That's constant use 24/7 for more than 100 years! According to the manufacturers, they are good for 10,000 insertions in your camera, and should be able to retain their data (and that's without an external power source) for something on the order of 11 years. Of course, with the millions of CF cards in use, there are bound to be a few lemons here or there.

Those mini-hard drives with a Compact Flash form factor are a special case. They really are hard disk drives with moving parts and are subject to the same kinds of failure that their bigger siblings inside your computer can suffer. You'll find many, many happy users of mini-disks who have never had a problem, but anecdotal evidence suggests that they do fail significantly more often than solid-state memory cards. Mini-drives are slower and their price and capacity advantages are fading, so I find little reason to use them for serious work.

Given the reliability of solid-state memory, though, it's more likely that your Compact Flash problems will stem from something that you do. Although they're not as tiny as the SD and xD cards a few other digital SLRs use, CF cards are still small and easy to misplace if you're not careful. For that reason, it's a good idea to keep them in their original cases or a "card safe" offered by Gepe (www.gepecardsafe.com), Pelican (www.pelican.com), and others. Always placing your memory card in a case can provide protection from the second-most common mishap that befalls Compact Flash cards: the common household laundry. If you slip a memory card in a pocket, rather than a case or your camera bag often enough, sooner or later it's going to end up in the washing machine and probably the clothes dryer, too. There are plenty of reports of relieved digital camera owners who've laundered their memory cards and found they still worked fine, but it's not uncommon for such mistreatment to do some damage.

Memory cards can also be stomped on, accidentally bent, dropped into the ocean, chewed by pets, and otherwise rendered unusable in myriad ways. It's also possible to force a card into your XTi's CF card slot incorrectly if you're persistent enough, doing little damage to the card itself, but bending the connector pins in the camera, eliminating its ability to read or write to any memory card. Or, if the card is formatted in your computer with a memory card reader, your XTi may fail to recognize it (try reformatting in your camera.) Occasionally, I've found that a memory card used in one camera would fail if used in a different camera.

Another way to lose images is to do commonplace things with your CF card at inopportune times. If you remove the card from the XTi while the camera is writing images to the card, you'll lose any photos in the buffer and may damage the file structure of the card, making it difficult or impossible to retrieve the other pictures you've taken. The same thing can happen if you remove the CF card from your computer's card reader while the computer is writing to the card (say, to erase files you've already moved to your computer). You can avoid this by *not* using your computer to erase files on a Compact Flash card but, instead, always reformatting the card in your XTi before you use it again.

What Can You Do?

Pay attention: if you're having problems, the *first* thing you should do is *stop* using that memory card. Don't take any more pictures. Don't do anything with the card until you've figured out what's wrong. Your second line of defense (your first line is to be sufficiently careful with your cards so that you avoid problems in the first place) is to *do no harm* that hasn't already been done. Read the rest of this section and then, if necessary, decide on a course of action (such as using a data recovery service or software described later) before you risk damaging the data on your card further.

Things get exciting when the card itself is put in jeopardy. If you lose a card, there's not a lot you can do other than take a picture of a similar card and print up some "Have You Seen This Lost Flash Memory?" flyers to post on utility poles all around town, unless you've remembered to record your name, phone number, or e-mail address on the back.

If all you care about is reusing the card, and have resigned yourself to losing the pictures, try reformatting the card in your camera. You may find that reformatting removes the corrupted data and restores your card to health. Sometimes, I've had success reformatting a card in my computer using a memory card reader (this is normally a no-no because your operating system doesn't understand the needs of your XTi), and *then* reformatting again in the camera.

If your Compact Flash card is not behaving properly, and you *do* want to recover your images, things get a little more complicated. If your pictures are very valuable, either to you or to others (for example, a wedding), you can always turn to professional data recovery firms. Be prepared to pay hundreds of dollars to get your pictures back, but these pros often do an amazing job. You wouldn't want them working on your memory card on behalf of the police if you'd tried to erase some incriminating pictures. There are too many firms of this type, and I've never used them myself, so I can't offer a recommendation. Use a Google search to turn up a ton of them.

A more reasonable approach is to try special data recovery software you can install on your computer and use to attempt to resurrect your "lost" images yourself. They may not actually be gone completely. Perhaps your CF card's "table of contents" is jumbled, or only a few pictures are damaged in such a way that your camera and computer can't read some or any of the pictures on the card. Some of the available software was written specifically to reconstruct lost pictures, while other utilities are more general-purpose applications that can be used with any media, including floppy disks and hard disk drives. They have names like Photo Rescue 2, Digital Image Recovery, MediaRecover, Image Recall, and the aptly named Recover My Photos. You'll find a comprehensive list and links, as well as some picture-recovery tips at www.ultimateslr.com/memory-card-recovery.php.

DIMINISHING RETURNS

Usually, once you've recovered any images on a Compact Flash card, reformatted it, and returned it to service, it will function reliably for the rest of its useful life. However, if you find a particular card going bad more than once, you'll almost certainly want to stop using it forever. In the case of CF card failures, the third time is never the charm. See if you can get it replaced by the manufacturer.

Replacing Your Clock Battery

In addition to the large rechargeable lithium ion battery that provides most of the power for your Canon Digital Rebel XTi, a second battery nestles in the same compartment to provide enough power to retain your current settings and preferences, as well as the local date and time. This coin-sized *clock* battery is a long-lived C2016 3-volt lithium manganese dioxide cell, located in a slide-out carrier near the hinge of the battery door, shown in Figure 9.7.

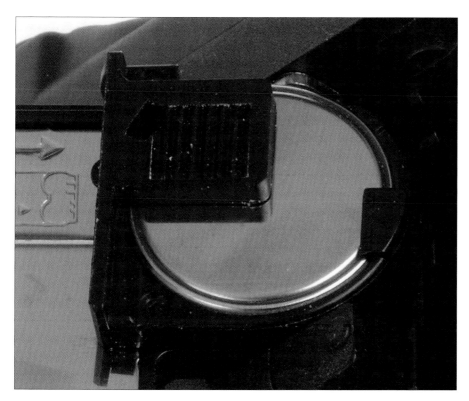

Figure 9.7 Your clock battery is located in the main battery compartment.

You may never notice this battery at all, as it may last several years without needing replacement. Your first clue will be when you switch on your XTi and a message on your LCD asks you to input the date and time. That's your cue to trot down to the electronics store and buy a new one.

To install it, just slide out the plastic carrier and remove the old battery. A pair of plastic tabs holds it in tight, and you may have to pry one up to free the dead cell. Then slide the new one in and return the carrier to your camera. When you turn on the power, you'll need to enter the current date and time and restore any other settings that have been lost. Don't forget to choose OK when finished; if you simply exit the settings screen by pressing the Menu button, your time setting will not be entered.

Clean Your Sensor

There's no avoiding dust. No matter how careful you are, some of it is going to settle on your camera and on the mounts of your lenses, eventually making its way inside your camera to settle in the mirror chamber. As you take photos, the mirror flipping up and down causes the dust to become airborne and eventually make its way past the shutter curtain to come to rest on the anti-aliasing filter atop your sensor. There, dust and particles can show up in every single picture you take at a small enough aperture to bring the foreign matter into sharp focus. No matter how careful you are and how cleanly you work, eventually you will get some of this dust on your camera's sensor. Some say that CMOS sensors, like the one found in the Digital Rebel XTi, "attract" less dust than CCD sensors found in cameras from other vendors. But even the cleanest-working photographers using Canon cameras are far from immune.

Fortunately, one of the Digital Rebel XTi's most useful new features is the automatic sensor cleaning system that reduces or eliminates the need to clean your camera's sensor manually. As I mentioned in Chapter 3, Canon has applied anti-static coatings to the sensor and other portions of the camera body interior to counter charge build-ups that attract dust. A separate filter over the sensor vibrates ultrasonically each time the XTi is powered on or off, shaking loose any dust onto a strip of adhesive adjacent to the sensor.

Although the automatic sensor cleaning feature operates when you power up the camera or turn it off, you can activate it at any time. Choose Sensor Cleaning: Auto from the Set-up 2 menu, and select Clean now (see Figure 9.8). If you'd rather turn the feature on or off, choose Set up instead, and then choose either Enable or Disable with the left/right cross keys. Press Set, and then press the Menu button to return to the Set-up 2 menu.

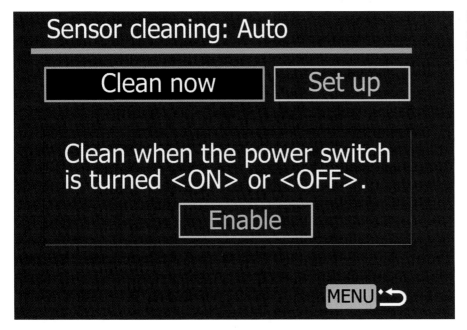

Figure 9.8 You can activate automatic sensor cleaning immediately, or enable/disable the feature.

If some dust does collect on your sensor, you can often remove it in software, using the Dust Delete Data feature in the Shooting Menu 2. Operation of this feature is described in Chapter 3. Of course, even with the Rebel XTi's automatic sensor cleaning/dust resistance features, you may still be required to manually clean your sensor from time to time. This section explains the phenomenon and provides some tips on minimizing dust and eliminating it when it begins to affect your shots. I also cover this subject in my book, *Digital SLR Pro Secrets*, with complete instructions for constructing your own sensor cleaning tools. However, I'll provide a condensed version here of some of the information in that book, because sensor dust and sensor cleaning are two of the most contentious subjects Canon Digital Rebel XTi owners have to deal with.

Here is a list of FAQs as an introduction to this section on what to do about sensor dust.

Dust the FAQs, Ma'am

Here are some of the most frequently asked questions about sensor dust issues.

Q. I see tiny specks in my viewfinder. Do I have dust on my sensor?

A. If you see sharp, well-defined specks, they are clinging to the underside of your focus screen and not on your sensor. They have absolutely no effect on your photographs, and are merely annoying or distracting.

Q. I can see dust on my mirror. How can I remove it?

A. Like focus-screen dust, any artifacts that have settled on your mirror won't affect your photos. You can often remove dust on the mirror or focus screen with a bulb air blower, which will loosen it and whisk it away. Stubborn dust on the focus screen can sometimes be gently flicked away with a soft brush designed for cleaning lenses. I don't recommend brushing the mirror or touching it in any way. The mirror is a special front-surface-silvered optical device (unlike conventional mirrors, which are silvered on the back side of a piece of glass or plastic) and can be easily scratched. If you can't blow mirror dust off, it's best to just forget about it. You can't see it in the viewfinder, anyway.

Q. I see a bright spot in the same place in all of my photos. Is that sensor dust?

A. You've probably got either a "hot" pixel or one that is permanently "stuck" due to a defect in the sensor. A hot pixel is one that shows up as a bright spot only during long exposures as the sensor warms. A pixel stuck in the "on" position always appears in the image. Both show up as bright red, green, or blue pixels, usually surrounded by a small cluster of other improperly illuminated pixels, caused by the camera's interpolating the hot or stuck pixel into its surroundings, as shown in Figure 9.9. A stuck pixel can also be permanently dark. Either kind is likely to show up when they contrast with plain, evenly colored areas of your image.

Finding one or two hot or stuck pixels in your sensor is unfortunately fairly common. They can be "removed" by telling the XTi to ignore them through a simple process called *pixel mapping*. If the bad pixels become bothersome, Canon can remap your sensor's pixels with a quick trip to a service center.

Bad pixels can also show up on your camera's color LCD panel, but, unless they are abundant, the wisest course is to just ignore them.

Figure 9.9 A stuck pixel is surrounded by improperly interpolated pixels created by the XTi's demosaicing algorithm.

Q. I see an irregular out-of-focus blob in the same place in my photos. Is that sensor dust?

A. Yes. Sensor contaminants can take the form of tiny spots, larger blobs, or even curvy lines if they are caused by minuscule fibers that have settled on the sensor. They'll appear out of focus because they aren't actually on the sensor surface but, rather, a fraction of a millimeter above it on the filter that covers the sensor. The smaller the f/stop used, the more in-focus the dust becomes. At large apertures, it may not be visible at all.

Q. I never see any dust on my sensor. What's all the fuss about?

A. Those who never have dust problems with their Digital Rebel XTi fall into one of four categories: those for whom the camera's automatic dust removal features are working well; those who seldom change their lenses and have clean working habits that minimize the amount of dust that invades their cameras in the first place; those who simply don't notice the dust (often because they don't shoot many macro photos or other pictures using the small f/stops that makes dust evident in their images); and those who are very, very lucky.

Identifying and Dealing with Dust

Sensor dust is less of a problem than it might be because it shows up only under certain circumstances. Indeed, you might have dust on your sensor right now and not be aware if it. The dust doesn't actually settle on the sensor itself, but, rather, on a protective filter a very tiny distance above the sensor, subjecting it to the phenomenon of *depth-of-focus*. Depth-of-focus is the distance the focal plane can be moved and still render an object in sharp focus. At f/2.8 to f/5.6 or even smaller, sensor dust, particularly if small, is likely to be outside the range of depth-of-focus and blur into an unnoticeable dot.

However, if you're shooting at f/16 to f/22 or smaller, those dust motes suddenly pop into focus. Forget about trying to spot them by peering directly at your sensor with the shutter open and the lens removed. The period at the end of this sentence, about .33mm in diameter, could block a group of pixels measuring 40 × 40 pixels (160 pixels in all!). Dust spots that are even smaller than that can easily show up in your images if you're shooting large, empty areas that are light colored. Dust motes are most likely to show up in the sky, as in Figure 9.10, or in white backgrounds of your seamless product shots and are less likely to be a problem in images that contain lots of dark areas and detail.

To see if you have dust on your sensor, take a few test shots of a plain, blank surface (such as a piece of paper or a cloudless sky) at small f/stops, such as f/22, and a few wide open. Open Photoshop, copy several shots into a single document in separate layers, then flip back and forth between layers to see if any spots you see are present in all layers. You may need to boost contrast and sharpness to make the dust easier to spot.

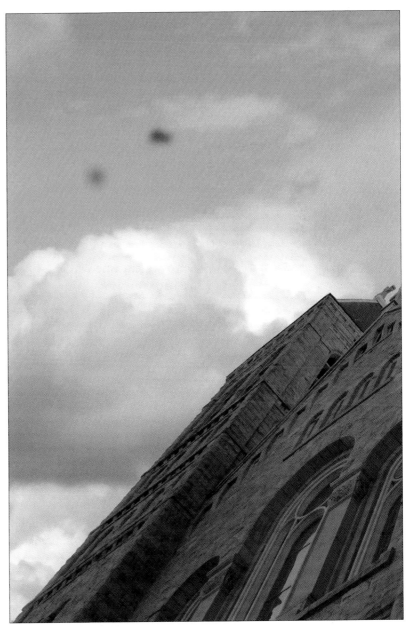

Figure 9.10 Only the dust spots in the sky are apparent in this shot.

Avoiding Dust

Of course, the easiest way to protect your sensor from dust is to prevent it from settling on the sensor in the first place. Some Canon lenses come with rubberized seals around the lens mounts that help keep dust from infiltrating, but you'll find that dust will still find a way to get inside. Here are my stock tips for eliminating the problem before it begins.

- **Clean environment.** Avoid working in dusty areas if you can do so. Hah! Serious photographers will take this one with a grain of salt, because it usually makes sense to go where the pictures are. Only a few of us are so paranoid about sensor dust (considering that it is so easily removed) that we'll avoid moderately grimy locations just to protect something that is, when you get down to it, just a tool. If you find a great picture opportunity at a raging fire, during a sandstorm, or while surrounded by dust clouds, you might hesitate to take the picture, but, with a little caution (don't remove your lens in these situations, and clean the camera afterward!) you can still shoot. However, it still makes sense to store your camera in a clean environment. One place cameras and lenses pick up a lot of dust is inside a camera bag. Clean your bag from time to time, and you can avoid problems.

- **Clean lenses.** There are a few paranoid types that avoid swapping lenses in order to minimize the chance of dust getting inside their cameras. It makes more sense just to use a blower or brush to dust off the rear lens mount of the replacement lens first, so you won't be introducing dust into your camera simply by attaching a new, dusty lens. Do this before you remove the lens from your camera, and then avoid stirring up dust before making the exchange.

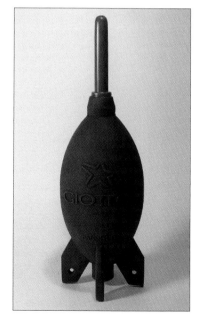

- **Work fast.** Minimize the time your camera is lens-less and exposed to dust. That means having your replacement lens ready and dusted off, and a place to set down the old lens as soon as it is removed, so you can quickly attach the new lens.

- **Let gravity help you.** Face the camera downward when the lens is detached so any dust in the mirror box will tend to fall away from the sensor. Turn your back to any breezes or sources of dust to minimize infiltration.

- **Protect the lens you just removed.** Once you've attached the new lens, quickly put the end cap on the one you just removed to reduce the dust that might fall on it.

- **Clean out the vestibule.** From time to time, remove the lens while in a relatively dust-free environment and use a blower bulb like the one shown in Figure 9.11 (*not* compressed air or a vacuum hose) to clean out the mirror box area. A blower bulb is generally safer than a can of

Figure 9.11 Use a robust air bulb like the Giottos Rocket for cleaning your sensor.

compressed air, or a strong positive/negative airflow, which can tend to drive dust further into nooks and crannies.

- **Be prepared.** If you're embarking on an important shooting session, it's a good idea to clean your sensor *now*, rather than come home with hundreds or thousands of images with dust spots caused by flecks that were sitting on your sensor before you even started. Before I left on my recent trip to Spain, I put both cameras I was taking through a rigid cleaning regimen, figuring they could remain dust-free for a measly 10 days. I even left my bulky blower bulb at home. It was a big mistake, but my intentions were good.

- **Clone out existing spots in your image editor.** Photoshop and other editors have a clone tool or healing brush you can use to copy pixels from surrounding areas over the dust spot or dead pixel. This process can be tedious, especially if you have lots of dust spots and/or lots of images to be corrected. The advantage is that this sort of manual fix-it probably will do the least damage to the rest of your photo. Only the cloned pixels will be affected.

- **Use filtration in your image editor.** A semi-smart filter like Photoshop's Dust & Scratches filter can remove dust and other artifacts by selectively blurring areas that the plug-in decides represent dust spots. This method can work well if you have many dust spots, because you won't need to patch them manually. However, any automated method like this has the possibility of blurring areas of your image that you didn't intend to soften.

Sensor Cleaning

Those new to the concept of sensor dust actually hesitate before deciding to clean their camera themselves. Isn't it a better idea to pack up your XTi and send it to a Canon service center so that their crack technical staff can do the job for you? Or, at the very least, shouldn't you let the friendly folks at your local camera store do it?

Of course, if you choose to let someone else clean your sensor, they will be using methods that are more or less identical to the techniques you would use yourself. None of these techniques is difficult, and the only difference between their cleaning and your cleaning is that they might have done it dozens or hundreds of times. If you're careful, you can do just as good a job.

Of course vendors like Canon won't tell you this, but it's not because they don't trust you. It's not that difficult for a real goofball to mess up their camera by hurrying or taking a shortcut. Perhaps the person uses the "Bulb" method of holding the shutter open and a finger slips, allowing the shutter curtain to close on top of a sensor cleaning brush. Or, someone tries to clean the sensor using masking tape, and ends up with goo all over its surface. If Canon recommended *any* method that's mildly risky, someone would do it wrong, and then the company would face lawsuits from those who'd contend they did it exactly in the way the vendor suggested, so the ruined camera is not their fault. If you visit Canon's website, you'll find this recommendation: "If the image sensor needs cleaning, we recommend having it cleaned at a Canon service center, as it is a very delicate component."

You can see that vendors like Canon tend to be conservative in their recommendations, and, in doing so, make it seem as if sensor cleaning is more daunting and dangerous than it really is. Some vendors recommend only dust-off cleaning, through the use of reasonably gentle blasts of air, while condemning more serious scrubbing with swabs and cleaning fluids. However, these cleaning kits for the exact types of cleaning they recommended against are for sale in Japan only, where, apparently, your average photographer is more dexterous than those of us in the rest of the world. These kits are similar to those used by official repair staff to clean your sensor if you decide to send your camera in for a dust-cleanup.

As I noted, sensors can be affected by dust particles that are much smaller than you might be able to spot visually on the surface of your lens. The filters that cover sensors tend to be fairly hard compared to optical glass. Cleaning the 22.5mm × 15mm sensor in your Canon XTi within the tight confines of the mirror box can call for a steady hand and careful touch. If your sensor's filter becomes scratched through inept cleaning, you can't simply remove it yourself and replace it with a new one.

There are four basic kinds of cleaning processes that can be used to remove dusty and sticky stuff that settles on your dSLR's sensor. All of these must be performed with the shutter locked open. I'll describe these methods and provide instructions for locking the shutter later in this section.

- **Air cleaning.** This process involves squirting blasts of air inside your camera with the shutter locked open. This works well for dust that's not clinging stubbornly to your sensor.

- **Brushing.** A soft, very fine brush is passed across the surface of the sensor's filter, dislodging mildly persistent dust particles and sweeping them off the imager.

- **Liquid cleaning.** A soft swab dipped in a cleaning solution such as ethanol is used to wipe the sensor filter, removing more obstinate particles.

- **Tape cleaning.** There are some who get good results by applying a special form of tape to the surface of their sensor. When the tape is peeled off, all the dust goes with it. Supposedly. I'd be remiss if I didn't point out right now that this form of cleaning is somewhat controversial; the other three methods are much more widely accepted.

Placing the Shutter in the Locked and Fully Upright Position for Landing

Make sure you're using a fully charged battery or the optional AC Adapter Kit ACK-DC20.

1. Remove the lens from the camera and then turn the camera on.

2. Set the Digital Rebel XTi to any one of the Creative Zone exposure modes. The shutter cannot be locked open in any of the Basic Zone modes.

3. You'll find the Sensor Cleaning: Manual menu choice in the Set-up 2 menu. Press the Set button to produce the screen shown in Figure 9.12.

4. Select OK, and press Set again. The mirror will flip up, and the shutter will open. The screen shown in Figure 9.13 appears on the LCD.

5. Use one of the methods described below to remove dust and grime from your sensor. Be careful not to accidentally switch the power off or open the Compact Flash card or battery compartment doors as you work. If that happens, the shutter may be damaged if it closes onto your cleaning tool.

6. When you're finished, turn off the power, replace your lens, and switch your camera back on.

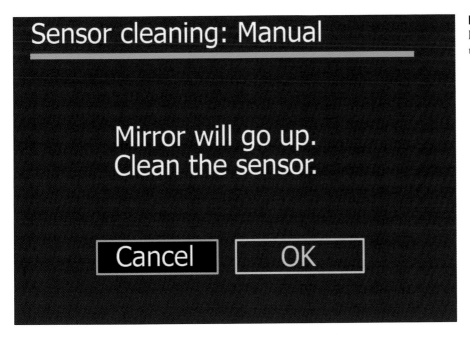

Figure 9.12 Select OK to lock up the mirror and open the shutter.

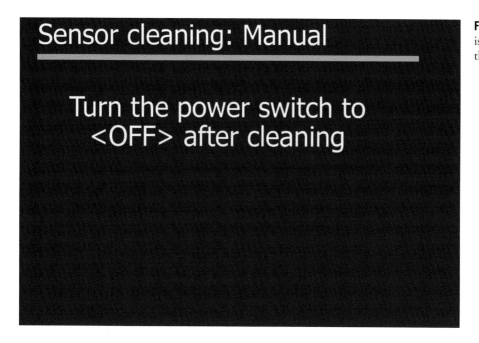

Figure 9.13 While the mirror is up, this message appears on the LCD.

Air Cleaning

Your first attempts at cleaning your sensor should always involve gentle blasts of air. Many times, you'll be able to dislodge dust spots, which will fall off the sensor and, with luck, out of the mirror box. Attempt one of the other methods only when you've already tried air cleaning and it didn't remove all the dust. In all cases, work in a clean environment, preferably with a high intensity light that allows you to view the innards of the camera.

Here are some tips for doing air cleaning:

- **Use a clean, powerful air bulb.** Your best bet is bulb cleaners designed for the job, like the Giottos Rocket shown in Figure 9.11. Smaller bulbs, like those air bulbs with a brush attached sometimes sold for lens cleaning or weak nasal aspirators may not provide sufficient air or a strong enough blast to do much good.

- **Hold the Digital Rebel XTi upside down.** Then look up into the mirror box as you squirt your air blasts, increasing the odds that gravity will help pull the expelled dust downward, away from the sensor. You may have to use some imagination in positioning yourself.

- **Never use air canisters.** The propellant inside these cans can permanently coat your sensor if you tilt the can while spraying. It's not worth taking a chance.

- **Avoid air compressors.** Super-strong blasts of air are likely to force dust under the sensor filter.

Brush Cleaning

If your dust is a little more stubborn and can't be dislodged by air alone, you may want to try a brush, charged with static electricity, which can pick off dust spots by electrical attraction. One good, but expensive, option is the Sensor Brush sold at www.visibledust.com, which has a video available that shows how to clean a sensor. A cheaper version can be purchased at www.copperhillimages.com. You need a 16mm version, like the one shown in Figure 9.14, which can be stroked across the short dimension of your XTi's sensor.

Ordinary artist's brushes are much too coarse and stiff and have fibers that are tangled or can come loose and settle on your sensor. A good sensor brush's fibers are resilient and described as "thinner than a human hair." Moreover, the brush has a wooden handle that reduces the risk of static sparks. Check out my *Digital SLR Pro Secrets* book if you want to make a sensor brush (or sensor swabs) yourself.

Brush cleaning is done with a dry brush by gently swiping the surface of the sensor filter with the tip. The dust particles are attracted to the brush particles and cling to them. You should clean the brush with compressed air before and after each use, and store it in an appropriate air-tight container between applications to keep it clean and dust-free. Although these special brushes are expensive, one should last you a long time.

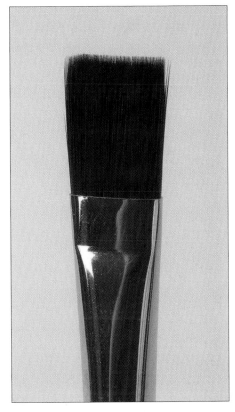

Figure 9.14 A proper brush is required for dusting off your sensor.

Liquid Cleaning

Unfortunately, you'll often encounter really stubborn dust spots that can't be removed with a blast of air or flick of a brush. These spots may be combined with some grease or a liquid that causes them to stick to the sensor filter's surface. In such cases, liquid cleaning with a swab may be necessary. During my first clumsy attempts to clean my own sensor, I accidentally got my blower bulb tip too close to the sensor, and some sort of deposit from the tip of the bulb ended up on the sensor. I panicked until I discovered that liquid cleaning did a good job of removing whatever it was that took up residence on my sensor.

You can make your own swabs out of pieces of plastic (some use fast-food restaurant knives, with the tip cut at an angle to the proper size) covered with a soft cloth or Pec-Pad, as shown in Figures 9.15 and 9.16. However, if you've got the bucks to spend, you can't go wrong with good-quality commercial sensorcleaning swabs, such as those sold by Photographic Solutions, Inc. (www.photosol.com/swabproduct.htm).

You want a sturdy swab that won't bend or break so you can apply gentle pressure to the swab as you wipe the sensor surface. Use the swab with methanol (as pure as you can get it, particularly medical grade; other ingredients can leave a residue), or the Eclipse solution also sold by Photographic Solutions. Eclipse (see Figure 9.17) is actually quite a bit purer than even medical-grade methanol. A couple

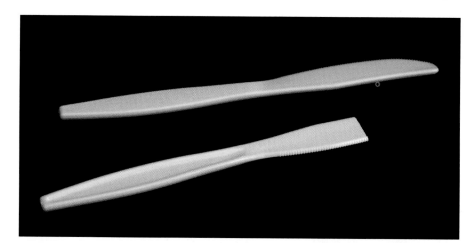

Figure 9.15 You can make your own sensor swab from a plastic knife that's been truncated.

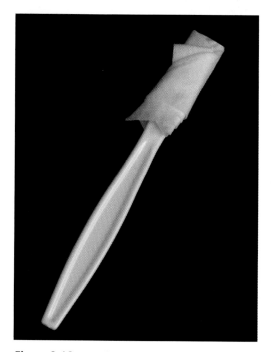

Figure 9.16 Carefully wrap a Pec-Pad around the swab.

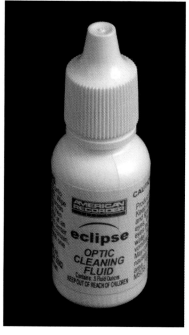

Figure 9.17 Pure Eclipse solution makes the best sensor cleaning liquid.

drops of solution should be enough, unless you have a spot that's extremely difficult to remove. In that case, you may need to use extra solution on the swab to help "soak" the dirt off.

Once you overcome your nervousness at touching your XTi's sensor, the process is easy. You'll wipe continuously with the swab in one direction, then flip it over and wipe in the other direction. Figure 9.18 shows a swab being lowered past the lens mount down to the sensor. You need to completely wipe the entire surface; otherwise, you might end up depositing the dust you collect at the far end of your stroke. Wipe; don't rub.

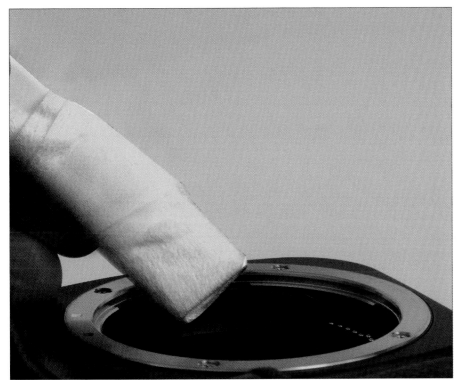

Figure 9.18 Carefully swab off the dust.

Tape Cleaning

There are people who absolutely swear by the tape method of sensor cleaning. The concept seems totally wacky, and I have never tried it personally, so I can't say with certainty that it either does or does not work. In the interest of completeness, I'm including it here. I can't give you a recommendation, so if you have problems, please don't blame me.

Tape cleaning works by applying a layer of Scotch Brand Magic Tape to the sensor. This is a minimally sticky tape that some of the tape cleaning proponents claim contains no adhesive. I did check this out with 3M, and I can say that Magic Tape certainly *does* contain an adhesive. The question is whether the adhesive comes off when you peel back the tape, taking any dust spots on your sensor with it. The folks who love this method claim there is no residue. There have been reports from those who don't like the method that residue is left behind. This is all anecdotal evidence, so you're pretty much on your own in making the decision whether to try out the tape cleaning method or not.

Glossary

Here are some terms you might encounter while reading this book or working with your Canon Digital Rebel XTi.

additive primary colors The red, green, and blue hues that are used alone or in combinations to create all other colors that you capture with a digital camera, view on a computer monitor, or work with in an image-editing program, such as Photoshop. See also *CMYK color model.*

A-DEP A Creative Zone mode that analyzes your scene and attempts to choose an f/stop and focus distance that will allow all the important subjects to be in sharp focus.

Adobe RGB One of two color space choices offered by the Canon EOS Digital Rebel XTi. Adobe RGB is an expanded color space useful for commercial and professional printing, and it can reproduce a larger number of colors. Canon recommends against using this color space if your images will be displayed primarily on your computer screen or output by your personal printer. See also *sRGB.*

AE/FE A control on the Canon Digital Rebel XTi that lets you lock the current autoexposure or flash exposure settings prior to taking a picture.

AEB Automatic exposure bracketing, which takes a series of pictures at different exposure increments to improve the chances of producing one picture that is perfectly exposed.

ambient lighting Diffuse, non-directional lighting that doesn't appear to come from a specific source but, rather, bounces off walls, ceilings, and other objects in the scene when a picture is taken.

analog/digital converter The electronics built into a camera that convert the analog information captured by the XTi's sensor into digital bits that can be stored as an image bitmap.

angle-of-view The area of a scene that a lens can capture, determined by the focal length of the lens and its crop factor. Lenses with a shorter focal length have a wider angle-of-view than lenses with a longer focal length.

anti-alias   A process that smoothes the look of rough edges in images (called *jaggies* or *staircasing*) by adding partially transparent pixels along the boundaries of diagonal lines that are merged into a smoother line by our eyes. See also *jaggies*.

aperture-priority   A camera setting that allows you to specify the lens opening or f/stop that you want to use, with the camera selecting the required shutter speed automatically based on its light-meter reading. This setting is represented by the abbreviation Av on the XTi's Mode Dial. See also *shutter-priority*.

artifact   A type of noise in an image, or an unintentional image component produced in error by a digital camera during processing, usually caused by the JPEG compression process in digital cameras.

aspect ratio   The proportions of an image as printed, displayed on a monitor, or captured by a digital camera.

autofocus   A camera setting that allows the Canon Digital Rebel XTi to choose the correct focus distance for you, based on the contrast of an image (the image will be at maximum contrast when in sharp focus). The camera can be set for ONE SHOT (generically known as *single autofocus* in which the lens is not focused until the shutter release is partially depressed), AI SERVO (known as *continuous autofocus*, in which the lens refocuses constantly as you frame and reframe the image), or AI AF, which allows the camera to switch back and forth between ONE SHOT and AI SERVO based on subject movement.

autofocus assist lamp   A light source built into the XTi that provides extra illumination that the autofocus system can use to focus dimly lit subjects.

backlighting   A lighting effect produced when the main light source is located behind the subject. Backlighting can be used to create a silhouette effect, or to illuminate translucent objects. See also *front-lighting* and *sidelighting*.

barrel distortion   A lens defect found at wide-angle lens focal lengths that causes straight lines at the top or side edges of an image to bow outward into a barrel shape. See also *pincushion distortion*.

Basic Zone modes   The Digital Rebel XTi's automated shooting modes, which select lens opening, shutter speed, exposure, and other parameters for you.

blooming   An image distortion caused when a photosite in an image sensor has absorbed all the photons it can handle, so that additional photons reaching that pixel overflow to affect surrounding pixels, producing unwanted brightness and overexposure around the edges of objects.

blur   To soften an image or part of an image by throwing it out of focus, or by allowing it to become soft due to subject or camera motion. Blur can also be applied in an image-editing program.

bokeh A term derived from the Japanese word for blur, which describes the aesthetic qualities of the out-of-focus parts of an image. Some lenses produce "good" bokeh and others offer "bad" bokeh. Some lenses produce uniformly illuminated out-of-focus discs. Others produce a disc that has a bright edge and a dark center, producing a "doughnut" effect, which is the worst from a bokeh standpoint. Lenses that generate a bright center that fades to a darker edge are favored, because their bokeh allows the circle of confusion to blend more smoothly with the surroundings. The bokeh characteristics of a lens are most important when you're using selective focus (say, when shooting a portrait) to deemphasize the background, or when shallow depth-of-field is a given because you're working with a macro lens, with a long telephoto, or with a wide open aperture. See also *circle of confusion.*

bounce lighting Light bounced off a reflector, including ceiling and walls, to provide a soft, natural-looking light.

bracketing Taking a series of photographs of the same subject at different settings, including exposure and white balance, to help ensure that one setting will be the correct one. The Canon Digital Rebel XTi allows you to choose the order in which bracketed settings are applied, or *bracket sequence.*

buffer The digital camera's internal memory where an image is stored immediately after it is taken until it can be written to the camera's non-volatile (semi-permanent) memory or a memory card.

burst mode The digital camera's equivalent of the film camera's motor drive, used to take multiple shots within a short period of time.

calibration A process used to correct for the differences in the output of a printer or monitor when compared to the original image. After you've calibrated your scanner, monitor, and/or your image editor, the images you see on the screen more closely represent what you'll get from your printer, even though calibration is never perfect.

Camera Raw A plug-in included with Photoshop and Photoshop Elements that can manipulate the unprocessed images captured by digital cameras, such as the Canon Digital Rebel XTi's .CR2 files.

camera shake Movement of the camera, aggravated by slower shutter speeds, which produces a blurred image.

CCD See *charge-coupled device (CCD).*

center-weighted meter A light-measuring device that emphasizes the area in the middle of the frame when calculating the correct exposure for an image.

charge-coupled device (CCD) A type of solid-state sensor that captures the image used in scanners and digital cameras.

chromatic aberration An image defect, often seen as green or purple fringing around the edges of an object, caused by a lens failing to focus all colors of a light source at the same point. See also *fringing*.

circle of confusion A term applied to the fuzzy discs produced when a point of light is out of focus. The circle of confusion is not a fixed size. The viewing distance and amount of enlargement of the image determine whether we see a particular spot on the image as a point or as a disc. See also *bokeh*.

close-up lens A lens add-on that allows you to take pictures at a distance that is less than the closest-focusing distance of the lens alone.

CMOS See *complementary metal-oxide semiconductor (CMOS)*.

CMYK color model A way of defining all possible colors in percentages of cyan, magenta, yellow, and frequently, black. (K represents black, to differentiate it from blue in the RGB color model.) Black is added to improve rendition of shadow detail. CMYK is commonly used for printing (both on press and with your inkjet or laser color printer).

color correction Changing the relative amounts of color in an image to produce a desired effect, typically a more accurate representation of those colors. Color correction can fix faulty color balance in the original image, or compensate for the deficiencies of the inks used to reproduce the image.

complementary metal-oxide semiconductor (CMOS) A method for manufacturing a type of solid-state sensor that captures the image, used in scanners and digital cameras such as those from Canon.

compression Reducing the size of a file by encoding using fewer bits of information to represent the original. Some compression schemes, such as JPEG, operate by discarding some image information, while others, such as TIFF, preserve all the detail in the original, discarding only redundant data.

continuous autofocus An automatic focusing setting (AI SERVO) in which the camera constantly refocuses the image as you frame the picture. This setting is often the best choice for moving subjects. See also *single autofocus*.

contrast The range between the lightest and darkest tones in an image. A high-contrast image is one in which the shades fall at the extremes of the range between white and black. In a low-contrast image, the tones are closer together.

Custom Functions A group of 11 different settings you can make to specify how the Digital Rebel XTi behaves, such as the function of certain controls, electronic flash features, and other customizable attributes.

dedicated flash An electronic flash unit, such as the Canon 580EX Speedlight, designed to work with the automatic exposure features of a specific camera.

depth-of-field A distance range in a photograph in which all included portions of an image are at least acceptably sharp. With the Canon Digital Rebel XTi, you can see the available depth-of-field at the taking aperture by pressing the depth-of-field preview button, or estimate the range by viewing the depth-of-field scale found on many lenses.

diaphragm An adjustable component, similar to the iris in the human eye, which can open and close to provide specific-sized lens openings, or f/stops.

diffuse lighting Soft, low-contrast lighting.

digital processing chip A solid-state device found in digital cameras that's in charge of applying the image algorithms to the raw picture data prior to storage on the memory card.

diopter A value used to represent the magnification power of a lens, calculated as the reciprocal of a lens's focal length (in meters). Diopters are most often used to represent the optical correction used in a viewfinder to adjust for limitations of the photographer's eyesight, and to describe the magnification of a close-up lens attachment.

equivalent focal length A digital camera's focal length translated into the corresponding values for a 35mm film camera. This value can be calculated for lenses used with the Canon Digital Rebel XTi by multiplying by 1.6.

exchangeable image file format (Exif) Developed to standardize the exchange of image data between hardware devices and software. A variation on JPEG, Exif is used by most digital cameras, and it includes information such as the date and time a photo was taken, the camera settings, resolution, amount of compression, and other data.

Exif See *exchangeable image file format (Exif)*.

exposure The amount of light allowed to reach the film or sensor, determined by the intensity of the light, the amount admitted by the iris of the lens, and the length of time determined by the shutter speed.

exposure values (EV) EV settings are a way of adding or decreasing exposure without the need to reference f/stops or shutter speeds. For example, if you tell your camera to add +1EV, it will provide twice as much exposure, either by using a larger f/stop, slower shutter speed, or both.

fill lighting In photography, lighting used to illuminate shadows. Reflectors or additional incandescent lighting or electronic flash can be used to brighten shadows. One common technique outdoors is to use the camera's flash as a fill.

filter In photography, a device that fits over the lens, changing the light in some way. In image editing, a feature that changes the pixels in an image to produce blurring, sharpening, and other special effects. Photoshop includes several interesting filter effects, including Lens Blur and Photo Filters.

flash sync The timing mechanism that ensures that an internal or external electronic flash fires at the correct time during the exposure cycle. A digital SLR's flash sync speed is the highest shutter speed that can be used with flash, ordinarily 1/200th of a second with the Canon Digital Rebel XTi. See also *front-curtain sync* and *rear-curtain sync*.

focal length The distance between the film and the optical center of the lens when the lens is focused on infinity, usually measured in millimeters.

focal plane An imaginary line, perpendicular to the optical access, which passes through the focal point forming a plane of sharp focus when the lens is set at infinity. A focal plane indicator is etched into the Canon Digital Rebel XTi at the left side of the pentaprism.

focus tracking The ability of the automatic focus feature of a camera to change focus as the distance between the subject and the camera changes. One type of focus tracking is *predictive,* in which the mechanism anticipates the motion of the object being focused on, and adjusts the focus to suit.

format To erase a memory card and prepare it to accept files.

fringing A chromatic aberration that produces fringes of color around the edges of subjects, caused by a lens's inability to focus the various wavelengths of light onto the same spot. Purple fringing is especially troublesome with backlit images.

front-curtain sync The default kind of electronic flash synchronization technique, originally associated with focal plane shutters, which consist of a traveling set of curtains, including a *front curtain* (which opens to reveal the film or sensor) and a *rear curtain* (which follows at a distance determined by shutter speed to conceal the film or sensor at the conclusion of the exposure). For a flash picture to be taken, the entire sensor must be exposed at one time to the brief flash exposure, so the image is exposed after the front curtain has reached the other side of the focal plane, but before the rear curtain begins to move. Front-curtain sync causes the flash to fire at the beginning of this period when the shutter is completely open, in the instant that the first curtain of the focal plane shutter finishes its movement across the film or sensor plane. With slow shutter speeds, this feature can create a blur effect from the ambient light, showing as patterns that follow a moving subject with the subject shown sharply frozen at the beginning of the blur trail. See also *rear-curtain sync.*

front-lighting Illumination that comes from the direction of the camera. See also *backlighting* and *sidelighting.*

f/stop The relative size of the lens aperture, which helps determine both exposure and depth-of-field. The larger the f/stop number, the smaller the f/stop itself.

graduated filter A lens attachment with variable density or color from one edge to another. A graduated neutral density filter, for example, can be oriented so the neutral density portion is concentrated at the top of the lens's view with the less dense or clear portion at the bottom, thus reducing the amount of light from a very bright sky while not interfering with the exposure of the landscape in the foreground. Graduated filters can also be split into several color sections to provide a color gradient between portions of the image.

gray card A piece of cardboard or other material with a standardized 18-percent reflectance. Gray cards can be used as a reference for determining correct exposure or for setting white balance.

high contrast A wide range of density in a print, negative, or other image.

highlights The brightest parts of an image containing detail.

high-speed sync A method for syncing Canon EX-series flashes at shutter speeds higher than 1/200th second by increasing the flash duration to match the speed of the focal plane shutter.

histogram A kind of chart showing the relationship of tones in an image using a series of 256 vertical bars, one for each brightness level. A histogram chart, such as the one the Canon Digital Rebel XTi can display during picture review, typically looks like a curve with one or more slopes and peaks, depending on how many highlight, midtone, and shadow tones are present in the image.

hot shoe A mount on top of a camera used to hold an electronic flash, while providing an electrical connection between the flash and the camera.

hyperfocal distance A point of focus where everything from half that distance to infinity appears to be acceptably sharp. For example, if your lens has a hyperfocal distance of 4 feet, everything from 2 feet to infinity would be sharp. The hyperfocal distance varies by the lens and the aperture in use. If you know you'll be making a grab shot without warning, sometimes it is useful to turn off your camera's automatic focus, and set the lens to infinity, or, better yet, the hyperfocal distance. Then, you can snap off a quick picture without having to wait for the lag that occurs with most digital cameras as their autofocus locks in.

image rotation A feature that senses whether a picture was taken in horizontal or vertical orientation. That information is embedded in the picture file so that the camera and compatible software applications can automatically display the image in the correct orientation.

image stabilization A technology that compensates for camera shake, usually by adjusting the position of the camera sensor or lens elements in response to movements of the camera.

incident light Light falling on a surface.

International Organization for Standardization (ISO) A governing body that provides standards used to represent film speed, or the equivalent sensitivity of a digital camera's sensor. Digital camera sensitivity is expressed in ISO settings.

interpolation A technique that digital cameras, scanners, and image editors use to create new pixels required whenever you resize or change the resolution of an image based on the values of surrounding pixels. Devices such as scanners and digital cameras can also use interpolation to create pixels in addition to those actually captured, thereby increasing the apparent resolution or color information in an image.

ISO See *International Organization for Standardization (ISO)*.

jaggies Staircasing effect of lines that are not perfectly horizontal or vertical, caused by pixels that are too large to represent the line accurately. See also *anti-alias*.

JPEG A file "lossy" format (short for *Joint Photographic Experts Group*) that supports 24-bit color and reduces file sizes by selectively discarding image data. Digital cameras generally use JPEG compression to pack more images onto memory cards. You can select how much compression is used (and, therefore, how much information is thrown away) by selecting from among the Standard, Fine, Super Fine, or other quality settings offered by your camera. See also *RAW.*

Kelvin (K) A unit of measure based on the absolute temperature scale in which absolute zero is zero; used to describe the color of continuous-spectrum light sources, and applied when setting white balance. For example, daylight has a color temperature of about 5500K, and a tungsten lamp has a temperature of about 3400K.

lag time The interval between when the shutter is pressed and when the picture is actually taken. During that span, the camera may be automatically focusing and calculating exposure. With digital SLRs like the Canon Digital Rebel XTi, lag time is generally very short; with non-dSLRs, the elapsed time easily can be 1 second or more.

latitude The range of camera exposures that produces acceptable images with a particular digital sensor or film.

lens flare A characteristic of conventional photography that is both a bane and a creative outlet. It is an effect produced by the reflection of light internally among elements of an optical lens. Bright light sources within or just outside the field-of-view cause lens flare. Flare can be reduced by the use of coatings on the lens elements or with the use of lens hoods. Photographers sometimes use the effect as a creative technique, and Photoshop includes a filter that lets you add lens flare at your whim.

lighting ratio The proportional relationship between the amount of light falling on the subject from the main light and other lights, expressed in a ratio, such as 3:1.

lossless compression An image-compression scheme, such as TIFF, that preserves all image detail. When the image is decompressed, it is identical to the original version.

lossy compression An image-compression scheme, such as JPEG, that creates smaller files by discarding image information, which can affect image quality.

macro lens A lens that provides continuous focusing from infinity to extreme close-ups, often to a reproduction ratio of 1:2 (half life-size) or 1:1 (life-size).

matrix metering A system of exposure calculation that looks at many different segments of an image to determine the brightest and darkest portions. The Digital Rebel XTi uses this system with its evaluative metering mode.

maximum burst A viewfinder indication of how many frames can be exposed at the current settings until the buffer fills.

midtones Parts of an image with tones of an intermediate value, usually in the 25 to 75 percent range. Many image-editing features allow you to manipulate mid-tones independently from the highlights and shadows.

mirror lock-up The ability of the XTi to retract its mirror to reduce vibration prior to taking the photo and to allow access to the sensor for cleaning.

neutral color A color in which red, green, and blue are present in equal amounts, producing a gray.

neutral density filter A gray camera filter reduces the amount of light entering the camera without affecting the colors.

noise In an image, pixels with randomly distributed color values. Noise in digital photographs tends to be the product of low-light conditions and long exposures, particularly when you've set your camera to a higher ISO rating than normal.

noise reduction A technology used to cut down on the amount of random information in a digital picture, usually caused by long exposures at increased sensitivity ratings. In the Canon Digital Rebel XTi, noise reduction involves the camera automatically taking a second blank/dark exposure at the same settings that contains only noise, and then using the blank photo's information to cancel out the noise in the original picture. Although the process is very quick, it does double the amount of time required to take the photo.

normal lens A lens that makes the image in a photograph appear in a perspective that is like that of the original scene, typically with a field-of-view of roughly 45 degrees, as opposed to wide-angle and telephoto lenses.

overexposure A condition in which too much light reaches the film or sensor, producing a dense negative or a very bright/light print, slide, or digital image.

pincushion distortion A type of lens distortion found at telephoto focal lengths in which lines at the top and side edges of an image are bent inward, producing an effect that looks like a pincushion. See also *barrel distortion.*

polarizing filter A filter that forces light, which normally vibrates in all directions, to vibrate only in a single plane, reducing or removing the specular reflections from the surface of objects.

RAW An image file format, such as the CR2 format in the Canon Digital Rebel XTi, which includes all the unprocessed information captured by the camera after conversion to digital form. RAW files are very large compared to JPEG files and must be processed by a special program such as Adobe's Camera Raw plug-in after being downloaded from the camera.

rear-curtain sync An optional kind of electronic flash synchronization technique, originally associated with focal plane shutters, which consist of a traveling set of curtains, including a *front curtain* (which opens to reveal the film or sensor) and a *rear curtain* (which follows at a distance determined by shutter speed to conceal the film or sensor at the conclusion of the exposure). For a flash picture to be taken, the entire sensor must be exposed at one time to the brief flash exposure, so the image is exposed after the front curtain has reached the other side of the focal plane, but before the rear curtain begins to move. Rear-curtain sync causes the flash to fire at the end of the exposure, an instant before the second or rear curtain of the focal plane shutter begins to move. With slow shutter speeds, this feature can create a blur effect from the ambient light, showing as patterns that follow a moving subject with the subject shown sharply frozen at the end of the blur trail. If you were shooting a photo of The Flash, the superhero would appear sharp, with a ghostly trail behind him. See also *front-curtain sync.*

red-eye An effect from flash photography that appears to make a person's eyes glow red, or an animal's yellow or green. It's caused by light bouncing from the retina of the eye and is most pronounced in dim illumination (when the irises are wide open) and when the electronic flash is close to the lens and, therefore, prone to reflect directly back. It can be minimized by a blinking light or pre-flash on the camera that causes the subjects' irises to contract. Image editors can fix red-eye through cloning other pixels over the offending red or orange ones.

RGB color model A color model that represents the three colors—red, green, and blue—used by devices such as scanners or monitors to reproduce color. Photoshop works in RGB mode by default, and it even displays CMYK images by converting them to RGB.

saturation The purity of color; the amount by which a pure color is diluted with white or gray.

selective focus Choosing a lens opening that produces a shallow depth-of-field. Usually this is used to isolate a subject by causing most other elements in the scene to be blurred.

self-timer A mechanism that delays the opening of the shutter for some seconds after the release has been operated.

sensitivity A measure of the degree of response of a film or sensor to light, measured using the ISO setting.

shadow The darkest part of an image, represented on a digital image by pixels with low numeric values.

sharpening Increasing the apparent sharpness of an image by boosting the contrast between adjacent pixels that form an edge.

shutter In a conventional film camera, the shutter is a mechanism consisting of blades, a curtain, plate, or some other movable cover that controls the time during which light reaches the film.

shutter-priority An exposure mode, represented by the letters Tv (Time Value) on the XTi's Mode Dial, in which you set the shutter speed and the camera determines the appropriate f/stop. See also *aperture-priority.*

sidelighting Applying illumination from the left or right sides of the camera. See also *backlighting* and *front-lighting.*

single autofocus An automatic focusing setting (One Shot) in which the camera focuses the image once as the picture is taken. This setting is often the best choice for stationary subjects. See also *continuous autofocus.*

slave unit An accessory flash unit that supplements the main flash, usually triggered electronically when the slave senses the light output by the main unit, or through radio waves.

slow sync An electronic flash synchronizing method that uses a slow shutter speed so that ambient light is recorded by the camera in addition to the electronic flash illumination. This allows the background to receive more exposure for a more realistic effect.

specular highlight Bright spots in an image caused by reflection of light sources.

sRGB One of two color space choices available with the Canon Digital Rebel XTi. The sRGB setting is recommended for images that will be output locally on the user's own printer, as this color space matches that of the typical inkjet printer fairly closely. See also *Adobe RGB*.

subtractive primary colors Cyan, magenta, and yellow, which are the printing inks that theoretically absorb all color and produce black. In practice, however, they generate a muddy brown, so black is added to preserve detail (especially in shadows). The combination of the three colors and black is referred to as CMYK. (K represents black, to differentiate it from blue in the RGB model.)

through the lens (TTL) A system of providing viewing and exposure calculations through the actual lens taking the picture.

time exposure A picture taken by leaving the shutter open for a long period, usually more than 1 second. The camera is generally locked down with a tripod to prevent blur during the long exposure.

tungsten light Light from ordinary room lamps and ceiling fixtures, as opposed to fluorescent illumination.

underexposure A condition in which too little light reaches the film or sensor, producing a thin negative, a dark slide, a muddy-looking print, or a dark digital image.

unsharp masking The process for increasing the contrast between adjacent pixels in an image, increasing sharpness, especially around edges.

vignetting Dark corners of an image, often produced by using a lens hood that is too small for the field-of-view, a lens that does not completely fill the image frame, or generated artificially using image-editing techniques.

white balance The adjustment of a digital camera to the color temperature of the light source. Interior illumination is relatively red; outdoor light is relatively blue. Digital cameras like the Digital Rebel XTi set correct white balance automatically or let you do it through menus. Image editors can often do some color correction of images that were exposed using the wrong white balance setting.

Index

Passionate about

photography...

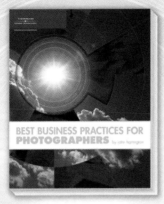

Best Business Practices for Photographers ■ 1-59863-315-5 ■ $29.99

Covers the essential business topics that professional photographers need to know in order to successfully meet important business objectives. This book focuses on best practices in client interaction, contract and license negotiation, and business operations. It serves as a roadmap for successfully navigating each of these issues, as well as many others faced by professional photographers.

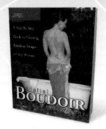 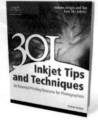 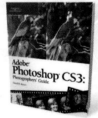 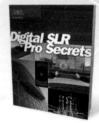

Digital Boudoir
Photography
1-59863-220-5 ■ $34.99

301 Inkjet
Tips and Techniques
1-59863-204-3 ■ $49.99

Adobe Photoshop CS3
Photographers' Guide
1-59863-400-3 ■ $39.99

Digital SLR Pro Secrets
1-59863-019-9 ■ $39.99

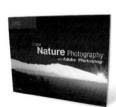 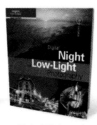 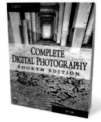 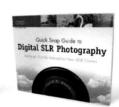 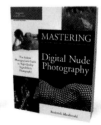

Digital Nature Photography
and Adobe Photoshop
1-59863-135-7 ■ $39.99

Digital Night and
Low-Light Photography
1-59200-649-3 ■ $29.99

Complete Digital
Photography, Fourth Edition
1-58450-520-6 ■ $39.99

Quick Snap Guide to
Digital SLR Photography
1-59863-187-X ■ $29.99

Mastering Digital
Nude Photography
1-59863-026-1 ■ $39.99

COURSE TECHNOLOGY
Professional ■ Technical ■ Reference

CHARLES RIVER MEDIA

Call 1.800.648.7450 to order
Order online at www.courseptr.com

Passionate about

photography...

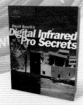

David Busch's
Digital Infrared Pro Secrets
1-59863-355-4 ■ $39.99

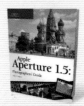

Apple Aperture 1.5:
Photographers' Guide
1-59863-340-6 ■ $34.99

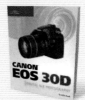

Canon EOS 30D
Guide to Digital SLR Photography
1-59863-336-8 ■ $29.99

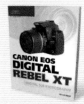

Canon EOS Digital Rebel XT
Guide to Digital SLR Photography
1-59863-337-6 ■ $29.99

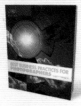

Best Business Practices
for Photographers
1-59863-315-5 ■ $29.99

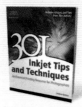

301 Inkjet Tips and Techniques
1-59863-204-3 ■ $49.99

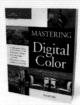

Mastering Digital Color
1-59200-543-8 ■ $39.99

Quick Snap Guide
to Digital Photography
1-59863-335-X ■ $29.99

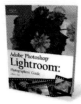

Adobe Photoshop Lightroom:
Photographers' Guide
1-59863-339-2 ■ $34.99

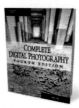

Complete Digital Photography,
Fourth Edition
1-58450-520-6 ■ $39.99

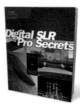

Digital SLR Pro Secrets
1-59863-019-9 ■ $39.99

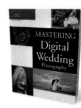

Mastering
Digital Wedding Photography
1-59863-329-5 ■ $39.99

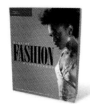

Digital Fashion Photography
1-59200-525-X ■ $34.99

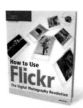

How to Use Flickr: The Digital
Photography Revolution
1-59863-137-3 ■ $24.99

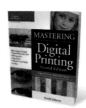

Mastering Digital Printing,
Second Edition
1-59200-431-8 ■ $39.99

Quick Snap Guide to
Digital SLR Photography
1-59863-187-X ■ $29.99

**COURSE
TECHNOLOGY**
Professional ■ Technical ■ Reference

CHARLES
RIVER
MEDIA

Call 1.800.648.7450 to order
Order online at www.courseptr.com